Fit after 40

Dr Sheela Nambiar is an obstetrician and gynaecologist, fitness consultant and a practitioner of lifestyle medicine. She runs an obstetric practice in Ooty and has a wellness/fitness programme called Training for Life (TFL) which she uses as an extension of her medical practice. Sheela is also the author of the books *Get Size Wise* and *Gain to Lose* (Rupa Publications). Her work can be found on her blog, sheelanambiar.wordpress.com, and her website, www.drsheelanambiar.com.

Fit after 40

DR SHEELA NAMBIAR

First published in 2018 by Hachette India
(Registered name: Hachette Book Publishing India Pvt. Ltd)
An Hachette UK company
www.hachetteindia.com

SRD

Copyright © 2018 Sheela Nambiar

Sheela Nambiar asserts the moral right to be identified
as the author of this work.

Illustrations by Pixtrics

All rights reserved. No part of the publication may be reproduced, stored in a
retrieval system (including but not limited to computers, disks, external drives,
electronic or digital devices, e-readers, websites), or transmitted in any form or by
any means (including but not limited to cyclostyling, photocopying, docutech or
other reprographic reproductions, mechanical, recording, electronic, digital versions)
without the prior written permission of the publisher, nor be otherwise circulated in
any form of binding or cover other than that in which it is published and without a
similar condition being imposed on the subsequent purchaser.

The views and opinions expressed in this book are the author's own, and the facts are
as reported by her and have been verified to the extent possible. The publishers are not
in any way liable for the same.

ISBN 978-93-5195-180-3

Hachette Book Publishing India Pvt. Ltd
4th/5th Floors, Corporate Centre,
Sector 44, Gurugram 122003, India

Typeset in Cardo 10/14
by InoSoft Systems Noida

Printed and bound in India by
Manipal Technologies Limited, Manipal

For two of the most amazing and inspiring people I know – Indira and Raghavan Nambiar

Contents

Introduction ix

Part 1: WHERE YOU ARE AT: AN HONEST ASSESSMENT

1. How Have You Been Doing So Far? 3
2. Assessing Your Wellness and Fitness Levels 19
3. Hormonal Changes with Age 34
4. Why Can't We 'Just Do It'? 49
5. Myths and Misconceptions about Your Body after 40 54
6. It's Never Too Late to Start 61

Part 2: UNDERSTANDING YOUR BODY AFTER 40 AND TAKING CARE OF IT

7. How and Why We Gain Weight 71
8. Turn Your Plate Around 88
9. Belly Fat and Gut Health 107
10. Cardio 126
11. Strength and Muscle 134
12. Flexibility 141

13.	Move More	152
14.	Essential Exercises	160
15.	The Importance of Posture	181
16.	Improving Balance as You Age	193

Part 3: UNDERSTANDING YOUR MIND AFTER 40 AND TAKING CARE OF IT

17.	Stress	207
18.	Sleep	230
19.	Relationships and Quality of Life	244
20.	Keeping the Brain Healthy	267
21.	Ageing Meaningfully	280

APPENDIX

Medical Conditions That Develop after 40	294
Bibliography	329
Notes	334
Acknowledgements	335

Introduction

As we grow older, things in our lives begin to crystallize. Perhaps the lens through which we view the world has changed over the years. Perhaps we are wiser, and are able to be more gentle towards ourselves and more accepting of those around us. We are also able to edit our lives, only worrying about what is truly important and not wasting time and effort on trivialities that needlessly exhaust us.

Well...at least that's how the narrative is supposed to play out. After all, all those years of experience must have taught us something?

That's not always the case, though I don't think there is ever a time when one is totally in control or entirely rid of old anxieties and habits. We are wiser, yes. We are also, hopefully, able to monitor our own reactions and interactions, understand them at a deeper level for what they really are, and manage our time and effort more effectively. Most importantly, we also appreciate that getting knocked down in life is inevitable. It's how we get back up that defines who we are.

From a physical perspective, we become conscious of our bodies in a more mature fashion. We suddenly become aware, for instance, that some things that seemed effortless when younger – multitasking, travelling, socializing and so on have become that much more challenging. We appreciate what our bodies are capable of rather than just what they look like. We are *respectful* of just how much abuse our bodies have withstood over the years. Fitness takes on a whole new meaning.

I say 'we are', but I'm fully aware that not all of us are. Some just lament the problems that come up but perhaps have done nothing about them in the past and have thus allowed themselves to get to this point. In that case, they still have a choice now to take stock and get moving.

I have learnt to value my body and mind now more than ever before. I am thankful for having taken up lifestyle medicine, not just as an extension of my medical practice and an alternate career, but also as a personal agenda. Having been able to prioritize my workout hour irrespective of circumstances, for the most part, I think has certainly given me an advantage. It hasn't always been easy, but it has certainly been worth it. There have been many times when I have struggled to sustain an exercise routine due to work or personal pressures. But I recognized the importance of maintaining a regular, disciplined fitness routine and of healthy eating very early in life and I made them non-negotiable for myself. This is how I have been able to work around most obstacles.

Over the years I have also recognized the dark side of exercise and fitness. Yes, there is a dark side! Sometimes (and this is especially true if one is already adept and entrenched in a fitness inclusive lifestyle) it may become habitual to use exercise as the only respite from just about everything. It becomes almost like the drug of choice to resolve other problems. Even though I do highly recommend a nice long walk or run when in the midst of emotional turmoil, it shouldn't be the only solution for sorting out our problems. You need other practices complementing your arsenal of strategies to deal with dilemmas. Work, hobbies, friends, relationships, meditation and relaxation should all form a part of it.

When I started teaching fitness and including fitness prescriptions in my day-to-day medical practice in the year 2000, I didn't even know that lifestyle medicine was a field of its own. (It was started in 1998 in the United States). All I understood was the obvious fact that everyone benefits greatly from a regular well-designed fitness and diet prescription and that the very important inclusion of psychological counselling facilitates the process.

Today, what is called 'lifestyle medicine', which involves looking at a person as a whole and not just as a body exhibiting symptoms of a particular disease, is seen as the way forward. Exercise, diet, stress, sleep and relationships are all part of the equation and need to be paid heed to while treating patients. It makes a lot of sense, doesn't it? Many diseases today are lifestyle-related, and can and should be effectively managed through lifestyle changes rather than merely treating symptoms with medicines.

I attended the first Asian conference on lifestyle medicine in Taipei in 2016 and was delighted to meet other doctors from around the world who were committed to this way of treating and managing patients. Following this conference, I was inspired to study positive psychology, another fascinating field and an offshoot of regular psychology, which deals primarily with the science of 'What Makes Life Worth Living'. Rather than focusing on disease and ill-health, it deals with helping people lead flourishing lives. It made a lot of sense to me. This is not to say that mainstream psychiatry or psychology are not relevant, for they are. They are more pertinent today than ever before. But I think positive psychology works as an effective supplement. In fact, the Indian chapter of lifestyle medicine is currently being created, spearheaded by a few of us who have been involved with this movement. In my first book, *Get Size Wise*, I quoted Thomas Edison, who said, 'The doctor of the future will give no medicines, but will instruct his patients in the care of the human frame, in diet and in the cause and prevention of disease.' This is more relevant now than ever before and is the essence of lifestyle medicine. Lifestyle medicine is truly the need of the hour given our (mostly) dysfunctional lifestyles.

Life comes full circle, they say. When I had to choose a speciality for my post-graduation, my first choice was psychiatry. Then, I reconsidered; I decided I would rather work in a 'happier' field, concerned mainly with women. I chose obstetrics, which, although extremely demanding, is also filled with the joy of new life and mostly happy endings.

You see, in those days, psychiatry was mainly concerned with mental health concerns, like depression, anxiety, schizophrenia, bipolar disorder and the myriad other mental disorders that I found very depressing in themselves. I was quite sure I wouldn't be able to survive them successfully on a daily basis. I have always been interested in the workings of the mind, however, and have implemented in my practice 'lifestyle counselling', which is inclusive of but not restricted to the motivation to exercise in order to stay healthy, and the management of life situations that impede a healthy lifestyle. Telling someone 'you need to lose weight' is not adequate. Understanding and helping them understand why he/she is overweight in the first place is far more effective. Now I use principles of positive psychology along with lifestyle counselling and have found it to be incredibly valuable both on a personal level and for my patients/clients. This book is a culmination of my experiences of working in these spheres.

As to why this book is important for you to read, I say this:

this book is not just about fitness; it is about good mental health for those over 40 – someone who, perhaps, has been through the whole 'quick-fix', 'fad-diets' rigmarole and is ready to finally listen to what staying holistically healthy really entails. It addresses more than just physical fitness, however. It explores the various aspects of our wellness, the symptoms of menopause, andropause and perimenopause and the medical problems one may encounter as we age; it looks at other components of our lives, including our relationships, stress, sleep and food, as well as at how we can improve resilience and flourish especially in the years when the body may not exactly be accommodating.

Every human being is unique. The principles in this book, however, are general and need to be used as such.

In the end, it's important to realize that 40 is really just a number. I know 30-year-olds who look and behave older than 50, through the neglect of their bodies and minds. Then there are the 80-year-olds who can put a 40-something person to shame!

If you haven't got your act together by now and are not sure how to start, then this book is for you. Begin with an evaluation of where you are at now in terms of holistic well-being and then take the next steps forward accordingly. Alternately, if you have most of it in place – that is, you already are an avid exerciser and only need to fine-tune the edges, understand food better, are anxious about hormonal changes in your body, or are concerned about medical conditions you may face as you grow older – then this book is for you too. In it, I have tried to address each problem you may face as holistically as possible. Hence, the chapters that deal with the physical body have been separated from those that address the mind. After all, how we deal with ageing begins in the mind. Growing older can be a wonderfully rewarding experience or a traumatic combination of physical and psychological setbacks. It all depends on how prepared we are and how much we do to prevent the deterioration of the body and the mind.

My own fitness philosophy is to focus on how I feel rather than how I look, and to stay consistent. I don't feel good when I don't exercise or eat healthy on a regular basis, for instance, so I listen to my body and maintain a regular healthy lifestyle. These days, I see more and more people following fad diets, sometimes endangering their own health and well-being in the hope of quick fixes. I believe our body is extremely clever and tells us exactly what it needs but we create contrary lifestyle habits and become immune to its warnings.

I am a keen believer in weight training to improve and increase muscle mass. This is especially important for the Indian phenotype (that has lower muscle mass to begin with). But I also firmly believe that yoga (or another serious stretching routine) should be a part of our fitness to improve flexibility, calm the mind and create an inward focus.

Writing this book has been a precious, personal and extremely educative journey for me. The research I did for the various chapters (like the one on keeping the brain healthy and ageing meaningfully, for instance) opened my eyes to many aspects of growing older. I have instinctively followed nearly all of the suggestions made in the book (such as having a learning mindset, connecting with nature, recognizing one's purpose, and so on), and while researching the chapter on sleep, I became more conscious of the serious importance of getting good quality sleep.

I hope you enjoy reading (and using!) this book as much as I have enjoyed writing it.

PART I

WHERE YOU ARE AT: AN HONEST ASSESSMENT

one

How Have You Been Doing So Far?

You may suddenly realize at 40 (or 50 or 60) just how negligent you have been of your physical self. This jolt could come from a simple health check-up revealing high blood sugar levels or weight that is off the charts. You may find that you are run down, anaemic or depressed. At the same time you may be doing well career-wise, might be financially secure and acing that promotion or pay raise when it's due. Perhaps you are a workaholic and haven't allowed yourself time to explore your emotional well-being, your creative side or to nurture relationships. Alternately, you may be in great physical shape, have an impressive social life and plenty of money, but might feel dissatisfied emotionally and empty spiritually. You may even be doing exceptionally well in all the aspects of wellness. If so, kudos to you! But most of us are probably somewhere in between.

So, let's begin by asking: **What have you been doing thus far? What have you done to better sustain yourself through the years?**

When you think about it, the answer to that question would be multifaceted. The response related to different areas of your life will be varied, with you scoring high in one aspect of wellness and abysmally low in others. That happens to everyone, but it is important to explore these aspects and understand oneself.

Divide your wellness into eight different categories:

- Physical
- Psychological/Emotional
- Spiritual
- Creative
- Intellectual
- Financial
- Social
- Environmental

PHYSICAL WELL-BEING

What have you been doing to stay healthy, fit and attractive? Nothing? Something? Or everything possible?

Different people turn to different means to do this. For some, it is exercise and meditation; for others, it is cosmetics and creams, surgery or botox, fillers, drugs, powders and pills.

For some, the trigger to maintain their health and physical well-being may be social pressure. A high-powered executive, for instance, is under pressure to 'look' presentable and attractive, dress well and so on, as he or she is often out in the public sphere. The motivation to stay that way comes from a need to achieve a certain level of 'presentability'. A man or woman who doesn't need to get out of the house, on the other hand, may believe there is nothing motivating him or her to 'look' better and may, therefore, see no reason to sweat it out or watch what they eat. This is not how it should be, of course, but it is unfortunately quite a common story. As much as one would love to be indifferent to the opinions of society, it influences our reasoning and actions. The good news is that as we age, appearances, other people's opinions and fads do not affect us as much as they once did. We can, therefore, begin to look at fitness and wellness just for ourselves. We can identify what is important to us and work towards achieving it.

Another reason for being (or not being) health- or fitness-conscious is sheer habit. For some, a healthy lifestyle may be a way of life, so to speak, so it's easier to make the necessary changes in their diets or include a different exercise routine when it is needed. This is especially the case for those who come from health-conscious families. When you are exposed to eating plenty of vegetables and exercising regularly from a very young age it becomes almost ingrained in your neural network. For others, this may not be the case. We may be forced to pay attention to our health or weight after a visit to our doctor.

Whatever be the reason that gets us motivated, adopting a healthier lifestyle is not easy. The key is to start slow but stay consistent. Following are a few key points you should follow:

- Don't be tempted to take shortcuts by going on fad diets for instance. Look at it as a lifestyle plan, something you can do without feeling completely overwhelmed for the rest of your life.
- Don't focus only on the weighing scale. Consider the feeling of well-being and healthy longevity as important side-effects.
- It helps to stay connected with like-minded people who may be going through the same situation. A motivating mentor/trainer and support from the family will always be helpful.

Depending on what you have been doing so far to stay well, you will have different learning curves for bettering your health, appearance and holistic well-being from here on. Many of you who are already on your journey simply need tweaks in your daily routine to enable you to get the best out of your hour of exercise and other efforts to stay fit and healthy. Others may require a complete overhaul of their lifestyle and/or mindscape.

If you already exercise every day, or at least several times a week, ask yourself the following questions:

1. Have you included weight training or any other form of strength training (such as using your own body weight to increase strength) at least twice a week?
2. Have you steadily been increasing the weights used during training sessions and thereby increased, or at least sustained, your overall strength?
3. Have you included anything to improve your flexibility? This could include traditional yoga or just simple stretches you do everyday.
4. How much cardio do you do? Have you improved in your timing, calories burnt or distance covered? Can you push yourself harder?
5. Have you started including balance training, coordination, agility, reaction time, etc. to your fitness routine?
6. Do you still feel challenged and invigorated by your fitness routine or has it become monotonous and tedious?
7. Have you consciously made an effort to include supplements like omega-3, calcium-rich foods and vitamin D in your diet?
8. Do you have a yearly gynaecology exam and see a physician to check your basic vitals like blood pressure and blood sugar?

> If you don't exercise, or have been very inconsistent with respect to your exercise and diet, ask yourself the following questions:
>
> - What am I willing to give in terms of time, money and energy?
> - Am I willing to implement a 'lifestyle' change or do I think this is a waste of time?
> - Do I prefer to dabble in short-term, quick-fix remedies or am I willing to go the whole nine yards and change my lifestyle completely to ensure change that is more permanent in nature?
> - How much do I really value my 'wellness' (not just my appearance)?
> - How important is this to me?

Once you've answered these questions, you can then decide on the course of action. I know several people who believe they are fine just as they are. In my clinic I try and reason with the women I meet to inculcate exercise habits and healthy eating when we discover abnormal test results because the patient is overweight with an unhealthy waist circumference. Some smile politely and give me random excuses for not being able to exercise. Others promise enthusiastically to start, but I can see that they are not yet in a position to begin the process of change. A third category is genuinely motivated and the people in this group readily start their journey to their fitter, better selves. Some of them are able to stay on the wagon, some fall off along the way and still others go back and forth between regular exercise and healthy eating, and an unhealthy lifestyle. In my second book, *Gain to Lose*, I have talked about the *stages of change* and how all of that plays out

Changing Perspectives

With age, different things become important. For instance, if you walk for exercise and can cover a great distance effortlessly in 40 minutes, that's wonderful. However, what will become more important for you as you age is not how fast you can walk but:

- If you can climb stairs without holding on to the banister.
- If you can go down a slope without being afraid of falling.
- If you can lift heavy stuff down from a shelf or up from the floor without needing help or ending up clutching your back with a pulled muscle.
- If you can shut your car door, holding your bag of groceries in one hand and phone in the other.
- If you can bend down to pick up something without ending up with a catch in the back.

These are the things that matter. No one is likely to test the speed of your one-mile walk. You will, however, be repeatedly tested in the little things that your body may slowly be giving up on unless you consciously train those areas.

You need to work not just on your stamina, strength and flexibility, which are the three main pillars of fitness, but also on your balance, your reflexes, your coordination and reaction time. As we go along, I will elaborate on these areas, which can be included into your own fitness routine.

Taking Stock

Shopping

What do you usually stock up on? Your shopping list should be mainly focused on perishable, fresh foods. Fruits, vegetables, poultry, fish, eggs, nuts, seeds, whole grains, pulses, different kinds of millets, various dried beans, milk, cheeses and good quality oils (like sesame, coconut, groundnut and olive, which are non-refined).

Ready-to-eat meals and dishes, boxed cereals, biscuits, cookies, fruit juices, sodas, packaged snacks and so on should simply not feature on your shopping list. If you buy it, you or your family are almost compelled to eat it. It's far wiser to prevent temptation altogether than have to use your will power to stop yourself from eating what's sitting right in front of you at home.

I know it's so much easier to just buy pre-cooked, easy-to-make food. It saves so much trouble! But keep in mind that anything that is packaged and has a shelf life is likely to have preservatives. I'm not talking about frozen vegetables, cheeses and things that are kept under refrigeration. Those are conveniences one can well afford. I am talking about ready-made curries, ready-made desserts and whole dishes that you are only required to heat up. I am also talking about packaged biscuits, chips and other delights that one can't stop eating once they start!

Shop at farmers' markets and local vendors who get the freshest food, if you can. Never shop when you are hungry. You tend to make bad choices.

Cooking

Who cooks at home? Who plans the meals? How much thought goes into it?

Even if you don't always cook all the meals yourself and have the luxury of help, you need to be invested in what goes into the meals. Using good quality ingredients is the foundation of great meals. Cooking simple yet tasty meals is the key to staying lean. Avoid cooking indulgences (like deep frying) through the week and allow yourself a treat or two over the weekend.

I often hear the complaint 'my maid cooks for me and she uses too much oil'. Here's the thing: if you have no control over what goes into your body on a day-to-day basis there's very little you can do to manage your health. One can't afford to be complacent about food any more.

I am no master chef but I taught myself to cook at a very young age. I make up recipes as I go along (I admit not all of them are stellar successes, but many are!). But I must say that with some common sense and imagination one can perform miracles when it comes to food. You can make delicious vegetable dishes with a vegetarian protein and good quality fat, for instance, and not have to depend on large volumes of breads or rice to satiate you.

I believe everyone needs to learn to cook. It's not rocket science. You may choose not to cook and only supervise, but you are in a better position to judge what goes into a dish and choose alternative ingredients if need be when you do your own cooking. Young people these days are reluctant to cook and would much rather eat out or order in. I am sometimes horrified when someone tells me they have no idea how to cook and, more importantly, doesn't have a basic understanding of food. You are quite literally delegating the responsibility of your health to someone else if you are always dependent on others to cook for you without that understanding of food.

Eating

Do you eat alone or with family and friends? Where? When?

Do you eat out a lot? How many times a week? Where? Are you cognizant of the food you order? Do you see it as an opportunity to indulge? Are you aware of what goes into the dish that you just ordered?

These are all variables you should be aware of. Eating has to be a very conscious and mindful act, not to mention, a joyful and fulfilling one.

> - Go through the list of questions to decide where exactly you find yourself today.
> - Understand your changing perspective. What about your physical self is important to you today (as compared to in your twenties)?
> - Explore how you shop, cook and eat.

Once you have evaluated these various aspects of your life to assess how your health and wellness could be affected, it's time to get started with some real-time interventions when it comes to your food and exercise routines to improve your body and overall well-being.

PSYCHOLOGICAL OR EMOTIONAL WELL-BEING

How does one ever know if one is truly psychologically well? I'm not sure there is a definitive answer to that question. How we feel changes and often depends on how we react to our circumstances and the world around us.

We are subject to a range of emotions. The balance of these emotions is more important in the overall scheme of things. Anxiety, fear, sadness and other negative emotions are not necessarily bad for us. They are, instead, signals for us to look at a situation and understand what to do about it. Instead of suppressing these emotions (which sometimes may result in many unwarranted repercussions like depression, post-traumatic stress disorder, loss of friendships, isolation and so on), use them as a reminder to look deeper.

There may be times when we feel terribly unwell within ourselves. Times of stress, family or work pressure or the loss of someone dear can upset our emotional/psychological equilibrium quite dramatically. There are other times when we are calm even under stressful situations.

Some of us are aware of these changes as we experience them and explore them to understand the motivations and delve into possible changes to implement. Some are quite naïve about inner well-being and its implications on health.

Think about it. Wouldn't you say that the range and complexity of your psychological inner life is just as much a reality as your physiological and physical body?

The Greek philosopher Socrates had said, 'An unexamined life is not worth living.' From time to time ask yourself what's going on in your mind. What do you think about life in general; your own life in particular? What meaning or purpose do you find? Are you happy, fulfilled, discontented or disinterested? What are the values that drive your attitudes to your existence? What brings you joy? What are your loves, your hates and your disappointments? Have you any idea as to who and what you are as an individual or how you are becoming your own person?

Self-awareness is key to growth. How can we move forward if we don't know where we are?

> Our emotional well-being is quite different from our physical well-being although they are intimately intertwined. While we can certainly improve mood and sense of well-being by incorporating regular exercise into our day, being 'well' emotionally requires other practices like deep contemplation, meditation, reflection and an understanding of our true motives and ourselves. It requires us to ask ourselves the question, 'What will truly make for a better life for me?'

SPIRITUAL WELL-BEING

Spirituality is a complex topic. It means different things to different people. To some, it is equivalent to religiosity. This may provide comfort and act as a support system for those who invest time and effort in religious pursuits, which include the social connections that exist as a result of the religious community.

To others, spirituality is not necessarily about religion but more about the profound questions you ask yourself concerning the 'meaning of life' and your existence and the role of your contribution to things and people around you.

Spirituality has been explained as, 'The search for transcendent meaning that can be expressed in religious practice or exclusively in relationship to nature, music, the arts, a set of philosophical beliefs, or relationships with friends and family.'[1]

To me, spirituality is a philosophy for life that acts as a framework to identify how to function effectively in the world. It is a sort of compass to negotiate the various alleyways of life, to help me understand how to prioritize what is important to me and how to live more meaningfully. I do believe we become more 'spiritual-minded' as we age. Perhaps we have more time and we see a deep inner need for such reflection.

Identify what spirituality means to you and ask yourself where you want to go with it. In a questionnaire I sent out to several women over the age of 40, it appears that many start to search for 'meaning' as they grow older. Some become more religious-minded or follow a leader of sorts (like a guru). A few abandon religion altogether and instead start on their own spiritual journey, questioning their existence and meaning of life through other means.

> Spirituality is not the same as religiosity. Explore your views on spirituality. Having meaning and purpose is important, especially as we grow older.

CREATIVE WELL-BEING

This refers to your creative or fun side. Here's where you develop something you love for the sake of itself. It could be a hobby or a recreational activity, a sport, a game, gardening, painting, music and so on. It taps into the lighter side of life. You may want to try learning how to swim, paint, write a book or read philosophy. Something that gives you satisfaction for no particular reason or monetary gain. It can, of course, spin off into a profession as often creative pursuits do. Alternately, you may be fortunate enough to be able to express your creativity in your current line of work.

Finding a creative outlet is immensely therapeutic and fulfilling. It allows us a reprieve from our daily routine. It also allows us to work better, be better parents, spouses and friends. Cooking and writing are my creative pursuits. I must admit I am not sure I would have been quite so excited about cooking had I been compelled to do it every single day. As it stands, I don't cook everyday so it is a pleasure to explore and experiment.

> Everyone is creative in his or her own way. Exploring our creativity brings out the part of us that we may have suppressed or ignored. It taps into part of the brain we don't always stimulate.

INTELLECTUAL WELLNESS/CAREER/WORK

Our intellect is stimulated by work, study, reading and other conscious efforts made to engage or stimulate the mind.

Many careers begin to peak when we are in our 40s. This can be both stressful and exciting. A great career is, of course, a wonderful way to keep your intellect challenged. But this doesn't mean that if you are not engaged in a career, you will inevitably be faced with declining brain function. There are myriad ways to improve brain function outside of a career. Reading books, joining groups that offer great talks, enrolling in online courses, playing games, voluntary work, etc. are available to do just that.

If the brain is not constantly stimulated, it tends to degenerate just like other muscles in the body. It is important, therefore, to ask yourself if you are doing things to keep the mind 'exercised' just like the physical body.

Are you constantly challenging your mind with new material?

- Are you happy with your mental growth?
- Do you read? Watch interesting material?
- Do you engage in stimulating conversation?
- Are you regularly learning something new?

If there is no conscious effort to stimulate the brain by learning and engaging in stimulating challenges it is very easy for the brain to deteriorate.

FINANCIAL WELL-BEING

If there is one aspect of 'well-being' I would happily delegate to someone else, this is it! But I do know it is critical to establish a semblance of financial structure and security in one's life. Understanding and managing your savings and spending give you a great sense of confidence and control. Many women leave the financial aspect of their lives entirely up to their husbands or the men in their lives. I know some who have no idea how a bank or an ATM works, how to deposit a cheque, and so on. This is especially true of large families where the male members manage finances. Learning these things, having your own bank account, managing your financial status and savings is just as important as earning money or building a career.

> Set yourself financial goals. Get help from others, even a financial advisor, if need be.

SOCIAL WELL-BEING

We are all social animals. We need to stay connected with those around us. We may not all wish to be highly sociable, but keeping connections going is crucial to overall well-being. While looking into some of the healthiest and oldest living people in the islands of Okinawa in Japan, Loma Linda in California and Sardinia in Italy, it was found that one of the commonalities in the lives of these centenarians was the presence of close connections with family and friends.

This is not always easy to sustain in today's fast-paced world, where everyone plays multiple roles and is constantly short on time. However, if you don't make an effort to sustain relationships early on, you may be at a loss for meaningful connections later. Besides, a lack of social connectivity is detrimental to emotional well-being and even heart health.

Not all relationships can or even should be sustained, of course. Some may need to be concluded for various reasons. There should, nonetheless, be at least two or three deep and authentic relationships in each of our lives that we can rely on at any cost. The security of these relationships paves the way to a certain level of happiness, besides bringing us moments of great joy.

Maintaining a relationship takes time and effort. It doesn't happen on its own, and many fall by the wayside simply because of lack of effort and neglect. It is finally about priorities. What you value most or believe to be the most urgent often takes precedence. For instance, bringing up children requires a lot of time and effort, and young mothers often find it hard to sustain relationships with friends or colleagues because of their commitments to family.

As we grow older, this pressure eases. You may find yourself making more time for extended family or friendships. Many women I questioned regarding their social well-being also spoke about a more confident and authentic social networking style. After a point, 'people pleasing' seems to be replaced with more productive connections and the 'need to explain oneself' is replaced with more confidence in oneself and what one is doing.

> Actively nurture relationships that you value.

ENVIRONMENTAL WELLNESS

This refers to your relationship with your environment and the understanding of how this affects your community and yourself. It includes protecting your environment and protecting yourself from environmental hazards. Leading a life that is respectful of your environment is the key to environmental wellness. Ask yourself:

- Do you segregate waste?
- Do you recycle?
- Do you save water?
- Do you plant trees?
- If you see a safety hazard, do you initiate steps to rectify it?
- Do you volunteer for worthy environmental causes?
- Are you aware of your surroundings and environmental hazards?

> Enabling a safe and sustainable environment is critically important. Small steps go a long way.

Explore the various aspects of wellness – physical, psychological or emotional, spiritual, creative, intellectual, financial, social and environmental and see where you stand and how 'well' you are doing in these eight dimensions. Focus on the ones you tend to neglect. Mostly, you will find that while you may be very good at one aspect of wellness, you may be neglecting another. Make a note of the steps you will take to improve each aspect of your wellness.

Well-being is more than just physical fitness. This is a realization that sinks in as we grow older. We have probably spent our second and third decades being so busy with our families and careers that we don't necessarily identify what we want to improve in our lives. Perhaps we haven't had the time to really think about it. Now would be a good time to start.

two

Assessing Your Wellness and Fitness Levels

So exactly how mentally and physically fit are you at this point in time? Starting with understanding where you are at this moment helps you understand where you have to go. The tests in this chapter are not just to determine your fitness levels but also to evaluate your overall health. Take this opportunity to visit your doctor and have the necessary tests done.

Here's what you need:

- A complete medical check-up
- Your weight
- Your fat percentage
- Your cardiovascular fitness
- Your strength
- Your flexibility
- Your balance

THE COMPLETE MEDICAL CHECK-UP

The Physical Activity Readiness Questionnaire, or PAR-Q, is the questionnaire that one would need to fill up before attempting to exercise. This is relevant for anyone between the ages of 15-69. (This questionnaire is usually filled up at your exercise facility. Carry a copy of it with you when you go to see your physician.)

The following sample of PAR-Q is from the National Academy of Sports Medicine NASM (ACE Personal Trainer Manual).

Data Collection Sheet

Name: _____

Date: _____ Height: _____ in. Weight: _____ lbs.

Age: _____ Physician's Name: _____

Phone: _____

Physical Activity Readiness Questionnaire (Par-Q)

	Questions	Yes	No
1	Has your doctor ever said that you have a heart condition and that you should only perform physical activity recommended by a doctor?		
2	Do you feel pain in your chest when you perform physical activity?		
3	In the past month, have you had chest pain when you were not performing any physical activity?		
4	Do you lose your balance because of dizziness or do you ever lose consciousness?		
5	Do you have a bone or joint problem that could be made worse by a change in your physical activity?		
6	Is your doctor currently prescribing any medication for your blood pressure or for a heart condition?		
7	Do you know of any other reason why you should not engage in physical activity?		

General and Medical Questionnaire

	Occupational Questions	Yes	No
1	What is your current occupation? _____		
2	Does your occupation require extended periods of sitting?		
3	Does your occupation require extended periods of repetitive movements? (If yes, please explain.) _____		
4	Does your occupation require you to wear shoes with a heel (dress shoes)?		
5	Does your occupation cause you anxiety (mental stress)?		
	Recreational Questions	Yes	No
6	Do you partake in any recreational activities (golf, tennis, skiing, etc.)? (If yes, please explain.) _____		
7	Do you have any hobbies (reading, gardening, working on cars, exploring the Internet, etc.)? (If yes, please explain.) _____		
	Medical Questions	Yes	No
8	Have you ever had any pain or injuries (ankle, knee, hip, back, shoulder, etc.)? (If yes, please explain.) _____		
9	Have you ever had any surgeries? (If yes, please explain.) ___		
10	Has a medical doctor ever diagnosed you with a chronic disease, such as coronary heart disease, coronary artery disease, hypertension (high blood pressure), high cholesterol or diabetes? (If yes, please explain.) _____		

11	Are you currently taking any medication? (If yes, please list.) _____ _____		

A medical check-up, which includes a thorough health history and a family history of disease, is helpful in planning your fitness schedule, diet and lifestyle change. Your risk for disease also needs to be assessed taking into account your age, weight, habits (like sedentary living, tobacco and alcohol), surgical and family history.

If you are 40 and above and if you have never exercised before, please have a complete cardiac evaluation. Your heart rate (pulse) and blood pressure are important measures of health. If you have filled up the Physical Activity Readiness Questionnaire (PAR-Q), show it to your physician. After the evaluation, seek advice from your physician on what type of activity is suitable for your current condition.

Even if you are already exercising regularly, you would still need to see your physician and a gynaecologist once you hit 40 for a general check-up and to detect any untoward problems that are otherwise easily missed. There are also some screening procedures that are important to include in order to prevent disease.

For Women

Visit your gynaecologist for the following:

Pap smear: To pick up very early signs of cervical cancer. It needs to be repeated once a year for the first three years, then every three years till the age of about 60.

Ultrasound: To visualize the ovaries, which are very hard to examine in a physical exam. Other internal organs like the kidneys and the liver can also be assessed. This is especially important if you have other medical problems like hypertension.

Gynaec examination and **breast** exam.

Mammogram: A mammogram is recommended at age 40. Follow-up mammograms depend on family history and the risk that you are up against.

For Men

A physician's examination for specialized tests like checking the prostate gland.

For Men and Women

A general physician's exam will determine the need for other specialized tests like a colonoscopy, gastroscopy, an MRI (in case of back or joint problems) and will need to be considered on an individual basis depending on the patient's need and complaints. A cardiologist may need to be consulted if your risk for cardiac disease is high.

A stress test to assess the status of your heart and lungs and their ability to cope with exercise is mandatory for anyone just over 40. A stress test, usually evaluated using the Bruce Protocol, is done in a hospital setting. It determines how well your heart and lungs perform when subjected to the stress of exercise. It also assesses the ability of your muscles to tolerate exercise and the added demand for oxygen.

You may occasionally need a pulmonary function test, especially if you are prone to asthma and allergies.

Biochemical tests that may be advised for both men and women

- Haemoglobin (to rule out anemia)
- Thyroid profile (to assess the working of your thyroid gland)
- Blood sugars (to check your body's ability to handle glucose)
- Lipid profile (to check levels of your cholesterol and lipoproteins)
- Serum calcium and vitamin D as and when required
- Other tests to determine risk of heart disease like:
  - Apolipoprotein-A1
  - Homocysteine
  - C-reactive protein or a CRP may need to be considered by your cardiologist when required

YOUR WEIGHT

Your weight is just a number on the scale. It helps to keep this in mind for the correct perspective. You may be very much within the averages according to height-weight charts. That does not imply that you are fit. You may also be over your standard weight and yet be in great physical shape.

The scale, therefore, could be misleading, so keep that in mind and use it with caution. It is a useful parameter to have as one of the (but not the only) markers of your health.

YOUR FAT PERCENTAGE

The ideal way to assess your fat percentage accurately is using the DEXA or body density scan, which is available in hospitals and diagnostic centers. This is an expensive test and is not required for everyone.

Fat percentage can also be evaluated using one of the fat percentage machines that use bioelectrical impedance and are available in a gym setting. They are certainly not 100 per cent accurate but they suffice to give you a rough idea and, more importantly, to keep track of your progress.

There are also several other tests available to evaluate fat percentage such as using girth measurements and/or skin fold thickness. These are simple tests that measure girth using an inch tape or measure the subcutaneous fat (under the skin) using a skin fold caliper.

There are also online sites that will help you measure your fat percentage. Quite frankly, many of them give quite varied results despite entering similar statistics. My advice is to measure yourself at various points on your body (waist, hips, thighs, chest and arms), on a regular basis (say, once a month) to understand where exactly you are losing fat.

YOUR CARDIOVASCULAR FITNESS

ONE-MILE WALK TEST/ROCKPORT WALK TEST

The one-mile walk test assesses your cardiovascular fitness. How well do your heart and lungs function with the demand of exercise?

This test assesses how long you take to walk one mile or 1.6 km. You may initially take over 15 minutes to cover this distance. With time and practice, this time can be improved as your capacity to walk faster improves.

Below is a chart showing a categorization of the timing of a one-mile walk test.[2] You can evaluate where you stand from the chart.

For Women

Age	40–49	50–59	60–69	70+
Excellent	<14.12	<14.42	<15.06	<18.18
Good	14.12–15.06	14.42–15.36	15.06–16.18	18.18–20.00
Average	15.07–16.06	15.37–17.0	16.19–17.30	20.01–21.48
Fair	16.07–17.30	17.01–18.06	17.31–19.12	21.49–24.06
Poor	>17.30	>18.06	>19.12	>24.06

For Men

Age	40–49	50–59	60–69	70+
Excellent	<12.54	<13.24	<14.06	<15.06
Good	13.12–14.06	13.42–14.36	14.06–15.12	15.06–15.48
Average	14.01–14.42	14.25–15.12	15.13–16.18	15.49–18.48
Fair	14.43–15.30	15.13–16.30	16.19–17.18	18.49–20.18
Poor	>15.30	>16.30	>17.18	>20.18

The one-mile walk can also ascertain the ability of your muscles to utilize oxygen well. Your heart rate at the end of the test is noted. A complicated formula is used to calculate Vo2max or Volume of Oxygen uptake, which is nothing but a numerical measurement of your body's ability to consume and utilize oxygen well. The following is a link to a website that can be used to calculate your own cardiovascular fitness level by entering all your values (time you took to walk one mile, your heart rate, age, weight and gender). https://www.exrx.net/Calculators/Rockport

Alternately, other cardiovascular tests like the Step Test, 1.5 Mile Run Test or Cycle Ergometer test may be performed.

> **A simple self-test:** While walking, aim to cover 2 miles or 3.2 km in 30 minutes. Obviously, as the incline is increased, your speed will automatically decrease and you may not be able to cover the same distance.

YOUR STRENGTH

How strong are you? There are several tests to assess the strength of various muscles. Each muscle or group of muscles performs certain actions like lifting, pushing, pulling and so on. You may be relatively strong in one area and weaker in others. You may have strong legs but a weak upper body, for instance.

You could perform about 8–10 basic exercises and identify how much weight you can lift in each of them. From there on, you move forward by increasing the weight you lift to build strength. For example, you could start with a bench-press and identify the weight you are able to lift to complete 10–12 repetitions. This is called your 12 rep max. Repeating the same exercise after four weeks to recognize how much more weight you are able to lift to complete 12 repetitions will indicate to you how much stronger your chest muscles (the pectoralis muscles) have become.

You can use the following chart with a few basic exercises to track your progress:

	Date	Current weight lifted	Next month weight lifted	Following month weight lifted
1.	Bench press/Pushups			
2.	Bent Over Row			
3.	Shoulder Press			
4.	Bicep Curls			
5.	Tricep Extensions			
6.	Ab Crunches			
7.	Leg Extensions			
8.	Leg Curls			
9.	Squats			
10.	Dead Lift			
11.	Calf Raise			

Plank

An important aspect of strength to keep in mind is your core strength. To test core strength, the plank is a great exercise. This tests the strength of your core muscles, namely:

- The deep pelvic muscles
- Abdominals
- The deep and superficial muscles
- The deeper and superficial lower back muscles

How long can you hold the plank? Aim for a minimum of a minute and work upward. (The method of performing the exercise is explained in chapter 14.)

Note down how much weight you can currently lift, how long you can hold the plank for or how many pushups you can do. Reassess yourself after a month. If you choose own-body-weight exercises like squats and pushups, determine how many repetitions you can do with good form and then reassess after a month. This gives you a goal to work towards.

YOUR FLEXIBILITY

SEATED FORWARD BEND

How far can you reach? Use this as a yardstick by which to measure the flexibility of your lower back and hamstrings and work towards improving it.

Different stretches assess different muscles. This is only one of the muscle groups tested. To test yourself more completely, perform all the flexibility exercises shown in chapter 12.

BALANCE

ONE-LEGGED STAND OR UNIPEDAL STANCE TEST (UPST)

Balance is probably one of the most overlooked aspects of fitness. However, it is a fact that your sense of balance progressively decreases with age due to various factors.

To test your balance, try to stand on one leg. If you are able to hold the position for more than a minute, you are doing really well. The ability to balance is controlled by three different systems. Your vision, your proprioception (your sense of your body's position in space), and the vestibular system or the middle ear.

During a study done at the Kyoto University in Japan, they asked older people to balance on one leg and found that those who struggled to balance even for 20 seconds had evidence of cerebral small-vessel disease (SVD) or problems with the tiny vessels in the brain (seen after an MRI), even though they weren't exhibiting any of the classic symptoms. Those with the shortest balance times generally had the lowest mental performance scores. A strong relationship was found between advancing age and declining balance.

It has been found that eyes-open balance stays in the 40-second range until age 50, then begins to drop by about 10 seconds for each decade after 60. Eyes-closed balance is a third of the duration of eyes-open balance and drops by about 4 seconds each decade after age 50.

TO TEST YOURSELF

1. Stand barefoot.
2. Cross your arms over your chest.

3. For the open-eye test, focus on a spot on the wall in front of you at eye level.
4. Raise one leg such that the raised foot is near but not touching the ankle of the standing leg.
5. Start the timer when the foot leaves the ground.
6. Stop the timer when you either 1) uncross your arms 2) move the raised foot away from the standing limb or touch it to the ground 3) Move the weight-bearing foot to maintain balance.
7. Repeat the test the same way with eyes closed; stop the timer if you open your eyes or if you lose your balance as mentioned above.
8. Record the best of three trials.

BALANCE AND CORE STRENGTH

Cross-Legged Sit and Stand Test

This is one test that is being used to determine your ability to age well. It is even said to predict your longevity. A simple assessment of how easily you sit down and rise from a cross-legged, seated position on the floor can tell you a lot about your balance, core strength and coordination.

The sitting-rising test (SRT) involves a score of 0–5 for each movement (sitting and rising), with a combined 10 being the highest score, awarded to those who can sit and rise from a cross-legged position (without uncrossing the legs during the course of the movement) without the help of their hands or knees.

Though it appears simple, it actually gauges a number of important factors, including your lower body strength, flexibility, balance and motor coordination, all of which are relevant to your functional capability and general fitness.

To perform the test, cross your feet and simply sit down on the floor cross-legged, and then stand up in the same cross-legged position, using as little assistance and support from your hands, knees or other body parts as possible. For each body part that you use or touch for support, you lose one point from the possible top score of 10. For instance, if you assist yourself with one hand on the knee or floor for support to sit down and then use a knee and a hand to help you get up, you lose three points for a combined score of 7. Research shows that the numbers strongly correlate with your longevity.

Don't be distressed if you are 40 years old and score a 5. It provides a place from where you can work to improve. This also gives an interesting perspective on the connection between mobility and health, and can provide encouragement for many to get in shape by developing specific areas in their fitness like their balance and core strength.

After undergoing the aforementioned medical and fitness tests, you are ready to start. Use this as a springboard from which to launch yourself into better fitness and wellness.

Set your goals and go for it!

> You can start by setting small goals for yourself like:
> - How much weight you want to lose.
> - How many inches you want to knock off from your waistline.
> - What kind of diet you need to follow.
> - How much you want to improve your flexibility.
> - How much you want to improve your strength.

Your goals should be followed by a detailed account of just how you intend to achieve those goals. For instance, 'I want to lose 10 kilograms' needs to be followed by:

- A plan of just how many days you will do cardio, for how long and at what intensity;
- How many days you intend to train with weights;
- What your diet is going to look like, and so on.

This will give you a roadmap to follow rather than just having a destination in mind with no idea of how to get there. We often set lofty goals for ourselves but fail to understand that to achieve those goals, we have to do the work.

The above are only some of the goals you could set for yourself. You may even want to add how much meditation you want to do in a day, etc. Ideally, you should have a professional fitness consultant guide you through your goals and help you set them and also advise you on how to go about achieving those goals. Then set a time frame in which you intend to achieve those goals and move forward.

Going through the rest of the book will give you a clear idea as to what you need to address and be aware of on your journey to better health and wellness.

three

Hormonal Changes with Age

With age, several hormonal changes occur in both men and women. Most of you will be familiar with the term **menopause** for women. In men, a similar time of change is called **andropause** or **male menopause**.

An awareness of these changes and the resulting change in the outlook or personality of both men and women will go a long way in understanding each other and improving interpersonal relationships.

ANDROPAUSE

In men, the levels of the male hormone testosterone begin to fall starting from the late 40s. A gradual dip in levels of the hormone may be seen even as early as the 30s. Testosterone is the hormone that makes men 'manly' (i.e. the one responsible for facial hair, deep voice, musculature, production of sperm and so on). Unlike menopause, however, andropause does not involve the complete shutdown of the male reproductive system. Men continue to produce sperm (albeit with a lower count) late into their lives. Some of the symptoms of andropause are:

- Lower energy levels
- Depression or sadness

- Decreased motivation
- Fat gain, especially around the belly
- Decreased libido, infertility and erectile dysfunction
- Decreased muscle mass (especially if not training with weights)
- Insomnia and difficulty sleeping
- Gynecomastia or development of breasts
- Decreased bone density or osteoporosis (although to a much lower degree than for women)

All the above symptoms may be the result of falling testosterone levels. The symptoms are more pronounced when long-term unhealthy lifestyle habits like smoking, alcohol, overeating and a lack of exercise accompany the ageing process. These symptoms, however, don't appear quite as dramatically as the symptoms of menopause appear in women. The drop in the levels of testosterone happens much more gradually than the decrease in estrogen in women.

A physician's visit, along with an evaluation of the level of testosterone, is warranted when such symptoms arise. However, the one way to arrest or slow down these symptoms is to manage your lifestyle by including exercise, especially weight training, and a change of diet. Adding other strategies like stress management, meditation, yoga, etc. will combat the symptoms and help you lead a productive, healthier life through your later years. Men could also consider hormone replacement therapy (HRT), but this is a controversial science and will need to be discussed at length with your physician.

MENOPAUSE

The term menopause quite literally means the cessation of one's menstrual cycle. You can be considered menopausal when you don't have a period for the time span of a year. The decreasing level of the female hormone estrogen is responsible for menopause.

This is a strange time of change. As a woman experiencing the onset of menopause, you may be convinced that everyone around you has an attitude problem. You may feel irritable, anxious and confused by what you are experiencing. You may sense a lack of control, both emotionally and physically. Your brain may feel like a sieve as you muddle through your day, forgetting important things. It doesn't help that you feel fat or bloated or that your bra seems not to fit well any more and you are considering buying elasticized pants.

But it's not all bad. This is also a great time of self-realization and acceptance. You become more assertive and less dependent on others' opinions. It's not uncommon for post-menopausal women to experience feeling empowered and poised, partly because of the biological changes that take place in perimenopause and menopause and partly because you have entered a certain phase of your life. Your children have grown older and more independent and you are free to pursue your professional and personal ambitions and go after what you want with a greater sense of independence and confidence. Having a sense of freedom from your periods or the risk of a pregnancy can also be liberating.

The actual progression of menopause, with all the physiological changes and symptoms, takes place over about two to five years, starting a couple of years preceding the menstrual cycles actually ceasing to a year or two after. The actual cessation the menstrual cycles can occur any time between the ages of 45 and 55. Perimenopause may last for a few years during that period. The actual age of menopause is partly determined by your genes. Many women experience it around the same time their mothers did. However, diet and lifestyle also play a role in the onset of menopause.

Menopause occurring before the age of 45 is known as early or **premature menopause** and needs special attention. Premature menopause poses a risk for osteoporosis, heart disease and other consequences of the lack of estrogen at an early age. Hormone replacement therapy is necessary to manage this problem.

SYMPTOMS OF MENOPAUSE

Some or all of the below symptoms may be experienced in varying degrees:

Hot flushes

Hot flushes or hot flashes, as they are sometimes called, are experienced by 75 to 85 per cent of women going through menopause. The frequency may vary from one or two per week to several per hour. Each hot flush may last from a few seconds to even five minutes. They are caused by hormonal changes (primarily the lowering of estrogen) affecting the levels of the neuro-transmitters in the hypothalamus of the brain.

- Neurotransmitters are substances that are important for transmission of signals from one nerve cell (or neuron) in the brain, to another.
- The hypothalamus is a part of the brain responsible for the secretion of various hormones that in turn control heart rate, metabolism, blood pressure, temperature, digestion, satiety, eating, memory, learning, sleep, etc.
- Norepinephrine and serotonin are two neurotransmitters in the brain which when lowered interfere with thermoregulation, or the control of body temperature.

Hot flushes have been described as an intense feeling of heat that seems to arise suddenly and at the most inopportune moments or at night from somewhere deep within the body to bathe the self in heat and sweat, and disappear just as abruptly. It is a most peculiar feeling. It can be quite frightening for those experiencing it for the first time. I remember a patient who would come to me claiming to have frequent panic attacks. In addition to the heat and sweating, she would experience difficulty breathing and had to rush to fling open the window and gasp for air. These hot flushes stop occurring quite naturally. For some they may last many months to years, while others don't experience them at all.

Being aware of them and being psychologically prepared could help matters. Although this is a terribly uncomfortable feeling, seeing the humour in it always helps. Positioning yourself under the fan, monopolizing the air-conditioning or even sticking your head in the fridge are all perfectly acceptable when experiencing flashes.

Hot flushes may be triggered by spicy food, stress, drinking alcohol or coffee, or eating certain kinds of food (like monosodium glutamate or MSG for instance). Or they may come on quite spontaneously.

If the flushes become intolerable, especially if they severely impair sleep, it may be worthwhile talking to your gynaecologist regarding hormone replacement therapy. When administered for a short while to relieve symptoms, it is perfectly customary and safe. If you do go on it, it is, however, important to follow up regularly with your gynaecologist.

Depression

Low moods, sadness and a lack of interest in things that used to be stimulating may all arrive as a compendium with the other symptoms of menopause. This is usually also a passing phase. Counseling, talking to friends or family, breathing, relaxation and meditation help in varying degrees. If uncontrollable, it may be a good idea to meet with a psychiatrist or psychologist to talk things through. Clinical depression may require treatment.

Worsening PMS

Some women experience worsening of their premenstrual syndrome (PMS) symptoms. This may include mood swings, pain, irritability; depression and so on, which come on just prior to the period and disappear once the period starts. The appearance of worsening of the symptoms of PMS may occur for a few months or years prior to the actual onset of menopause.

Frequent mood swings

The exact cause of mood swings is not known. It may be the plummeting estrogen levels or even the presence of hot flushes and other symptoms that just make you physically uncomfortable and irritable. You may suddenly find your family and friends tip-toeing around you and your husband agreeing with almost everything you say!

Irregular or heavy periods

Your cycles become irregular, scanty or heavy as you near your menopausal years. If the bleeding is very heavy, do see your gynaecologist.

Difficulty in sleeping or restless sleep

Sleep appears to be disturbed mainly due to the hot flushes. Depression may compound the problem. The result is worsening fatigue and mood control.

Forgetfulness

On some days, it will seem as though your brain is a sieve. You walk into a room and suddenly wonder why you are there. You open a cupboard and can't remember what you wanted. You leave your car keys in the fridge. You forget names or faces. However, this is temporary and should lift post menopause. Your memory recovers once the menopausal period is over.

Bloating

You may find yourself uncomfortably bloated even after eating small meals. You may also develop strange allergies to foods like lactose, wheat and so on during this time. Be mindful of how your body responds to what you put in it and respect that. Make the necessary changes in your diet.

Discomfort during sex from vaginal dryness

The thinning of the vaginal mucosa leads to some degree of discomfort during sex. Using lubricant jelly will help. You may also develop malodourous discharge.

Decreased libido

There may be a decrease in libido during these years. It is a combination of the moods, thinning mucosa leading to discomfort, hot flushes and the whole gamut of symptoms that you are battling with. Sex may be the last thing on your mind.

Tender breasts

Breasts start to lose fat and become tender or painful. Any discharge, lumps or puckering of skin needs to be addressed immediately by your gynaecologist. Well-supported, good quality inner garments are essential, of course, especially during exercise.

Dry skin and hair

Hair becomes brittle and the skin turns dry. Hair fall, increased wrinkles are signs of aging and may seem very pronounced when the estrogen levels begin to drop. Hopefully, by now you have a good moisturizing and skin care routine in place. You may want to invest in good quality products to keep the skin well hydrated and nourished.

Age spots and sunspots

Your facial skin, which was once smooth and supple, begins to change. Discolouration and redness of the skin and sunspots may occur. The skin becomes thinner and is easily damaged. Using a good sunscreen is helpful in managing these symptoms.

Strange allergies

You may find yourself allergic to things you were not allergic to before. You may develop bloating and discomfort with milk and milk products, for instance. Carbs may make you uncomfortable, especially the processed kind. Your skin may start to react to synthetic fabric. The soap or cream you are accustomed to may unexpectedly cause a reaction. Be mindful of these changes and observe your body's reaction to the things you use.

Loss of muscle mass and tone

It seems as if your flesh has begun to sag! You start to lose muscle pretty much from age 30, if not before, especially if you lead a sedentary life. The area behind your upper arms, your belly and inner thighs are the most affected. This is one reason it is important to build muscle and firm up those sagging arms and legs. This can only be done with weight training.

Accumulation of fat around your middle

Weight gain typically occurs around the midriff. This is, as explained in the chapter on belly fat, the most dangerous kind of fat and needs to be battled at all costs. The combination of muscle loss in the limbs and accumulation of fat around the middle changes the whole body structure of a woman as she ages. It should be addressed using exercise by building the large muscles of the body (the torso, arms and legs). The fat around the middle responds to weight training, cardio and diet. It's not easy, but it is possible.

Gastrointestinal symptoms

You may find that you develop acidity, gastritis, bloating and other gastrointestinal symptoms that you never experienced before on a regular basis. You will have to rethink your food habits and change your menu. Foods that you could earlier tolerate may become intolerable. This is particularly true of processed food. Processed meats, flour, oil and packaged goodies fall in this category.

Urinary incontinence

As the tissues of your vagina and urethra lose elasticity, you may experience frequent, sudden, strong urges to urinate, followed by an involuntary loss of urine (urge incontinence), or a loss of urine with coughing, laughing or lifting (stress incontinence). You may have urinary tract infections more often. Strengthening the pelvic floor muscles with Kegel exercises and using a topical vaginal estrogen may help relieve symptoms of incontinence.
All in all, menopause results in a strange amalgamation of symptoms. Some are so subtle you can't quite be sure if you are actually experiencing them or just imagining them. It doesn't help that you feel bewildered and the people around you are unaware or inconsiderate of what you are going through.

It's important to remember that not everyone experiences the whole range of symptoms and many don't experience anything at all. For some women, the transition into the postmenopausal years is astonishingly smooth.

The Physiology of Menopause

The primary cause of the symptoms during this period is the falling levels of the hormone estrogen that is produced by the ovaries. As we age, ovarian function gradually declines producing eggs less frequently. With dwindling ovarian function, the hormones produced by the ovaries – estrogen and progesterone – begin to drop. The symptoms enumerated above are caused by the fluctuation of these hormones.

In addition to the lowering of estrogen, the levels of androgen, or the male hormone, tend to increase and the working of other hormones like leptin, insulin and thyroid, to name a few, starts to change. All of these changes are responsible for the various physical changes, feelings and emotions experienced by women at this stage.

Dealing with Menopause

The following remedies can help alleviate the stress menopause brings with it:

- **Medical and natural remedies:** Acute symptoms may be managed using hormone replacement therapy, which may be given in the form of tablets, injections or patches. Follow-ups with your gynaecologist are imperative if you go on HRT. HRT is given only for a short term to relieve symptoms. The Women's Health Initiative, or WHI, a long-term study done to determine the heart protective effects of HRT, failed to prove this effect and in fact found estrogen to be detrimental in the long term in some cases.

- **Plant-based therapy:** This kind of therapy, which is often advertised as 'natural and safe', needs a special mention here. While plant-based therapy may be natural, it does not mean that it will have no side effects, especially when taken over a long period of time. Soy and flax seeds, for instance, do have estrogen-like substances (and precursors to estrogen which finally convert to estrogen in the human body), which will eventually produce symptoms and reactions within the body similar to those of estrogen if taken in large quantities. Moreover, several studies done with plant-based supplements, especially soy, have had mixed results in the alleviation of symptoms. It is important, therefore, that you mention to your gynaecologist any plant-based treatments or other medications you are taking.
- **See a therapist:** Going into counseling with a good therapist is useful during this transitional phase. Sometimes, family and friends may not be the best people to help you, in fact, they may find it stressful to do so. Talking things through with a good therapist who is especially skilled at dealing with older women helps put things in perspective.
- **Lifestyle change:** If you haven't already started the process of making the right changes in your life, you should start now. Diet and exercise become critical.
- **Rid yourself of clutter:** This includes clothes you haven't worn in over a year. You may be storing these hoping to get into them one day. All those kitchen gadgets you have collected has led to the creation of a graveyard of gadgets. Identify the ones you will never use and give them away. Emotional clutter, digital clutter even spiritual

clutter has been found to undermine well-being. More on that in chapter 17.
- **Stop processed foods:** Eat more wholesome foods with more vegetables and fruits.
- **Eliminate sugar completely:** The human body does not require added sugar. Besides being highly addictive, sugar is detrimental for the teeth, heart, blood vessels and, of course, weight.
- **Increase protein intake:** This could be plant-based protein like legumes, nuts, seeds and a variety of vegetables. If you are a non-vegetarian, poultry, eggs and meat are high in protein.
- **Take a calcium and omega-3 supplement:** Supplementing calcium helps maintain bone mass to a degree. Foods rich in calcium include leafy vegetables, fish, nuts and dairy. Omega-3 (found in fish oils), meanwhile, helps curtail hot flushes somewhat. Calcium is even more important if you have weaned yourself off dairy as a result of a reaction to dairy products.
- **Start training with weights:** This is one simple change you should include to dramatically improve health and well-being. Osteoporosis (frail bones) and decreasing muscle mass are hallmark symptoms of menopause. Weight training will help prevent both of these problems.
- **Move more:** Our tendency these days is to be sedentary, sit a lot, and watch TV. You may be awkward about venturing out for fear of a hot flush. A low mood may keep you moping at home. Moving more through the day not only improves well-being but also prevents weight gain.
- **Explore various options for cardio:** You may enjoy different kinds of cardio like walking, cycling, aerobics and so on. Sustain regular aerobic activities to ensure you keep the

heart and lungs healthy. You may need to decrease your intensity for a while or even change the kind of cardio that you do to something more fun or motivating. Ensure you maintain cardiovascular activity on a regular basis, however.

- **Do your Kegels:** One of the most embarrassing symptoms of menopause (besides the hot flushes, which can be more annoying than embarrassing), is urinary incontinence or the sudden leakage of urine when you strain, cough, sneeze or just want to go. Strengthening your pelvic floor with Kegel exercises is hugely helpful. This is explained further in chapter 14.
- **Explore the various aspects of wellness:** Don't focus on physical well-being alone. Explore all the aspects of wellness. Develop and nurture more meaningful relationships. Friendships and close connections matter more with age. You should also engage in mindful practices such as meditation, relaxation, massage, yoga, Tai Chi. They are all very useful to stay calm and focused. Improve your creative and intellectual well-being by finding something interesting to learn and do. Learning a new language, taking up a musical instrument and even pottery are great choices.
- **Ask for help:** It's not just about going to see your gynaecologist to be treated for hot flushes. It may be required for you to ask to be excused or take a break at work if you feel quite overwhelmed. Many working women find this hard to do for fear of being judged as weak or inefficient. This is made worse by the fact that we don't really discuss menopausal symptoms openly or feel empathetic towards those going through it.

- **Find the humour:** Finally, do see the humour in it all. Knowing this is a passing phase helps you laugh about it. It also makes it easier for other people to deal with you.

As I mentioned earlier, not all women experience every one of the symptoms. Those that do, do so in varying degrees. Interestingly, those who exercise in a balanced, sensible way, and eat well (by that I mean those who eat healthy, wholesome, non-processed food and are not starving themselves into some misguided ideal size), seem to have either less disconcerting symptoms or are able to manage them better. Perhaps it is the mindfulness that has already been established by individuals practising a healthier lifestyle, or perhaps it is the endorphins that are released during regular exercise that mitigate some of the unpleasant menopausal symptoms. Or perhaps it is the fact that they have better control over their weight that helps them through. Multiple studies examining the association between obesity and menopausal symptoms have shown that women with an elevated body mass index (BMI) report more severe symptoms than women with a healthy BMI and that obese women are at greater risk of depression.

Whatever the reason, regular exercise is certainly beneficial in managing menopause. It helps not only with weight control and menopausal symptoms but also to sustain brain functions.

In a study published in the *Journal of the American Medical Association* (JAMA), it was found that lifestyle concerns and psychosocial factors have an impact on how symptoms of disruptive hormonal imbalance (during menopause, for instance) is perceived. In other words, science has found that if you suffer from stress, especially distress in other areas of your life, it is more likely to show up in the form of negative symptoms in your physical body and more pronounced menopausal symptoms. This is true of physical pain or emotional vulnerability. Negative stress only compounds the sensitivity to the symptoms or the problem.

Women who lead productive, meaningful lives are also less likely to experience severe symptoms of menopause. Or, perhaps, they are able to handle it better.

Both menopause and andropause are phases in one's life that cannot be avoided. If one is privileged to live long enough to go through this time, all one needs is an understanding of the hormonal changes that account for the symptoms and the knowledge that it is only a passing phase. How you deal with it is certainly under your control. Just as adolescence is a phase, so is this. The only difference is that we are older and (hopefully) wiser and, therefore, better capable of handling it. Some of the symptoms may need short-term treatment and your physician can work that out with you. We can, however, mitigate most of the other problems with the choices we make. How much we exercise, what we eat, what we do to actively find ways to lead more purposeful lives, all influence our experience of this phase.

four

Why Can't We 'Just Do It'?

You want to lose weight, you know you need to exercise, you know you need to cut back on the food, alcohol or cigarettes. So why can't you, as the famous Nike ad says, 'Just Do It'? Here's the caveat: while you do need to think about and act on health and wellness, we need to define what the 'it' in 'Just Do It' means. It certainly does not mean crash-dieting, excessive exercise or an obsession with the physical self. What it does mean is a holistic approach towards well-being.

Here are some reasons we are unable to get moving with our goals, or are sometimes unable to set the required goals:

- **We believe it's too late:** In the next chapter, I explain why it's never too late to start a good habit. You may think to yourself, 'What's the point? I am 40, 50, 60, 70 or 90 years and it's too late.' But it isn't. Even starting as late as in your 90s has been found to be helpful.
- **We think we are indestructible:** It is inherent in human nature to believe we are indestructible and can get away with our indulgences. After all, we know of that guy who ate all he wanted, drank habitually, smoked a pack

a day and lived to be 80, right? So, maybe, at the back of our minds, we believe we can be that person too. It's a juvenile and self-indulgent approach to health and wellness, but there it is – a feeling of infallibility.

- **We create the most ingenious excuses for ourselves:** We tell ourselves we are really not *all that* overweight. Just a few pounds that we could very easily be rid of if and when we so desired, which apparently we don't. Or maybe we tell ourselves we only smoke a pack a week, which is not too bad at all, really. Or likely, we convince ourselves we *like* ourselves plump or curvy (never mind the lack of fitness). And then there is the eternal reckoning with age. After all, one is expected to gain weight with age or develop diabetes or any of the other diseases one hears of these days. So it seems perfectly okay that we consume a regular diet of pills and potions, which get us through the day.

- **We blame our bad genes:** Our parents were diabetic; one can't escape that destiny so why even bother to try? The fact is, **genes are not our destiny.** There is a lot we can manipulate in our lifestyle to improve not just our own health, but also the very structure and health of our genes, and even that of our progeny. If that's not an exciting thought, I don't know what is!

- **We are not inspired enough:** This is a strange reason but it is amazingly prevalent. I speak to women who say they really don't see the point of it. Oh yes, staying 'healthy' is all very well, but to what end? They are not inspired to put themselves through the ropes every day in order to feel better or even look a certain way. They think refusing cake is not worth the results it is supposed to produce. Besides, that cake is too delicious to pass up.

I suspect this has more to do with a penchant for self-indulgence and instant gratification than an indifference to the results of a healthier lifestyle, a sort of 'habit' of indolence when it comes to exercise or healthy eating. There is also a social context. Very often, it is the society we live in that influences our lifestyle. Being surrounded by health-conscious people makes one want to attempt to live a healthier life. If one is surrounded by friends and family who make no attempt at regular exercise or if one is faced with unhealthy food choices all the time, it is far more difficult to stay on track. The last reason that one may not feel at all inspired is when one is depressed. While exercise itself is a form of treatment for depression, starting an exercise programme is not easy for someone who suffers from it. Severe clinical depression needs medical treatment. Regular physical exercise is, however, the treatment of choice for low-grade depression, low mood or just 'feeling down'.

▸ **We believe we have more important things to do with our time:** Exercise can wait until we are successful in business, or when your career is well established. It can wait till we get that pay raise. It can wait till we are over this stressful time in our lives. It can wait till the kids get to college. It can wait till the parents or in laws are in better health. There always seems to be something more important to do. The point here is, however, exactly that. There will always be something that appears more important than an hour of what seems to be aimless running or pumping iron. But it is about **finding the time.** You will never become less busy or have more time. You will have to make do with the time you have and manage it better. Sometimes you may not be able to fit in a whole hour but even twenty minutes of some heart-pumping exercise sets the stage for a great day.

There have been times when I have lain in bed thinking maybe today I will skip that walk; after all, I have surgery scheduled in an hour at the hospital and I could do with a lie-in. But I have never regretted getting out of bed, into some warm clothes and getting out into the cold air in Ooty for a morning walk. It is one of the most exhilarating experiences of my day, one that makes it so much more positive and productive.

- **We honestly don't believe we have it in us to stay motivated:** We hear all this talk of 'no pain, no gain', 'stay the course, come what may', 'persistence and dedication are the cornerstones of success', and we think, well, we can't hang in there! I know of clients who come in believing they will falter on motivation. It's almost like a self-fulfilling prophecy. As a result, they get de-motivated at the slightest setback. This is probably a pattern in their lives.

  Women often tell me, 'You have to keep me motivated.' Well, I am not around you all the time to do that, am I? While I can provide inspiration, meet with you at regular intervals, get my trainer to take you through your routines and push you when required, eventually, this is an inside job! The more you tell yourself you are *just* not motivated to exercise, the more likely it is that you won't be!

- **We believe we are too far gone for any kind of redemption:** We are far too overweight, or our health problems are far too advanced for recovery. The truth is that it is almost never too late. I say almost, because on the rare occasion that one has many or all the above problems, it would truly be difficult to make a turnaround.

- **We get easily distracted:** We often start off with good intentions but at the slightest hiccup – whether it is someone catching a cold at home, the arrival of a guest or a change in weather – we tend to slide right off the wagon. We may resume over and over again, but the tendency to slide is almost written into the script. We anticipate our next reprieve from exercise and, sure enough, there it is!

Despite all the possible excuses, I find that most people can be converted, even in extreme cases of ill-adjusted thought process. Some of the excuses may seem very valid to the person concerned and it takes a great deal of persistence, motivation and counselling to help them turn that crucial corner. If you happen to have a great coach, it would indeed be an enormous help not just to teach you exercises and provide dietary instructions, but also to help maintain perspective.

five

Myths and Misconceptions about Your Body after 40

There are a number of myths that permeate the realm of fitness, diet and wellness that are presented as 'solutions' for the various problems one faces as they age.

MYTH 1: 'Fat-burning' foods

Some of the miracle foods that are frequently listed as foods that will help you get slim, as they are 'fat-burning' foods, are: lime juice and honey, green tea, green coffee, spices like cumin and cinnamon, grape fruit, cucumber, yogurt, quinoa, oatmeal, spicy food…and the list goes on.

Here's the thing. Eating a certain types of food cannot and will not help to 'burn fat'. I truly wish it were that easy! In order for fat to be burnt, it has to be used as fuel. Increasing expenditure of energy by moving and exercising more is the only way to do this. Yes, some ingredients like caffeine, spices and garlic increase the rate of metabolism in the body for a brief period of time following their consumption and can lead to a temporary, marginal increase in calorie burn, but this does not amount to much in the long term.

All foods, when consumed, require energy for digestion. This is called the **thermic effect** of food. Some foods, like protein, have a greater thermic effect than others, like simple carbs. Just consuming them, however, will not lead to any significant fat loss.

All the above foods are beneficial by themselves. They have some key nutrients that are important for the proper functioning of the body. They will also help keep your digestive tract healthy by improving the gut microbes and so on. But, they will *not* burn fat.

Lime juice and honey early in the morning is great, especially in hot weather. Neither lime nor honey, however, has the ability to miraculously burn fat. What they could do is limit your intake of tea and coffee with added sugar, thereby limiting calories. As for green tea, the only way it helps you lose fat is if you actually climb that mountain and pick the leaves yourself! Green tea has beneficial antioxidants called catechins, which are known to lower blood pressure and cholesterol and improve brain and heart health, so it is good for you, but drinking copious amounts will not tip the weighing scales in any way. If you ate only grapefruit all day long, there is a good chance you could lose weight, but this is not because of a miraculous property of the fruit itself but a result of the general lowering of calorie intake. When eaten as part of a healthy, balanced diet, all the above mentioned foods can provide great benefits. If they also prevent you from indulging in processed or fast foods with additives and sugar, then they will be even more beneficial and will certainly help you lose fat.

Here's the hard truth – nothing will help you lose fat unless you eat a healthy, balanced diet, exercise regularly and move more through the day. The simplest solution is often the most suitable, especially in the long term, and burning fat to lose weight is accomplished by increasing energy expenditure by moving or exercising more. This often seems rather prosaic and oversimplified, so we feel the innate need to try more fascinating methods to 'burn fat' – and one of them is labelling what we eat as 'fat-burning' foods. It also makes for a great marketing tactic. A label that says 'burns fat' attracts a great deal of attention. Companies that produce and market these products have mastered the art of advertising a convenient solution for something that we desperately want – to lose fat – and they package it beautifully and sell it to us. Take green tea, for instance. The chances of you buying a tin of expensive green tea are infinitely greater if it says 'helps burn fat' on the label as opposed to 'helps improve the brain and heart'. Who wants to improve the brain and prevent the onset of Alzheimer's? Losing pounds is what we want!

The list of diets that include these 'fat-burning' foods is long and impressive. You tend to believe that it is that particular combination of exactly one-and-a-half teaspoon of honey with the juice of exactly two limes is what will result in weight loss. Most of us like to believe in these miracle cures, especially when it comes to weight. It pleases us to think that something beyond our control has led to our weight gain and, therefore, we NEED something extraordinary to help us get rid of the excess baggage. As I explain in the chapter on why we get fat, there certainly are some external factors like food cues and added flavours that drive us to eat more than we need to. The solution is not to be drawn to even more gimmicks, but to understand our drivers and work around them.

The thing to remember is this: **We really don't need other people telling us what to eat. We know what to eat – wholesome healthy food, mostly plants, in moderate quantities!** It's really that simple. Instead of focusing on weight alone, improving health, mood, overall wellness and fitness levels by incorporating a regular, sound exercise programme, a healthy balanced diet (that could very well include all the 'fat-burning' foods), along with the management of stress, sleep and relationships will most certainly bring better, more long-lasting results.

MYTH 2: Exercising to get healthy after you cross 40 is pointless as decline with age is inevitable and weakness sets in.

While some decline in health and fitness with age is inevitable, you can pretty much control how you age through fitness, food and lifestyle changes. Many people are still doing phenomenal things with their bodies at ages 70, 80 and even 90. Weakness results from a lack of muscle strength. Building muscle is the sensible solution to improve strength. 'Frail' is a term commonly used to describe older people. The reason for frailty is loss of muscle, which will certainly cause weakness and prevent you from performing simple daily tasks. The solution is to build muscle. Exercise does not just aid in improving physical well-being but also prevents dementia and physical weakness and improves memory, balance and posture, all of which deteriorate with age.

Your body will most definitely age. It can, however, age gracefully.

MYTH 3: It is unnecessary for slim people to exercise.

This is also a common misconception across ages. There are people who proudly pronounce that they have 'maintained' their weight over the years despite not exercising. Weight on the scale could very well be fat weight. You will most certainly lose muscle mass with every decade that you don't actively train to preserve it. You may, therefore, be the 'same weight' on the scale as you were years ago, but the composition of your body – fat versus muscle – would have undeniably changed for the worse.

Exercise is not only for weight loss. It has so many other benefits for the aging body and mind that it would be sheer foolishness not to include it in your daily routine.

MYTH 4: Once you cross the age of 40, there are many kinds of exercises you should not do as they are not good for you.

While I would never advise anyone starting an exercise programme to go into a fitness regime all guns blazing, I would certainly hope their purpose is to feel fitter and stronger. In order to achieve this you need to build your body's capability, which means you need to challenge yourself as you progress. If you begin with boot camp, HIIT (High-Intensity Interval Training), zumba, running and so on, all of which have a higher impact on your joints, the potential for injury will be very high. If you are already fit, understand your body well and have a strong foundation of strength, then you could most certainly vary your fitness routine with the above kinds of exercise for fun and for a challenge.

If you are a beginner, after going through a basic fitness and medical assessment, you should start a beginners' exercise routine, adding a low-impact activity like cycling or walking and including weight training and yoga so that you cover all the pillars of fitness. With time, you will get stronger. Your muscles will start to grow in size and strength as you build a strong foundation for your fitness. It is important to build strength in your muscles first and then explore other possibilities for cardio. You can then include just about anything you like into the cardio segment of your fitness to vary your routine – HIIT, aerobics, stepper, zumba, and so on.

You don't necessarily NEED to do various different kinds of cardio. All you need is to increase your heart rate. The heart cannot differentiate between muscles working on a run and muscles working to complete a cycling or dance routine. It pumps harder to provide those muscles the oxygen they require to work irrespective of the kind of work the muscles are engaged in.

Anything you hear about a 'miracle workout' that burns more fat is purely a result of the workout being of a higher intensity, which leads to an increased heart rate and number of calories expended. It is not the specific form of exercise (for example, zumba versus cycling) that is responsible. In effect, you can get just as good a workout using your good old bike as you would attending a new-fangled class with a fancy name. Just like a lot of other things in today's world, packaging and marketing play a huge role in how certain things are perceived as being better and more effective than others.

Having said that, adding variety to mitigate boredom is always helpful. So if you are strong and flexible enough to attend a variety of classes and different cardio sessions without injuring yourself (which means you need to be strengthening with weights and stretching simultaneously), do so if it keeps you motivated to continue to exercise.

MYTH 5: Gyms are for people in their 20s and 30s

This is quite untrue. The gym, with its equipment, trainers and safety measures, is the place to go to if you need to be guided and taught the exercises in a safe environment. I often find people trying to do things on their own by watching videos online or reading books and magazines. This is perfectly acceptable if you are already equipped with enough body intelligence to know intuitively if you are doing something wrong. If you are a beginner or haven't bothered to pay attention to just how your body works in the past, it's best you work under a qualified professional until such time that you can manage on your own without injuring yourself. Having said that, do choose a good gym with qualified trainers who understand your requirements and your body.

MYTH 6: As you grow older, you cannot train with weights as you may injure yourself.

Nothing could be further from the truth. Studies done at the University of Navarra in Spain on 90-year-olds who started weight training at that advanced age have found benefits in strength gains. Benefits of weight training include improvement of functional status, health and quality of life among older adults.[3] In fact, weight training is probably the safest form of exercise there is and provides a multitude of benefits. If you haven't started already, do so now!

MYTH 7: People suffering from thyroid-related problems, diabetes, arthritis, and so on, can't/shouldn't exercise.

Exercise is probably the one thing that will help any and all of the problems associated with aging. Lifestyle diseases are not an excuse to avoid exercise. Most of these diseases are better controlled using exercises that help build muscle mass and strength and lose fat. Pain and disability that is associated with arthritis, for instance, can be circumvented through the right exercises.

There are many more related myths that should just be ignored. I urge you to be discerning about the source of information when you read articles and other material on health and wellness. Check with a specialist and then arrive at the best solutions for yourself.

six

It's Never Too Late to Start

Myths, misinformation and the limitations we set on ourselves all come in the way of us living better lives.

I often meet clients who are in quite a bad way physically and emotionally. They may have gained a lot of weight, developed various medical problems and are suffering the consequences. Many feel there is no way out of this sad predicament and almost give up. When one is extremely overweight or has several medical issues (as a result of excess weight or a certain lifestyle) making a change may seem like an insurmountable problem. It is not. There's always a way around everything. It depends on how you approach the problem, and the steps you take to move forward. Some of us truly believe that we are not capable of anything more than what we are currently doing, achieving or the lives we are leading. We imagine this is the most we can do. We may feel overwhelmed, stressed and short on time and energy.

This is a self-fulfilling prophecy. We become what we believe of ourselves. I've seen it happen over and over again to those who, in my opinion, are certainly capable of better health, of being better able to control disease and lead better quality lives. The truth is, we are far more remarkable and capable than we think we are, and this applies to our ability to get fit and strong just as it does to anything else.

So here are a few winning strategies to remember as you prepare to make the necessary changes in order to be strong and healthy for your life ahead at any point in time.

Perspective is everything

Instead of saying 'no pain, no gain', **a slower, more cautious approach** for someone who is already apprehensive about the various pitfalls of exercise may be more sensible.

Quality trumps quantity

Understanding that 'quality of life' is as important, if not more important than longevity, may make sense to someone who feels indestructible. How well you live and enjoy your life is closely related to your health and fitness levels. It's not just about longevity, but also about quality living.

Thoughts don't burn calories

Just *thinking a*bout knocking off the 'few extra pounds' won't cut it. We actually have to do the work.

It's not just about weight

It's perfectly all right to be comfortable with our weight. Being slightly overweight is not the problem, lack of exercise and poor nutrition is. So, defocussing from weight on the scale to a better, healthier body may be a way of working around one's defensiveness about weight.

Growing fat with age is not okay

Age does slow down one's metabolism. This is particularly true if one does not consciously make an effort to maintain and increase muscle mass through weight training while younger.

But excessive weight gain with age is certainly not a given. There are ways of curtailing and managing that weight gain and, of course, it takes effort.

Your lifestyle molds your life

Epigenetics is a wonderful new field that studies how our lifestyle molds our lives. An appropriate lifestyle modification can even change the proclivity for a disease such as diabetes. The amazing thing is this happens fairly quickly once the change is implemented.

Studies have shown that the body adapts to better lifestyle habits and begins to change its very molecular structure in even as short a time as six weeks.

Find the inspiration

I can understand the 'not inspired enough' argument. Habits are hard to break. If you are used to living a certain way, eating a certain way and not putting your physical body through any kind of rigorous routine, it could be hard to see the upside of changing those habits. I have had the opportunity of working with women who seem on the face of it, not to want to be inspired to make a change. Yet, this is so just on the surface, because **I have found that they most often want to find the inspiration at some deep level**, even though they may not acknowledge it. Once they do, they are amazed not just at what such a lifestyle change can do for their bodies, but also for their minds and emotional landscape. They may or may not achieve phenomenal bodies or reach incredible levels of fitness (although some do), but many do stay on track, gaining comfort in their newfound discipline.

Here's the thing, though – if you are looking for inspiration from outside, chances are even if you find it in someone or something in the initial stages (to get you started, for instance), unless you start to find it from within yourself at some point, relapses are common. No one can continue to inspire you indefinitely. Not even your coach/trainer. You have to feel it from within to make a lifestyle change.

The interesting thing is this is exactly what exercise does for you. Random spells of exercise cannot produce this level of motivation; in fact, it can be quite counter-productive in that it can lead to injury, pain and then, of course, the return to a feeling of 'it's just not worth it!'. Regular exercise, however, makes you feel more positive and confident about yourself from the inside. **It is an amazingly self-perpetuating model of behaviour.** So while it may seem absurd that you would want to go to a gym or for a run or any other form of exercise to go through what *appears* to be a torturous ordeal for the body, it is that very thing that keeps you going back. You need to, however, **do it often enough and frequently enough** to avail of this benefit. It needs to become a habit.

Moderation is key

Here's the thing. One does need to be disciplined, but that does not necessarily mean a highly restrictive or almost punishing lifestyle. We do, after all, also need to enjoy the various pleasures life has to offer. The key is moderation.

In the initial stages, when you have a lot of weight to lose, it requires a great deal of change and adjustment in various small things through the day including how you shop, what you buy, how often you eat out or order in, understanding food and so on. As the weight comes off and you start to get fitter and your understanding of food and health improves, the whole process becomes easier.

Take it slow

In the initial stages, take it slow. For instance, start walking just five minutes a day for the first week. Then increase it to 10 minutes the following week, 15 the next and so on, until you can walk about 30 to 40 minutes a day on a regular basis. It doesn't matter that your neighbour is running a marathon or the gym bunny is sprinting on her treadmill. You have to listen to your own body and go easy.

The same holds for weight training. Learn all the exercises first using light weights so the chances of injury are less. Then gradually move up to lifting heavier weights as you start to feel stronger and more confident.

Don't go to a yoga class that is for advanced students where everyone seems to be bending themselves into pretzels with ease. It can be very intimidating. Once again, start with beginner poses that gently push your body to becoming more flexible. Learn the breathing, which is essentially the most important part of yoga. Once you begin to get more comfortable with the routines, move forward.

Go to a qualified professional

This is probably the most important aspect of training. Go to someone who knows the human body, understands your particular problems and is eager to listen to you and help you deal with them. A cookie-cutter approach will not work.

I know there are a lot of 'qualified' trainers out there who probably know how to perform an exercise and how to avoid injury, but the question to ask is whether that particular exercise is the safest and best for you? Has he/she taken into consideration that you may have high blood pressure or diabetes? Is he/she aware you have had surgery in the past?

The other thing to consider is that our priorities change with age. Or rather, they should. While exercising to keep looking good is a great way to persist, a greater emphasis needs to be placed on the *performance of the body* in ways that will benefit or affect us as we grow older.

Don't look for a quick fix

Most people want and expect a quick-fix solution to their problem. Unfortunately, problems like weight, lifestyle change and food are not easily solved. It's quite unlike taking a course of antibiotics for an infection. Sustainable weight loss and improved health and well-being cannot be achieved with a short course of medicines or a fad diet for a couple of weeks.

This is particularly true if you are a beginner, are extremely overweight or have other medical problems. Most fads have general principles that may not be applicable to your body. Fad diets do cause rapid weight loss. This kind of weight loss does not last, however, and you may well not be able to sustain the rigorous rules involved with the diet.

Be patient with yourself

It's easy to **want** to lose 10 kilos in a month. But is that advisable? Is it good for your body? Is it feasible in the long run? Can such weight loss be sustained over time?

If you have spent much of your life being sedentary then you will have to respect your body. It cannot become athletic overnight. With patience, however, you can become extremely fit, lean and healthy, and reverse many of your medical problems like high blood pressure and diabetes once you have lost the extra weight and become fitter.

Be mindful of your body

The most important person in this whole journey to a better, fitter self is **you**. Only **you** can listen to the signals your body sends you. Only **you** can tell if you are truly hungry or are eating because of anxiety. Only **you** can identify if the workout prescribed is too much or too easy. Most importantly, only **you** can be completely honest with **yourself**.

Be consistent

Consistency is the holy grail of wellness. You cannot do something for a few days or weeks and then stop or become highly inconsistent with it and expect results. Daily dedication to what you commit to do is critical.

I see this happen quite often. People start quite enthusiastically. Then they have a slight hiccup, like a travel schedule or additional work for a day or two, and then, instead of getting right back on the wagon, they stop altogether.

While there may be some setback with short spells of inconsistency, you should not be completely derailed. So get back to the exercise and diet as soon as you can and stay with it.

Find the right motivating partners

You do need encouragement and motivation. Find the right fitness buddies to hang out with. They should be able to motivate and not discourage you.

I recall a client who started exercising with us and was fairly regular and succeeded in losing a lot of weight. Then she moved to the US to pursue her education. She mailed me from there saying she had found a fabulous running partner and would train regularly with her.

A few months later when we had a Skype chat, she said she had stopped exercising altogether. Her running partner apparently had been so good that this poor girl couldn't keep up. As a result, instead of stepping back and working to her capacity, or perhaps finding someone else to run with, she stopped completely.

'There's no way I can run as much as her,' she said to me. But the point is, she didn't have to!

You can train at your own pace. The fitness buddy you choose to train with has to motivate you to push your boundaries and keep you company. Sometimes it's fun to have someone to train with. Other times you may want to work on your fitness on your own. You cannot hold the other person responsible for your success or failure.

It's the same with a fitness class. Find one that motivates you enough to keep improving. It has to have the right balance of careful instruction and the gentle push in the right direction.

And, finally, be kind to yourself

While you need to push yourself, improve, lose weight, get fitter and so on, it's also important to be kind to your body. Understand that many of your own life choices may have gotten you to this place in your life. Respect your body enough to not abuse it with punishing routines you cannot tolerate or with diets that almost kill you. Being kind to yourself also means continuing to do everything you can to improve your state of well-being.

PART II

UNDERSTANDING YOUR BODY AFTER 40 AND TAKING CARE OF IT

seven

How and Why We Gain Weight

As we age, we notice our bodies showing signs of something new and strange. Even those of us who have exercised for the most part of our lives and eaten sensibly find, to our utter horror, that fat settles on our tummies and waist!

So is weight gain inevitable with age?

For many people it is. If you are extremely cautious about your habits (exercise, food and lifestyle) then it can be controlled to a large extent. That's not to say you will weigh and look exactly the same as you did in your 20s. Clearly that's not feasible. Your body and mind see several changes as they age, and one such change is the accumulation of fat.

In this chapter, we will explore how and why this happens, and at the end I will explain some of the things one can consciously do to circumvent weight gain and build a better body with age.

But, let us first begin with what we put into our body.

HOW IS EATING CONTROLLED?

Did you know that how much we eat, what we eat and when we eat is pretty much controlled by the brain? The brain initially drives us to eat for survival. We need the energy and so we consume calories in the form of food. Once our hunger is satisfied and our survival needs are met, the stimulus to eat stops. A newborn baby will feed only until it is full. Once its stomach is full and the hunger signal is turned off, it stops feeding. As we grow older, we believe that food can satisfy us in many other ways besides just satisfying our hunger. Even children learn this very early in life when they are given too much to eat in too many varieties. Eating, thus, becomes more than just a hunger-satisfying survival strategy.

Ask yourself:

- When was the last time you were truly hungry?
- Do you eat indiscriminately? If so, why?
- Do you eat to assuage hunger or do you eat out of habit?

The Different Kinds of Eating

There are two kinds of eating we participate in: **homeostatic eating** and **non-homeostatic eating.**

Homeostatic Eating

Homeostatic eating is controlled by **real** hunger. The body identifies hunger (much like our internal thermostat identifies our body temperature), and initiates eating behaviour.

When we eat, the sensors in our mouth, stomach and intestines measure the volume and composition of what we eat. Hence, homeostatic eating is controlled by:

- Stretch receptors in the stomach and intestines that send messages to the brain to signal fullness.
- Certain peptides released in the intestines that send signals to the brain stem through a nerve called the vagus nerve to tell the brain what *kind* of food was eaten.

- The hormone **dopamine** that is released in the brain in response to food intake.

All of this enables the calories, palatability and energy density of the food to be noted and registered by the brain. The brain stem sets your level of fullness, which usually remains stable. This means that most people have a standard amount of food they eat after which they tend to feel full and stop eating. If you continue to overeat over long periods of time, this **set point for the level of fullness** is altered and you can continue to eat large quantities of food.

Non-homeostatic Eating

Non-homeostatic eating, on the other hand, is what most of us are quite accustomed to. When we eat for various reasons other than hunger, such as boredom, stress, anxiety, depression, social pressure and also for fun and celebration at social occasions, it is called non-homeostatic eating.

Non-homeostatic eating is rarely controlled.

It's clear, therefore, that if it were only hunger that you were trying to appease, you would stop eating as soon as you were full. We know, however, that there are several other factors behind our eating far more than is required. By now, you may have figured out what drives you to indulge in that late-night binge. It may be anxiety, loneliness or stress and pressure. **Whatever the reason, once you identify the connection, it will be possible for you to relearn how you deal with it.** If you become much more 'mindful' of your eating habits, and manage your emotions with the appropriate response (other than eating), you can prevent overeating. This is the fundamental strategy for preventing non-homeostatic eating.

Food and Our Brain

The **hypothalamus**, which is a tiny almond-shaped structure in our primitive brain, controls our body temperature, sleep, sexual urges, hunger and mood. Certain peptides released from the hypothalamus regulate our food intake and are responsible for body fat. The brain tells us when we are 'full' – not only from the volume of food we consume, but also from the level of satiety or satisfaction the particular food provides. It signals us to eat more or less. It also determines what kind of foods we reach for.

We appear to have a preference for **calorie-dense** food, which seems to be the result of evolution. Let me explain. Food that packs more calories per unit volume is called a calorie-dense food. For instance, pizza would certainly be more calorie-dense than broccoli (volume for volume). Humans seem to be naturally drawn to such food. We clearly prefer a slice of pizza and a bar of chocolate to a bowl of broccoli, don't we?

In talks I give on this topic, when I show pictures of slices of pizza, chocolate, dessert, cheesy pasta, yummy biryani and so on, instead of a bowl of fresh green salad, and ask the question, 'Which would you most likely choose?', most of the audience chooses the former, though some do opt for the latter. Now, this is a choice they make after just a visual representation of these foods. So you can well imagine what we would choose when actually faced with the various kinds of food. Clearly, there is a reason why most people tend to veer towards tasty, calorie-dense food.

You see, our ancestors, the hunter-gatherers, hunted for food, and sometimes went days without a kill or finding berries or plants to eat, depending on their skills as hunters. Their brain, therefore, was wired to search for and be attracted to calorie-dense food. This enabled them to survive during the longer periods of scarcity.

This hardwiring of our ancestral brain has an influence on how we reach for calorie-dense food today. This would mean foods rich in fats, starch, salt, sugar and protein, like pizza, chips, fried food, creamy pastas, and so on. The difference, of course, is that there is an abundance of such food available to us at any given time today so there is no question of starvation, at least not for those of us fighting weight gain! We can eat as much calorie-dense food as we choose, whenever we choose – and that's what we do. Our ancestors did not have additives, flavouring, colouring or preservatives added to their calorie-dense food. Food then was limited but fresh and came straight from nature. Our ancestors were also far more physically active than we choose to be today.

Research has shown that our hunter-gatherer ancestors searched for ripe fruit with a sweet taste, which provided instant energy.[4] Fruit provides not only calories, but the necessary vitamins and minerals, and this was perhaps innately recognized. This has been shown to be true even today as we find people of any age seem to prefer sweet foods over others. Human beings inherently seem to have a tendency to be attracted to sweet, high fat, calorie-laden foods. While this may be true, the environment we live in and the food we are repeatedly exposed to in our early lives greatly influence our eating habits as we grow older.

If you are a parent, you have the responsibility of feeding your children. This means preparing different kinds of meals that appeal to them. This is a huge window of opportunity to educate and influence children on how to eat. A home environment where parents are consistently conscious of consuming plenty of vegetables, some fruit, legumes and unprocessed foods enables kids to imbibe that as a part of their lifestyle. Their taste buds can be educated at a young age to actually like these foods.

I've often heard the excuse, 'But the kids will never go for that (vegetables), they need sweets, rice, chips, etc.' But this is not wholly true. In reality, your child's preferences depend on:

1. What you train their palates to enjoy.
2. How you (the parents) view food and what you eat.
3. How strongly you (the parents) feel about the food that is served.

There are plenty of dishes made with vegetables and unprocessed foods that are absolutely delicious. 'Treats' can remain just that – an occasional indulgence, both for you and your family. Ordering in or eating out at restaurants does not need to be a habit and when you do it, making conscious choices about healthier options should become the default setting.

However, it's never too late to change your food habits. You can programme your taste buds as you create habits for yourself. If you insist on eating a sugary treat after every meal, your palate becomes accustomed to enjoying that flavour and your brain expects to eat that sweet after every meal. It becomes an ingrained habit that you then proceed to make a part of your lifestyle, one 'that you just can't do without'. To undo such habits, you may be required to completely abstain (like quitting cold turkey) to rewire the brain. Abstaining for months, even a year is required for the brain to actually 'forget' that gratification you believed you experienced from that treat.

You may then say, why would I deprive myself of that treat if I enjoy it so much? Why can't I eat what I like? After all, life is short...and so on and so forth. I have sat through many such conversations. That's a choice you make. If you do decide you want to make the change, then the amazing result of abstaining is an actual change of preference for the kind of food you enjoy eating. You actually stop enjoying a sweet indulgence after every single meal. You may enjoy small portions occasionally, but it certainly is not at the top of your list of 'must eats'. This happens once you are past the initial struggle of abstinence.

How Is Our Environment Responsible for Our Weight?

Added to the hardwiring in our brain, advancement in **food science and technology** has enabled the extremely clever manipulation of many foods that are mass-produced and marketed.

It all started back when women started to go out to work in the 1960s in the West and had little time to cook for the family. This brought with it the inevitable ideas of neglect and guilt that women encounter when dividing their time between their own interests and the family's. Big food companies stepped in at this very opportune moment to say, 'Oh hey, we'll help you, don't worry. You go to work, we will make ready-to-eat, reheatable dinners and lunches for you.'

At first, this appeared to be a blessing. Except that it wasn't. In country after country, we have now become used to buying ready-to-cook dishes so we can save time on cooking. Sure, it's easy and convenient. But the fact is that the dishes are also loaded with preservatives, sugar, salt and added flavours (the names of most of which we cannot even pronounce). When the ingredient list in a packaged dish is as long as a laundry list, you've got to wonder what's in it.

Ready-to-eat food has to be flavour-enhanced and what exactly is added is anybody's guess. Salt, sugar, corn starch, high fructose corn syrup, additives and flavourings are included in such foods to enhance flavour. Flavour enhancement has one end goal – to make the food irresistible. Food companies are hugely successful at that. Who doesn't love the wonderful taste and texture of the cereal we empty into our bowls with all those nuts and sweet bits of flavour? What about those sinfully rich, chocolate-filled cookies? Who doesn't relish conveniently emptying a can of admittedly delicious food to be heated and eaten with none of the labour of cooking involved? Added to this, these ingredients also give the foods an **addictive quality**. Do you see why we can't stop at just one chip, as the ad for Pringles rightly says? You really can't, not because you are devoid of will power, as one is likely to believe, but because the food itself is addictive.

Those who largely depend on packaged, commercially-prepared food are at the mercy of the food companies. The ingredient list at the back of any package is enough to frighten any biochemist. Not only do you need a magnifying glass to read it, but when you do manage to decipher the strange words, they are also mostly incomprehensible. Quite honestly, some of it is not even food! There are hundreds of such additives that are added in packaged, processed foods. Some of them are:

- Food colouring;
- HFCS (high fructose corn syrup) and aspartame, used to sweeten foods (which may conveniently be labelled 'no sugar added');
- MSG or mono sodium glutamate that imparts the 'umami' or meaty taste to foods to enhance flavour;
- Sodium benzoate, used as a food preservative;
- Sodium nitrite, used for curing meat;
- Trans fats, seen in 'partially hydrogenated oils' or vegetable fats, to which hydrogen has been added during the manufacturing process. Trans fats are typically found in commercially baked and deep fried foods, margarine and vegetable shortening. Small amounts of trans fats are also naturally found in animal foods.

- BHA and BHT (E320) or butylated hydroxyanisole and butylated hydroxytoluene are preservatives found in cereals, chewing gum, packaged potato chips, candy and jello. They are used to retain colour and flavour;
- Sulphur dioxide (E220), found in beer, soft drinks, juices, wine and vinegar;
- Potassium bromate, added to white flour to add volume while making bread, rolls etc.

While choosing what to eat, it, therefore, becomes incredibly important to watch out for **highly palatable and addictive food**. Added sugars, salts, monosodium glutamate, while adding flavour, also make it difficult for us to stop eating.

The reason so many people overeat is because food is easily acceptable, available and affordable.

- **Acceptable** because one hardly raises an eyebrow when someone piles his/her plate or indulges in a second and third helping. Unlike alcohol or drugs, eating large quantities of food is completely acceptable in society.
- Packaged food is so easily **available**. Even small supermarkets stock an unimaginable array of foods, especially those with long shelf-lives.
- Food companies have also made food very **affordable**. This is especially true of processed, packaged food. Unprocessed foods at good quality restaurants or foods made from scratch will be more expensive, because the ingredients cost more and there is more effort involved in the making of the dish.

We seem, therefore, to be struggling against everything around us. Advertisements scream for our attention. We are reminded of delicious easy-to-buy, cheap food at every street corner. The supermarkets are filled with things we can stock up on for a rainy day – except that it doesn't have to rain, does it?

The Role of Society, Family and Friends

Depending on where we live and with whom we associate, we either tend to either focus a great deal on body size and appearance or not. Families that consider it completely acceptable to be overweight tend to encourage indulgence on good food, drink and a sedentary lifestyle.

Food habits develop from what we learn to eat from our families. Certain kinds of food become more acceptable, and indeed preferable, depending on what we are accustomed to. Children who grow up in families that focus on plenty of vegetables, legumes and freshly-made food, and eat in smaller quantities, are encouraged to do the same. Similarly, if packaged, take-away or very rich food is the norm at family dinners, the offspring will think nothing of continuing with the habit as they move out to make homes of their own.

When young people start living away from their family, pressures of work and time may make cooking every day more difficult and less appealing. This is when old habits kick in. An extra effort to eat healthy comes more naturally to those who are familiar with it.

Peer pressure can work both ways. If all your peers are lean and watch their weight, it's likely you will focus on your weight too. Exercise myths and fad diets are also perpetuated through societal pressure.

Be aware of these roles of society, family and friends. They are a great influence on how we lead our lives.

The Role of Food Cues

We like to believe we are in complete control of our decisions regarding our food choices. Unknown to us, however, subtle food cues in our environment encourage us to eat more or make unhealthy choices. Here are some food cues we need to be aware of.

Advertising: The most obvious, of course, is **advertising**. Ever been in a situation where you are watching a perfectly boring late-night movie on TV after a satiating dinner and during the commercial break an enticing ad for an ice cream brand comes on? Your mind is instantly drawn to your freezer where you had stored a tub of your favourite ice cream that you had completely forgotten about. Advertisements are meant to seduce you into believing you need that particular food right away. So you head straight to your fridge for a midnight snack. Picture driving down a highway, not really hungry, and you see a huge billboard for 'freshly baked bread and pastries' or a 'juicy burger' or any number of mouth-watering delicacies. How likely are you to stop and buy something?

Placement of items in a grocery store: Processed, packaged food is usually placed in the middle aisles of a store while the fresh, whole foods are placed along the periphery. Sweets and chocolates are often placed near the checkout counter and, if you notice, may even be at a child's eye-level. When you are waiting at the checkout in that never-ending queue, your child may be restless and insist on that candy bar. If you refuse, he or she threatens a tantrum and it is likely that you cave in. Those things are placed there deliberately for this very reason.

The sound and smell of food: In an experiment by Professor Brian Wansink, a researcher of consumer behaviour and nutritional science and the director of the Cornell Food and Brand Lab at Cornell University in the United States, showed that people tend to eat more when they are exposed to other people eating. Just the sound and smell of food and it being prepared or eaten is enough to trigger such behaviour, even if you are not hungry.

The colour and size of your plate or bowl, and lighting in a restaurant: The ambience in which food is served to you plays a role in how much you eat. Fast food restaurants are deliberately painted in bright colours to stimulate hunger, while sober colours and low lighting soothe the brain, causing you to eat slower and in smaller quantities. The **size of your plate** determines how much you eat. A larger plate encourages you to pile on more food. In another experiment, called the 'Bottomless bowl experiment', Professor Wansink showed that when research subjects were given self-refilling bowls (the soup bowls refilled slowly and imperceptibly without the participants noticing), they tended to consume more soup than those eating from normal soup bowls. However, despite consuming up to 73 per cent more, they did not believe they had consumed more, nor did they perceive themselves as more sated than those eating from normal bowls.

A larger variety of food being served: A buffet encourages you to eat more even if you take only a small helping of each dish you want to sample. A buffet, therefore, is a recipe for an overeating disaster.

The Role of the Workplace Environment

In a working environment, you have to either depend on food from the canteen at the workplace or carry your own food. The kind of food available in most canteens is definitely not of very high quality or healthy.

When I talk to corporates regarding weight issues and point out that the available food in the workplace has to encourage healthy eating, I am always told, 'But this is what everyone wants.' Perhaps many or most employees want to eat deep fried, refined or processed, taste-enhanced food. But today, many also want the option of eating healthy and that should be accounted for. In fact, it should be mandatory in all companies to provide such food options for employees. The health of the employee is critical for the company, after all. Some corporates are certainly making inroads to better the health of their employees. They even ask about the necessary changes to be made in their canteen. This invariably happens only when the philosophy of the company and the senior management truly centres around better health of their employees.

How Are Our Hormones Responsible for Our Eating Behaviour?

There are several hormones involved in the eating process. The most important of these are:

- Leptin, which causes us to stop eating and controls long-term fat accumulation.
- Ghrelin, which induces short-term hunger and is secreted from the stomach.
- Dopamine, which is secreted in the brain to create the motivation to eat and is particularly associated with the learned behaviour to be attracted to a certain kind of food.
- Insulin, which is secreted from the pancreas following a glucose-rich meal to control blood sugar and direct it to the liver or muscle.

- Estrogen, which is responsible for our moods and also sensitizes the brain to other hormones.

Leptin

Of the above, leptin could possibly be one of the most important hormones that control eating and fat storage in our bodies. This hormone is released from fat cells. The amount of leptin secreted depends on the amount of fat cells we have.

The increase in fat cells leads to an increase in the secretion of leptin, which sends a signal to brain that says that the fat stores are adequate and eating can now stop.

In those who start to accumulate fat, this signalling seems to go awry. The brain appears to become resistant to leptin. In some people, even large quantities of the hormone released from fat stores seem unable to elicit the appropriate response to stop eating. The individual becomes insensitive to leptin signalling and continues to eat. Obese individuals may be leptin resistant and, alternatively, leptin resistance leads to obesity.

The factors that increase leptin resistance are:

- High-calorie intake for prolonged periods of time.
- Low-grade inflammation in parts of the brain that recognize leptin (possibly as a result of high-fat, processed meals).
- Certain drugs like antipsychotics.
- A very gradual increase in fat mass over a period of time increasing the body's 'set point' of leptin sensitivity and fat accumulation.

Estrogen

The all-important female hormone estrogen has a significant role to play in the maintenance of our weight. As mentioned in an earlier chapter, the level of estrogen begins to drop in the female body from the early 40s, and sometimes even in the late 30s. Estrogen serves some very important functions as far as weight is concerned.

- It sensitizes the brain to the hormone leptin, which is important in the control of fat accumulation.
- It is important for mood and well-being. Mood swings are notorious precursors to binge-eating behaviour which, in turn, leads to weight gain.
- It is important for good quality sleep. As you will read in the chapter on sleep, lack of sleep leads to the likelihood of overeating, eating indiscriminately and not being able to exercise due to the accompanying fatigue.
- Estrogen is also important for our body's sensitivity to the hormone insulin, which manages our blood sugars. Insulin resistance and diabetes increases with age, more so when one is overweight.

Dopamine

This is the hormone that triggers reward-seeking behaviour. It is involved in learning and motivation. It is connected intimately with food consumption, social connections, physical comfort and parenting.

When we eat certain kinds of food (hyper-palatable foods with starch, sugar, salt, fat and other added flavourings), the hormone dopamine is released in the brain. It encourages the brain to remember the taste, smell, sight, flavour and texture of the preferred food, such as a pizza or chips. This information is saved for later referral. When exposed to even the sight or smell of that particular food at a later date, dopamine is released in the brain to motivate us to seek out that food that provides the reward, which is the temporary pleasure of eating it. Picture driving past your favourite pizza joint. Just the memory of a pizza eaten earlier that week or month is sufficient to make you crave the experience again.

To forget this reward-seeking behaviour then, we need to break the cycle of the memory of the food. Completely abstaining from hyper-palatable foods as a lifestyle is the only way to unlearn this behaviour. It is similar to stopping smoking or quitting any other addictive substance. The addiction lies in memory recall. Refrain from eating these addictive foods for long enough and you actually forget the flavour and addiction.

How Can We Eat and Still Stay Lean?

The person who cooks or plans the meals for the family is called the **'nutritional gatekeeper'** of the family. This word was coined as far back as 1945. This person, usually but not always the woman of the house, has the colossal responsibility of the health of the entire family. There is much she or he can do to control what goes into the meals prepared. Cooking for others and yourself should be a well-thought-out effort.

Healthy food doesn't necessarily have to be unpalatable or inedible. Wholesome food with the right amounts of protein and good quality fat is highly satiating. The key is to find the right balance. Fortunately, the custom of cooking from scratch has not completely disappeared from our country. We still largely eat and believe in eating home-cooked meals.

If one is ordering in, it makes a lot of sense to order from places that use high-quality ingredients and are conscious of food science, rather than from a fast-food outlet. Instead of buying ready-to-eat, packaged food, it is far better, for instance, to order from home chefs who have now sprung up in many cities in India. Having sampled dishes from various friends who have such businesses I know this is a great option. Many of them put in a lot of effort into the kind of ingredients that go into their dishes, providing healthy choices for their patrons.

So What Is the Solution?

After reading the chapter this far you may think, so what's the point of even trying to prevent weight gain? Everything seems stacked against you. Your brain is hardwired to eat high-calorie food, your hormones play all kinds of games, and the environment you live in isn't exactly supportive of a healthy lifestyle.

Don't lose heart! There are ways to circumvent these problems – and that's what the next chapter is all about.

eight

Turn Your Plate Around

The question of what one should eat and how they should choose the right food categories for their health are uppermost in the minds of most people I meet.

WHAT IS THE HEALTHIEST DIET FOR YOU?

The word 'diet' itself conjures up thoughts of restriction, elimination and struggle. Instead of focusing on what you can't eat, read on to understand what you *can* eat.

Many of you may have read the currently raging debates about cholesterol levels, statins, high-fat diets, paleo, keto, and so on, and that may have left you quite confused. In my practice, the one question I seem to run into the most often is: What do I eat? And, related to this: Should I not eat carbs? What about fats? Which are the high-protein foods that are meant for me?

Until now, the only diet proven to actually reverse heart disease is the Whole-Food Plant-based Diet as researched and documented by Dr Dean Ornish in his landmark study that was published in *The Lancet* journal in 1990. He showed that a Whole-Food Plant-based Diet actually reversed heart disease.

In this study, he also introduced exercise and meditation, which would certainly have played a role in the reversal of heart disease. Such a diet would comprise of foods that are primarily plant-based (vegetables, fruits, seeds, nuts and whole grains) with the complete elimination of all animal products like meat, fish, eggs, dairy and processed food. It is essentially a vegan diet but the stress is on whole-food plant-based foods.

'Vegan' could mean anything from potato chips to samosas, so simply following a vegan diet is no indication of just how healthy it is. It is indeed possible to eat a very unhealthy vegan diet. According to Dr Ornish's study, the stress needs to be on plant-based whole foods with a very low percentage of fat (less than 10 per cent).

Many Indians are vegetarian or even vegan. So, you will ask, how do we account for the high incidence of heart disease and diabetes in our country? The reason lies in the huge volumes of refined carbs and the excessive quantities of fat we consume in the form of refined vegetable oils. In addition to this, we have also adopted the fast food and junk food culture of the West, which worsens the situation.

The question, then, is what kind of diet should you follow.

I think Michael Pollan, the author of *The Omnivore's Dilemma*, *Cooked* and many other brilliant books, summed it up very well when he said, 'Eat food, not too much, mostly plants.' I would add to that by saying, 'Eat *whole* foods, not too much, mostly plants.'

What are Whole Foods?

Whole foods are foods that are unrefined and unprocessed, foods that are fresh and real and not a mixture of unrecognizable ingredients put together cleverly, enhanced with flavours to make them more addictive and sold in packages. Vegetables, fruits, seeds, nuts, whole grains and legumes all come under this category. Animal products can be whole foods too as long as they are not processed in any manner. For example, it is far better to eat free-range chicken to a chicken sausage. Cold cut meats, smoked meat, cured meat, corned beef are other examples of processed meats.

Here is a very rough guide to what an average person who exercises could eat. You need to personalize this, however, based on your lifestyle, weight, gender and activity levels.

Food group	Examples	Quantities/day
Bread/cereal/grain/starch	Cereal, rice, wheat, millets, ragi, tapioca, potato, or any product made from the above.	Keep to the minimum. Two to four servings in a day is plenty. One serving would be half a cup of any of the cooked cereal/rice/wheat/millets or a small-to-medium potato.
Vegetables	Any vegetable except potato and corn, which belong to the bread/cereal group.	As much as you want in a day. Make sure you include greens.
Fruit	Any fruit. Eat a variety of them.	2 to 4 fresh fruits a day.

Protein	Meat, poultry, fish, eggs, nuts, seeds, legumes, peas.	4 to 7 ounces a day. – Half a cup of cooked beans or legumes is approximately an ounce of protein. – A chicken breast is about 3 ounces. – ¼ cup of nuts is an ounce. – ½ cup seeds is one ounce.
Dairy	Milk, yoghurt, cheese, paneer (cottage cheese).	1 to 2 servings a day. One serving would be: – A cup of milk – A cup of yoghurt – A slice of cheese – About 30g of paneer.

Important tips to remember

- When you keep the bread/cereal group to about two to three servings a day, you start to automatically increase the intake of vegetables, protein and fruit.
- Every meal should include protein and fibre (in the form of vegetables).
- What about fats? Seasoning or cooking what you eat with good quality, filtered or cold-pressed oil is perfectly fine. Adding a teaspoon of ghee on occasion is acceptable too. Do you need to slather on the butter? Certainly not!
- If you are vegan and do away with animal products entirely from your diet it would mean that you need to compensate

with more vegetables, nuts, seeds and vegetarian protein like legumes and beans.

Basic Food Principles

We don't seem to dwell enough on the mental work that goes into staying well, fit, lean and healthy.

Here are some principles I have learnt along the way to make fitness and wellness a **lifestyle** rather than something one does for an hour or two a day and then forgets about for the rest of the day.

Turn Your Plate Around

In our country we consume way too much from the bread/cereal/grain group. Every meal is accompanied by either bread, in the form of naans and rotis, or rice in its various avatars. Various other millets also feature abundantly. It's not that whole, unprocessed grains are bad for you, for the most part, but given the volumes we consume, it certainly plays a significant role in the evolution of various lifestyle-related diseases we are prone to, like diabetes, cardiac disease, high triglycerides and metabolic syndrome (which is a combination of at least three of the following five medical conditions – abdominal obesity, high blood pressure, high blood sugar, low HDL cholesterol and/or high triglicerides). Metabolic syndrome has become more prevalent globally and is a major cause of heart disease.

Simply adopting a diet that restricts or eliminates entire food groups is not the answer. For instance, if you stop eating carbs altogether, you will develop cravings that will either drive you to eat more or frustrate you as you expend more energy and time trying to resist them. The key is to eat smaller quantities (about two to four servings from the bread/cereal/grain group per day) and include more plant-based foods, protein and good-quality fats.

In essence, what I'm recommending is that you turn your plate around.

It's a simple process. Instead of serving yourself several spoons of rice first and then dotting your plate with miniscule quantities of vegetables and a little protein, as we are accustomed to do, when you serve yourself:

1. First serve yourself your vegetables;
2. Add your protein (in the form of a meat or a legume, depending on whether or not you are a meat-eater);
3. Add a small portion of the bread/cereal/grain in the far corner of your plate.

Extreme Dieting

Extreme dieting is not a long-term proposition. While you may lose weight initially with an extremely low-calorie diet, you are unlikely to sustain it. Women who go on and off diets, called yo-yo dieting, tend to lose and gain weight cyclically. That's an awful way to live. You often tend to gauge your self-worth with that number on the scale. So you feel great one season because you've lost a few pounds and then feel dreadful after the holiday season simply because you've gained it all back, and with interest! Punishing diets can also lead to eating disorders like anorexia, bulimia and binge eating. Even yo-yo dieting itself is a form of an eating disorder. All these have repercussions on your health. So it's not just about your weight on the scale but about how you feel about yourself, your energy levels, level of positivity, productivity and your quality of life. Your objective should be not just to lose weight, but also to be healthier and fitter with more energy to truly live the life you want.

Intermittent Fasting

Intermittent fasting has been practised in many cultures around the world, including our own, for centuries. Every religion follows some form of fasting at certain times in the year. I think, however, that the more we understand food, the better we will be able to understand what we should eat during non-fasting periods. So there is no point in fasting for 16 hours a day if you are going to go on a food orgy at dinner.

There are various forms of intermittent fasting. You can devise your own. Your fast (not eating or drinking anything except water) can last twelve hours or longer. You can do this in various ways. For example:

- Eat your first meal of the day around 8 a.m. and your last meal around 6 p.m. and nothing after that. That gives you a 14-hour fasting period.
- Delay your first meal of the day to 10 a.m. and eat your last meal by 6 p.m. and you get a 16-hour fasting period.
- Fast one day a week where you drink only water for 24 hours.
- Fast every three days.
- Go on a liquid diet twice a week. This could include vegetable juices, clear soups or very thin buttermilk.

Intermittent fasting is not difficult and once you get the hang of eating only within a certain time-frame (for instance, between 8 a.m. and 6 p.m.), it becomes a habit. It has several benefits.

- It improves your metabolic profile or the ability of your body to handle glucose (that is, provided the meals you eat are not loaded with sugar and high glycaemic carbs).
- It boosts insulin sensitivity so the cells become very sensitive to the available insulin and metabolize the blood sugar better.

- It improves the ability of the cells, especially nerve cells, to repair themselves.
- It enhances brain health by reducing oxidative stress, inflammation, blood-sugar levels and insulin resistance.
- It increases the levels of brain-derived neurotrophic factor (BDNF), which is important for the growth of the brain cells. The same effect is produced by regular exercise.
- It has beneficial effects on genes related to diseases like Parkinson's Syndrome and Alzheimer's disease.
- It aids weight loss, provided the total calories consumed during the non-fast period are lower than the total calorie expenditure.
- It improves heart health by reducing blood pressure, weight, and inflammation of cells and tissues.
- Promising evidence from animal studies shows that intermittent fasting may protect us from cancer.
- Finally, intermittent fasting may increase lifespan (shown in animal studies).

Intermittent fasting can be adopted as a way of life. You could, for instance, eat just two meals a day every day, restricting these two meals between 9 a.m. to 7 p.m., to make it a 14-hour fast, or between 10 a.m. and 4 p.m. to make it a 16-hour fast. You could also follow this through the week and extend the feeding time a little over the weekend. This means that you continue your normal activities during your fasting and non-fasting hours or days. If you are unable to sustain normal day-to-day activities and your exercise during this time, you may need to scale back and shorten the time of the fast.

Work to gradually increase the time of the fast and you will find that it is possible. The important thing is the quality of the food you eat during the non-fasting period. It should contain enough vegetarian protein and good-quality fat to sustain you through the fast. Legumes, nuts, vegetables, fruit, eggs, whole grains and millets can feature in your diet. Make sure you don't overeat during the non-fasting times, as that would defeat much of the purpose of the fast.

Your Attitude to Food

In the end, what really matters is your attitude to food. Does it control you or do you control your food? For some people, food is almost a drug of choice. This will not play out well, especially when one is trying to lose fat.

Eating is probably the one act that can test our levels of self-discipline on a daily basis. At every stage we are in a position to make either the right or the wrong choice. We are exposed to a variety of foods several times a day so there is that level of constant enticement. If you really think about it, we need very little food to sustain a regular lifestyle. Athletes and those who lead hugely physically demanding lives will require more energy in the form of calories, but the majority of us need far less than we actually think we do and consume.

In the previous chapter, I have explained the various factors that make it difficult for us to sustain a healthy diet or maintain our weight. There are so many external cues and internal factors that seem to control how much and what we eat. Our brain is the main motivator for our food intake. It controls everything, including the way we eat. Changing our eating habits has to, therefore, start with making the necessary changes in our mindset.

It's not enough just to understand the influence of our environment, food cues and so on. We have to **internalize** that understanding. Every time we are subjected to and enticed by an advertisement, for example, we need to stop and recognize that it is the visual cue of the advertisement that generates the urge to eat and ask ourselves whether we **really** want or need that treat. Are we **really** hungry? Or, if we are sitting around eating with a group of friends, we must acknowledge that we don't necessarily have to keep pace with the others or continue to eat until everyone else is done. We can listen to our own bodies and refuse food when we know it is time to do so.

There are many people who shuttle from one dietician to another in the hope of finding the magic diet that will bring about the weight loss they seek. There's no secret there. I suspect they too know that. In fact, they already know if they are eating wrong or eating too much. While gaining control over eating is not necessarily easy, we don't have to make it more difficult for ourselves.

Waypower over Willpower

Most people believe they are completely responsible for their food choices. Yet, as described in the previous chapter, temptation is all around you. It's easy to be sucked into the lure of attractive, easily available food. After a while, most people give in and go with the flow, and even justify their unhealthy eating habits. They take the easy way out, adapt to weight gain and just change their wardrobe.

The objective, then, should be not to have to struggle with your willpower to fight cravings everyday – and exercise that could prove exhausting and futile. There is nothing more frustrating or demoralizing than losing a battle with yourself. Suggestions such as 'go for a walk', 'take a bath', 'listen to music', and so on, don't always work as a diversion once the cravings strike.

What you need to do is re-haul your environment – kitchens, pantries and workspaces – and make them accessories not enemies of your attempts at good eating. This means you should set up your environment in such a way that it is easy to eat healthy. Keep healthy and delicious food within reach and keep the avoidable foods out of the house. It will become impossible to binge-eat if you can't find the food in the first place. Stocking tempting and harmful foods in the house is the first step towards sabotaging your efforts towards eating clean.

This will also ensure that the children in your house are also exposed to good-quality food at home from an early age and imbibe the habit as a lifestyle. After all, how we approach food in our formative years establishes lifetime habits. Once a particular eating habit sets in, it will come naturally to them to reach for a fruit rather than for a biscuit or a piece of pizza.

That being said, having to exercise willpower all the time is exhausting. You have only a limited amount of it. Much of it is expended in just to get through your day– to get to work on time, to exercise, meet a deadline, or to be patient with your child, your household help, or restraining yourself from shouting at the person who cuts you off on the road.

Initially, such a paradigm shift may seem challenging. How can you keep refusing food offered to you? How can you not stop at the sweet store to pick up that box of sweets (supposedly for you in-laws)? How can you not stock up on fried chips and savories (supposedly for your partner)? How can you not order pizza (supposedly for your children)? Well, you can and you must! You can make the right decisions at the preliminary stage in order to avoid the concern of then having to resist those temptations. In short, use your **waypower** instead of having to fight with your **willpower**.

The Dichotomy of Control

It is clear by now that your body is not always under your control. While you can choose to exercise, eat healthy and the rest of it, much hinges on your genetic propensity. You may be genetically prone to be a larger-built person. What is important is that you be a fit larger-built person.

While you may not have control over all the events around you, you can certainly control how you react to them. For instance, you don't need to react to a stressful event by overeating. The eating part is under your control. What you stock in your home is under your control. What kind of food you eat is under your control. How you cook your food is under your control. Rather than wishing for an ideal situation with no temptations, stress, anxiety or even unhappiness, you can learn to deal with the situations as they are with equanimity and respond appropriately.

Given below is a short list of things you can and cannot control. These are just examples of ways of looking at situations.

What you can't control	What you can control
Advertising that makes food appear attractive and calls out to you.	The understanding that this is just an advertisement designed to tempt you and asking yourself if you are truly hungry without giving in to temptation.
Other food cues like the smell of food, sight of other people eating, buffets with a wide variety of food.	The understanding that food cues trigger cravings. Asking yourself if you are truly hungry. Knowing the extent of your willpower and deciding whether or not to go to a place serving a buffet in the first place.
Stress, anxiety, sadness.	How we react to such emotions. Food does not need to be the answer to every problem. Once again, recognizing that you perhaps use food as a form of therapy will help you deal with it and learn other coping mechanisms.

Exactly how much weight or how much weight you lose and in how short a time. (This is largely dependent on genetics.)	How much you exercise, how well you eat, how you manage stress, sleep and relationships.
What your hostess serves at a dinner you're invited to.	What you choose from the items that are served.
How much other people like you or how popular you are.	Your behaviour towards others.
How successful you are in your career.	Your work ethic, your commitment to your work, your enjoyment of it.
How happy other people make you.	How happy or content you make yourself by exploring all the avenues for wellness.
An extremely busy work or travel schedule preventing you from exercising regularly.	Controlling what you eat, getting in short spells of exercise and moving more through the day.

The above are only some examples of what you can and cannot control. You can add to the list as you go along and create alternative solutions to the things you can't control.

Here are some questions you might want to ask yourself and come up with your own solutions:

- How would you make living well a 'lifestyle'?
- How would you sustain making the right choices?
- What happens when you can't exercise?
- What happens if you are injured and have to rest?
- What happens when the foods you are recommended are not available?
- What happens when you do gain some weight?
- What happens when you get depressed or sad and feel unmotivated?

In ancient Greek philosophy, there is a wonderful analogy of an archer who is preparing to hit a target. He prepares his bow, gets the best arrows, practises hard and then shoots at the target. Once the arrow has left his bow, he has no control over it. External factors like the wind or movement of the target may well prevent the arrow from hitting it. The archer, however, has done his very best, and that's all that really matters. His obsessing about hitting the target and then being distraught if he doesn't is not helpful to him.

In a similar vein, doing our very best is all that is really required of us. I mean *truly doing our best.* I say that because many a time we make excuses for doing what we do or don't do and justify our actions. We then become preoccupied with not having achieved the results we sought. The results are not truly within our control, only our own actions are. But don't be upset with the results you didn't get from the work you didn't do. How can you expect results if you haven't worked for it?

How Do You Enjoy and Sustain Healthy Eating?

Willpower aside, here are some practical pointers that will help you control what you eat and make eating healthy an enjoyable experience.

Prepare in advance: The one thing that is helpful in sustaining a commitment to healthy eating is to plan in advance. It is far more difficult to make decent choices when we are hungry and as we near meal time. Be well-prepared for the following day's meals. By keeping pre-cooked beans, chopped vegetables, vegetable or chicken stock, and so on, in the fridge and planning the menu ahead of time, it is far easier to make choices when required.

Planning ahead about what to choose when you go out to eat or when you travel and making such choices easier by going to the appropriate restaurant, carrying nuts or fruit in your travel bag, etc., makes the process of clean eating attainable. By not preparing in advance we often set ourselves up to be caught unawares and make poor choices when at the mercy of our hunger.

Plan for travel: One of the most common complaints I encounter is that of healthy diets getting upset when one is travelling or after a long day out of office, in the field, or even a long commute to work. When you know you are likely to travel or be outside of your normal environment, the sensible thing to do is to carry suitable snacks with you. Why set yourself up for likely temptation or even extreme hunger, which then precipitates a binge?

Eliminate sugar from your diet: If there is one thing you can do to help you improve your diet and become healthier, it is to eliminate sugar completely from your diet. By this I mean all forms of sugar like honey, jaggery, palm sugar, etc. They are better options than sugar, but are certainly not required as part of a healthy diet. So a dessert made with jaggery, while healthier than one made with refined sugar, is not an absolute requirement from a health perspective. As an occasional indulgence, they are better options than refined sugar. Please remember that there is added sugar in almost every packaged, commercial food available on the supermarket shelf. Be aware of that when you consume these foods.

Abstain from the offending foods for a period of time: As I have mentioned in the previous chapter, you can retrain your palate to eat and enjoy the right kinds of food. To alter habits, you need to abstain from the offending foods in order to actually 'forget' their flavour. After a period of time (this could take months or years, depending on your body), the retrained palate is very comfortable eating more complex carbs, protein and good fats as opposed to excessive simple carbs, sugary treats and processed fast food.

This is something I have witnessed among my own patients. Even those from traditional backgrounds who are accustomed to eating large volumes of rice are able to retrain their palate to enjoy more vegetables and protein and less refined carbs when they have to change their diet to manage diabetes, during pregnancy, for instance. Many of them then proceed to continue such a diet post-pregnancy and admit they are very comfortable with it.

Eat mindfully: There are a few rules you should follow before you eat everyday.

- Be **conscious** of what and how much you eat every single time.
- Be aware of the numerous **food cues** in your environment. They are there to subtly influence your food choices. If you know about them and are conscious of them, then you are less likely to be influenced.
- Don't eat on autopilot or out of habit. You don't have to eat at 'lunch time'. Eat when you are hungry.
- Avoid eating in front of the TV or with your mind engaged by various electronic gadgets that distract you from the eating process itself.
- Recognize your body's signals of hunger and satiety.
- Be cognizant of your emotional state, which may easily influence your eating.
- Understand food and food groups, and be conscious of how many servings of each group you eat.
- Serve yourself on a smaller plate.
- Ensure you eat in a calm environment. If you are stressed, stop and breathe. Drink a glass of water. Ask yourself

if you are really hungry or if you can wait till you feel calmer.
- Write a food journal for several weeks to identify the triggers for your cravings. Once you are aware and consciously decide to deal with them, the process itself will become easier.

Keep your environment healthy-food friendly: This can be done by following a few simple steps.

- Stock up on veggies, fruits, eggs, poultry, beans, nuts, yogurt, etc., which form the essentials of a healthy meal.
- Always have healthy fats available in your home and around you.
- Don't keep processed, packaged food at home. You will be tempted to eat it.
- While travelling or at work keep nuts, seeds or fruits with you. If you get hungry you will not tempted to stop at the nearest bakery or order in a bread pakoda or some other oil-soaked snack.

Be a responsible nutritional gatekeeper: As I mentioned before, being a nutritional gatekeeper is an overwhelming job if you take it seriously. Being well-prepared for meals with the right ingredients is the key to making eating healthy simpler.

- Include plenty of plant-based foods at every meal. They are filling and delicious. There are a variety of vegetables to choose from. Experiment with new ones every week. Cooking them also need not be elaborate or time-consuming. Vegetables cook extremely quickly, and prepared as such retain much of their nutrients and flavour rather than when they are completely annihilated by overcooking and over-seasoning.

- Fruits, nuts, seeds and legumes are also very satisfying and high in fibre. This creates a feeling of being full, preventing overeating.
- Meat, poultry, eggs and fish have a place in your meal as they provide good quality protein. How much you can consume will need to be calculated on an individual basis depending on your weight, gender activity levels, exercise and so on. A vegetarian diet, however, is quite capable of providing us with adequate protein for our daily needs and even for the recreational exerciser.
- Vegetarian sources of protein are plenty and most plants also provide protein.
- Eliminate processed foods like sugar, white flour and tinned meat completely from the diet.
- Change over to better-quality oil like olive oil, coconut oil, sesame oil, groundnut and mustard oil to cook with rather than vegetable oils like sunflower oil.

Exercise regularly: There's no getting away from the fact that regular exercise is absolutely necessary to stay lean and fit. This should include both cardio and weight training, as explained in the chapter on essential exercises.

Build enough muscle: Building muscle is important in order to prevent fat gain. In my book *Gain to Lose*, I have elaborated on that in great detail. The entire book is, in fact, about gaining muscle to lose fat! Suffice to say here that you simply must start to train with weights for you to keep fat from accumulating. **Building enough muscle is probably one of the most important strategies in sustaining fat loss.**

Move more: Movement through the day (even if you exercise regularly) is critically important for weight management. Many people believe that exercising for an hour a day exempts them from moving the rest of the day! This couldn't be further from the truth. Try and capitalize on opportunities to move as much as possible through the day. Climb stairs, walk to the neighbourhood market instead of ordering in your groceries, walk around your office communicating with your colleagues instead of sending emails or calling.

Manage your lifestyle better: This includes the management of stress, sleep and relationships that I have elaborated on in relevant chapters later in the book. Don't underestimate the importance of these aspects of your life for your general well-being and also to control your weight.

While it may seem like you are destined to grow fat with age, that is not necessarily inevitable. Your body will certainly change with age. Building enough muscle will keep the curves in the right places while combating fat accumulation around the middle. Mindful eating, being conscious of your environment, and aware of your food triggers will allow you to better manage your weight.

nine

Belly Fat and Gut Health

Many of us notice that we gain weight as we age. At the least, our bodies change in shape as a strange phenomenon plays out with the accumulation of fat around the waist. You may also notice the limbs get thinner (as we lose muscle in the extremities), so generally it's not a happy picture.

Why we gain overall fat is explained in detail in the relevant chapter. Fat accumulation around the waist is a separate topic and also a cause for great concern in more ways than one. The anxiety involved with not being able to button your jeans is quite justified, as that fat around your waist is more than just an aesthetic problem.

MEASURING BELLY FAT

Measuring belly fat is easy. All you need is an inch tape.

Measure your waist around the belly button. In Asian populations, the upper limit for waist circumference **for women is 80 cm or 31 inches. For men it is 34 inches.** This is the absolute upper limit for waist circumference.

The standard has been set lower for Indians because we seem to be at a higher risk for developing diabetes and heart disease above these values for waist circumference.

WHY BELLY FAT IS MORE THAN JUST SKIN-DEEP

The trouble with belly fat is that it's not limited to the extra layer of padding located just below the skin (subcutaneous fat). It includes **visceral fat** — which lies deep inside your abdomen, surrounding important internal organs.

Visceral fat is otherwise called **toxic fat** and is the worst kind to amass. Heavy thighs or hips are not quite as dangerous to health and well-being as a large waistline. So an apple shape with a larger waistline is more dangerous than a pear-shaped body with larger hips but a relatively small waist.

Although subcutaneous fat certainly poses cosmetic concerns, visceral fat is linked to far more dangerous health problems, including:

- **Metabolic syndrome:** A dangerous combination of a large waistline, high cholesterol and diabetes.
- Heart disease.
- **Type 2 diabetes:** It is far more likely when you have a wide abdominal circumference.
- High blood pressure.
- Abnormal cholesterol.
- **Sleep apnea:** Inability to breathe as you sleep causing snoring and sudden obstruction of the breath for short periods of time.
- Increased risk of **premature death**.

Regardless of overall weight, some studies have found that even when men and women were considered of normal weight based on standard body mass index (BMI), a large waistline increased the risk of dying of cardiovascular disease. The reason? Fat in the abdominal cavity is not just present as a storehouse of energy but as an active tissue. This means that it behaves almost like an endocrine organ releasing inflammatory substances that lead to all the above mentioned problems.

For women, hormone levels (specifically estrogen) start to drop in their 40s and the body begins to handle fat differently. While it is true that with age, lowering of estrogen and a slightly lower metabolism rate contribute to the increasing waistline, there are steps we can take to prevent or at least manage this problem.

- Gut health
- Eating right
- Exercise
- Stress
- Sleep

Gut Health

Your gut does more than just digest food and expel waste. The health of your gut is of utmost importance to many things happening in your body including your weight. Did you know that your gut is called your **'second brain'**. For good reason, too, as it appears that the gut controls your moods to some extent and has been implicated in depression, multiple sclerosis, perhaps even autism, and is certainly responsible for eating and weight. I'm sure you've heard of the expression 'gut feeling'? That's not just an arbitrary phrase arising from nowhere.

The intestines are connected to a large number of neurons or nerve cells (about a hundred million), which connect to the real brain inside your skull. This system is called the enteric nervous system. These nerves and nerve cells naturally produce neurotransmitters, just like within the brain, and so the intestines do much more than just aid digestion. That pang you feel when nervous (often called 'butterflies in the tummy') is the result of the blood supply and nervous connections to and from the gut being activated as a physiological response to stress.

Of course, the second brain is not the seat of any intelligent thought or cognition. What it does, however, is enable you to literally 'feel' things.

- Ever been in a new environment and felt distinctly uneasy?
- Ever met someone for the first time and felt an instant like/dislike for the person?
- Ever felt a certain unexplainable 'vibe'?
- Ever felt queasy when you receive bad news or even good news?

All the above 'gut instincts' arise as a result of the flourishing nervous stimulation of the gut and the bacteria that reside within the gut.

The gut controls moods as a result of the serotonin, one of the neurotransmitters, formed from the intestinal neurons. Depression has been related to the presence of abnormal gut bacteria and their interaction with these nerve cells. Irritable bowel syndrome, which is often triggered by stress and anxiety, is the result of too much serotonin in the bowels.

Our intestines contain trillions of bacteria. In fact, there are more bacteria in our intestines than the total number of cells in the entire human body. Think about that for a second. It does sound a bit gross, but it's really quite astonishing! These bacteria are not the harmful kind that lead to infections in the body. Instead, they are the important organisms within our body that are responsible for digestion and seem to actually communicate with the nerve cells in the intestines.

These bacteria play an important role in our immunity. This is why **probiotics,** which are dietary supplements that contain potentially beneficial microbes, help us improve immunity. The bacteria also aid in digestion, help to fight disease, create B vitamins and soothe inflammatory conditions.

When these bacteria are altered or depleted in any way, all kinds of health problems may arise.

How Is Gut Health Connected to Belly Fat?

Studies have found that the kind of gut flora or bacteria differs for those who are obese and diabetic than that of people who are of normal weight with no metabolic disorder.

One possible reason for this may be that different bacteria have different effects on not only appetite and food intake, but also on the metabolism, causing some people to store more fat. Some kinds of gut bacteria may cause us to absorb more fat from the intestines. This may mean that someone with bad gut flora may eat the same number of calories as someone with good gut flora but absorb more of the calories consumed to be stored as fat. Bad gut bacteria can also increase the production of insulin and lead to insulin resistance, which, as I have explained in the previous chapter, is one of the causes of obesity.

Did you know that babies that are not breastfed and are born to mothers with bad gut flora (as a result of various unhealthy lifestyle habits) develop bad gut flora and have a tendency for obesity later in life? Babies born of a vaginal birth also seem to have more beneficial gut flora than those born by Caesarean section.

So, essentially, what this means is that you are programmed for obesity (or the opposite) later in life as a result of maternal habits. This would mean, then, that if you have these disadvantages from birth, rewiring the whole system, so to speak, would take a lot more effort and commitment. This is also possibly why some people find it far easier to knock off excess weight while others struggle interminably.

Yes, by now you must be rolling your eyes and saying, 'Whatever next? We're at the mercy of bacteria?'

Well, the point is we do control what kind of bacteria colonize in our gut by virtue of what we eat and other lifestyle habits. We can also alter our gut bacteria to the better kind by implementing lifestyle habits that keep them thriving. So, in essence, we can control, to a large extent, the quality and health of our gut.

> Foods that improve the quality of these gut bacteria include fermented foods like fermented yoghurt, apple cider vinegar, sauerkraut, kefir, cruciferous vegetables like broccoli, cauliflower, kale and cabbage.

The objective should be to maintain the health of your gut. The following deplete and alter the microbiome in our gut:

- Stress, especially if prolonged and chronic
- Chronic inflammation or infection
- Sugar
- Processed foods
- Steroids
- Antibiotics
- Quitting smoking

A word on the last point, in case you're thinking taking up smoking is a good idea! In an observational study written by researchers Luc Biedermann et al., it is suggested that the reason those who quit smoking tend to gain an average of about five to seven pounds over the observational period of nine weeks is not their increased calorie intake. Instead, it is because of the altered bacterial flora within the gut after quitting smoking that leads to weight gain. I've had women tell me they are scared to quit smoking for fear of gaining weight. Well, the toss up is between lung cancer and a few extra pounds (which you can easily work off with exercise or control by altering what you eat), so the choice is restrictive indeed!

> **To Aid and Improve Gut Health**
>
> - Manage stress.
> - Get enough rest.
> - Eat whole foods with plenty of vegetables, fibre, protein and good quality fats.
> - Give your digestive system a rest once in a while. Intermittent fasting is one way to do this.
> - Include fermented foods in your diet.
> - Take a probiotic supplement, if required.

The importance of gut flora has been recognized to be so critical that scientists have isolated the beneficial flora from the faeces of humans and consider it to be the future of treatment for obesity, several intractable gut infections and even diabetes. (Yes, you read that right!)

'Faecal microbiota transplantation (FMT) transfers intestinal bacteria by a "stool transplant" from a healthy, lean person to a person with obesity,' says Elain W. Yu of Massachusetts General Hospital who is leading the research. So, essentially, 'poop pills' from a lean individual may be one way forward for the management of obesity!

EATING RIGHT

Food is the number one culprit in the belly fat story.

Do you need to go on a particular 'diet' with a fancy name in order to lose belly fat? No, you don't. What you do need to do is find an eating plan that works for you and that you can sustain for life.

Are you one of those people who gets excited by the latest fad 'diet' or product that promises a flat stomach? The most common mistake people make is to start on a fad diet that works well initially and produces weight loss. As time goes by, they are either unable to sustain the diet or start to plateau on their weight. What you should do instead is follow an eating plan that you can sustain for life with the below suggestions (some of which has been elaborated upon in the previous chapter):

- Cut out the sugar completely.
- Eat more protein.
- Cut refined carbs from your diet.
- Consume more fibre.
- Avoid processed food.
- Use simple ingredients whose names you can actually pronounce, put together in elegant ways. These always make for the best meals.
- Use good quality, filtered and cold pressed (not refined) oils like coconut oil, groundnut oil, sesame oil, mustard oil and olive oil.

- Be mindful when eating out. Keep in mind that eating out, socializing etc. give us the license to overeat or eat very high calorie food. Be wary and extremely mindful of what you eat at those times.
- Drink water instead of soda or fruit juice.
- Respect your body's signals; eat only when you are hungry. Learn to listen to your body.
- Keep a food journal for a couple of weeks. This will help you identify exactly where you are going wrong.
- Watch your alcohol. While it is true that a serving or two of alcohol a day may be good for the heart, do remember that alcohol has a lot of empty calories. Seven calories per gram to be exact. Added to that, the habit of snacking along with your drink and the lowered inhibitions after alcohol allowing you to eat more can all add up on your waistline. If you want to cut calories, it's best you abstain at least until you've knocked off that belly fat.
- Watch out for foods that don't agree with you. At this point in your life, you may find that what you used to eat doesn't work anymore. You may even discover foods that downright don't agree with you. You may need to cut back on meat or stop wheat or milk completely. Paying attention to just how your body reacts to foods is the key to understanding your body and its needs.

Bloating

Do you feel good after you've eaten? Do you feel uncomfortably bloated even if you have only eaten a little? Sometimes a bloated belly may just be gaseous distension. Eating the wrong kind of food can cause this. Besides processed food, sugar and aerated drinks, certain foods may trigger gaseous distension for you. Milk and milk products or wheat can do it for some people.

Pay close attention to your food and correlate that with what it does to your body.

Signs of bloating should not be taken lightly. If, after making the necessary dietary adjustments, you still experience bloating (especially if it's associated with weight loss), do see your doctor. Bloating is one of the symptoms of many forms of cancer, irritable bowel syndrome, Crohn's disease and liver disease.

EXERCISE

You may have been exercising for a while now. Perhaps you are doing a couple of hours of cardio every week? What do you do? Do you walk at a moderate pace for about 45 to 60 minutes? Do you participate in marathons and practise your running? Do you do yoga? Do you cycle? **The best results for a toned midriff come from a combination of clean eating, high intensity cardio, weight training and abdominal exercises to tighten the muscles.**

Ab Exercises

Most women believe that performing hundreds of crunches will flatten the stomach. It certainly will tighten the abdominal muscles, or the rectus abdominis muscle, which runs vertically from the lower end of your chest to your pubic bone, and the obliques, which constitute the sides of your waist. However, the fat over the muscles (just under the skin) and the fat inside the abdominal cavity can only be addressed with diet, cardio and weight training.

So while you should continue to do your abdominal exercises, doing them to the exclusion of the rest of the pillars of fitness is not the answer.

Some abdominal and lower back exercises to include are:

- Crunches
- Plank
- Side plank
- Reverse crunch
- Bicycle

These are great for the abdominal muscles. I've explained these in the chapter called 'Essential Exercises to Follow'.

To strengthen the lower back, include **back extensions.** It's important to add lower back exercises to your abdominal routine. This prevents muscle imbalance.

Research has found that while moderate intensity, longer duration cardio, lasting 45 to 60 minutes, is beneficial for overall health, it has been found that a much shorter duration, higher intensity routine like **High Intensity Interval Training** or **HIIT** is more advantageous, particularly for belly fat.'[5] This should be done about twice or thrice a week. Lasting only about 20 minutes, HIIT is hugely time conserving. Your stamina/cardio aspect of fitness, therefore, has to include HIIT routines twice a week.

You may have concerns about pushing your intensity fearing that your heart may not withstand the stress. A clearance from your physician with an exercise stress test is mandatory. The intensity you progress to in HIIT can be completely individualized. You don't have to start off pushing your limits in the challenge phase of the exercise. You could work up to higher intensities once you are comfortable with that level of exercise. HIIT has been explained in the chapter on cardio.

Weight Training

Weight training to build muscle is perhaps the *most significant* thing you can do to burn fat. Weight training is often considered as unnecessary, cumbersome, something that creates bulkiness or manliness and so on. All the above are inaccurate. If there is one thing you should do in your later years, it is weight lifting.

Muscle is critical tissue. Unless you work it against resistance, it is likely to deteriorate and atrophy.

Muscle is also the most active tissue in the body, demanding large quantities of fuel for its functioning. It makes sense, therefore, that if you build enough muscle, you will burn more fuel (fat stores), leaving very little to accumulate as fat. In my second book, *Gain to Lose*, I have elaborated on how exactly fat is 'burnt' with muscular activity. Do give that a read.

When I say weight training, I also do mean using enough weight to actually build muscle. This means observing your routine and progressively increasing the weights used till you see muscle mass building. Playing with very light dumbbells really doesn't do much for building muscle or improving strength.

Weight training is terribly empowering. Anyone who has tried it will endorse this. It gives you the strength to do so many simple things in your day-to-day life. Activities like lifting, pushing, climbing stairs, rising from a low chair, are controlled by the strength, stability and balance of the muscles.

Recreational exercisers should aim to train with weights at least twice a week. All the muscles in the body should be addressed using different exercises at least twice a week. The exercises themselves could be different to break the monotony, but every muscle should be worked in both sessions. A serious body builder, on the other hand, will follow a different routine but I won't go into that.

Flexibility

How does improving flexibility help you lose belly fat, you may ask? Flexibility helps rid you of abdominal fat in a rather circuitous manner.

One reason is that the relaxation produced following any breathing and stretching routine is highly beneficial in reducing stress. Stress, as we know, is a very important reason for weight gain, especially around the waist.

Stretching properly is also important for other reasons, namely:

- **It prevents a tight back and abnormal posture:** Sometimes your belly sticking out may be just a case of having a tight lower back and hamstrings and poor abdominal tone. Stretching these muscles is important for ideal posture.
- **It prevents injury:** Not stretching and having tight or imbalanced muscles can lead to injury. You know what happens as a result of injury! You stop exercising because you've been told to rest and then everything goes into a tailspin. You start to gain weight again as you 'rest', you start to get depressed and frustrated, you start your comfort eating and, eventually, you find yourself back where you started.
- **It prevents muscle soreness:** Stretching properly after a workout, especially weight training, prevents muscle soreness. Delayed Onset Muscle Soreness (DOMS) is one of the reasons people avoid continuing to exercise. It can also prevent you from being able to exercise effectively the next day. Such a compromised 'form' of exercise can then lead to injury and further pain and the rest is history.
- **It addresses deep muscles:** Deep muscles like the hip flexors and the iliopsoas, which link the torso to the legs, are

difficult to stretch with the brief cursory stretches we do for a few minutes post our regular routine. These muscles are important for posture, among other things. Stretching them properly will prevent the misalignment of the pelvis, which is important to avoid a protuberant tummy.

To avoid unnecessary setbacks, it's best to include a good stretch routine into your workout. It doesn't have to be long or arduous. Even a 10-minute stretch works wonders.

Here are a couple of stretches that help align the pelvis and prevent tight muscles in that area. This, in turn, will keep the spine aligned and, along with abdominal and back exercises, will help you with the right posture for a flat stomach:

The hip flexor stretch: This releases the hip flexors, which help you lift your entire leg. These muscles tend to get tight with constant use (as in running) or if you sit for long periods of time, as most of us do.

To do this stretch, kneel on the floor. Next place the right foot on the floor and lean forward, stretching the hip flexors of the left leg. Repeat with the other leg.

The deep glute stretch: The muscles deep within your pelvis are difficult to stretch. Lie on your back. Bend the knees and place your feet on the floor. Place your right ankle on your left knee with the right knee opened out to the side. Now, bend the left leg, pulling it towards your chest. This produces a deep stretch in the right glute area. Repeat on the other side.

Stretching the IT band: The iliotibial band runs along the side of the thigh from the hip bone to the side of the knees. This can often get tight, leading to misalignment and pain.

To stretch it, lie on your back with legs stretched out. Bend your left knee and, with the leg bent, drop in on to the right ride of your body using your right hand to assist it. To stretch further, turn your neck to look over your left shoulder keeping both shoulders on the floor. Hold for about 20 to 30 seconds and repeat on the other side.

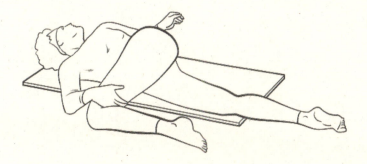

Cat stretch: This stretch mobilizes your spine and keeps it flexible. I have described it in detail in the chapter on posture.

Pigeon pose: This is a wonderful stretch for the deep pelvic muscles.

First, get into the downward dog position, forming an inverted V with your body, palms and soles flat on the ground in front of and behind you, head lowered, buttocks in the air. Feel the stretch along your spine and the back of your thighs and calves.

To get into the pigeon pose from the downward dog, bring your left leg forward between your hands, bend the knee so it is on the floor and aligned with your hip socket (not bending out) and sit on your left buttock and thigh. The other leg remains stretched out behind you. Your spine should be stretched as straight as you get in this position.

STRESS MANAGEMENT

The better you deal with stress, the better the handling of weight, especially belly fat. The stress hormone **cortisol** has been found to be a key player in the accumulation of abdominal fat.

Anything the body finds stressful will cause the release of cortisol. Certain kinds of stress (like a deadline) are beneficial for some to improve productivity. Pressure at work is often a driver of better work, up to a point. Then, it becomes 'distress' and detrimental.

Stress can come in many forms. Something that is not stressful for one person may turn out to be incapacitating for another. All of us face stress in some way or another. How we manage it is another story altogether. Habits die hard, so if we are in the habit of overreacting, acting out, ruminating, being angry or resentful over stressors, then this tends to be our way of operation. These are not helpful strategies and it is worthwhile looking at your behaviour to see if anything can be changed to make it more manageable.

Low level, unspoken stress in the form of dissatisfaction with life situations is probably the worst kind of stress that you may experience at this stage in your life. Perhaps you had an *expectation* of who you would be or how much you would have achieved 'by the time you were, (let's say) fifty'. Feeling frustrated about not achieving what you had anticipated could be a huge stressor.

This may be a time to rethink what you want to do and move forward in another direction. Perhaps it's time to learn something new or start a new venture. Or perhaps what you really need to do is relax and let go a little.

Stress management should take on a whole new meaning for you. Go through the chapter on stress to learn more about this aspect of your well-being.

Sleep

There is an entire chapter on stress and sleep in this book. That's how important these two aspects of our well-being are. Do refer to those chapters for more details on the subject. Suffice here to say that **good quality sleep** is imperative to health. Losing sleep for one night or a couple of nights may not necessarily harm you, but when you sleep poorly on a regular basis, it becomes a hindrance to well-being.

So how does losing sleep lead to belly fat?

- Have you ever tried making decisions when you are sleep-deprived? Quite challenging, isn't it? Your brain is fuzzy, you feel irritable and are uncomfortable within your body. Imagine making a decision to eat or not to eat ice cream (or any one of your favorite foods) in such a situation. Not an ideal scenario. You tend to make poor food choices when you are sleep-deprived. **The body is unable to distinguish hunger from sleep deprivation and fatigue.** The tendency to overeat, eat at night and indulge in sugary, carb-loaded foods is more when sleep deprived.
- Sleep deprivation causes abnormal and erratic eating habits. Sleep helps maintain a healthy balance of the hormones that signal hunger (ghrelin) or satiety (leptin). When you don't get enough sleep, your level of ghrelin rises and the level of leptin goes down. This creates feelings of hunger and food-seeking behaviour.
- It's a catch-22 situation. Sleep deprivation leading to obesity can lead to further sleep deprivation when obese individuals suffer from sleep apnea, etc. that hinder good quality sleep.

- Your gut is your best friend in keeping your belly fat under control. Eat foods to improve gut health and eliminate those that destroy the gut microbiome.
- **Eating mindfully** is key to eating the right foods, keeping within your calorie requirement and preventing weight gain
- **Exercise is non-negotiable** and what kind of exercise is just as important. Include abdominal and back exercises.
- **HIIT** should feature in your cardio routine to rev up your metabolism.
- Start training with weights to **build muscle mass**.
- **Manage stress** better — identify your stressors. Address them individually.
- Include **breathing and relaxation** techniques and **yoga** in your daily routine.
- **Sleep** enough to avoid the problems associated with sleep deprivation, one of which is weight gain.
- **Stay busy and productive**. It's not enough to be randomly busy with 'no time'. What you need is to be productively occupied with meaningful activities.

ten

Cardio

By now, you may have experimented with various forms of fitness. Perhaps you've tried zumba or crossfit or stepper. Maybe you prefer to run or walk. Maybe you only do yoga. Dividing your fitness into different 'pillars' makes it easier for you to try and accommodate all the pillars, which will help you improve all round rather than focus on any one pillar of fitness, as is the tendency.

Most of us are creatures of habit. If we are accustomed to using walking as our mode of exercise, for instance, we prefer to continue to do so especially as we grow older. We may feel unsure about including any other form of cardio. There are ways to make your walking routine more effective, however.

Stamina/cardio is the first pillar of fitness. Anything you do to increase your heart rate and rate of breathing will improve your cardiovascular endurance.

This happens in two ways:

- The ability of your heart and lungs to transfer oxygen to the blood in order for it to supply the rest of the body will improve.

- The ability of the larger muscles of your body (legs mostly, but arms and torso as well) to absorb the oxygen from the blood and dispose carbon dioxide or waste from working muscles back to the blood for it to be disposed from the lungs will improve.

Both these capabilities of the body are enhanced by cardiovascular activities like walking, running, cycling etc. Some forms of training where you use weights but perform the exercises in rapid succession (supersetting and circuit training) or with no rest between exercises (boot camp) will also increase the heart rate and improve cardiovascular fitness. The harder you push the body, the greater the development of these functions and capabilities. Remember, though, that if you are not fit enough to perform exercises at a fast pace or with no rest, the chances of you injuring yourself are far greater. So, while bootcamp-type workouts may be great fun and attractive, the 'form' or the method of performing individual exercises is not always addressed and focused on. Instead, more attention is given to 'pushing harder', 'working out till you drop' and such tactics, which don't play out well for many people.

The heart is a muscle of a special kind. It is called **smooth muscle and is not controlled voluntarily**. The more intense the exercise, the harder the heart muscles have to work to supply blood, both to the lungs and to the rest of the body. The heart muscles, therefore, become stronger. There will be an improved capacity of the heart with every beat, including more blood pumped with every contraction (called stoke volume). As you get fitter and the heart muscle gets stronger and bigger, it needs to contract fewer times per minute to supply the same, if not more, oxygenated blood to all the working muscles.

A slower heart rate, therefore, is indicative of higher fitness levels. Keep a record of your resting heart rate (as soon as you wake up, before getting out of bed) to evaluate progress. (There are some other reasons for a slower heart rate also – such as while on some blood pressure medication – that needs to be kept in mind.)

We may choose to continue to do the cardio routines we enjoy such as the walks or a cardio class with all our fun fitness buddies. It's important to remember, though, that our bodies start to acclimatize to routine exercise. While a routine class or your regular walk will certainly serve you well to keep you moving, burn some calories and sustain motivation, it's also necessary to include higher intensity workouts through the week. This is particularly important as you get fitter. A workout that used to be a challenge proves not to be after a point. That's the amazing power of the human body. So you will need to challenge it differently.

HIIT

High Intensity Interval Training, or HIIT, is a great way to add intervals of higher intensity to your routine a couple of times a week. The advantage of a HIIT routine is its shorter duration. You can complete an entire routine in about 20 minutes, burning more calories than you would from your usual 40-minute, steady-state walk. You will also increase cardiovascular fitness levels using HIIT.

An HIIT routine could typically look like this:–

- ▸ Warm up for three to five minutes.
- ▸ Walk at a moderate pace for a minute.
- ▸ Increase the pace to as fast as you can walk for the next 20 to 30 seconds (also called the **challenge phase**)

- Return to your **recovery phase** and walk at a moderate pace again for another minute (or two to three minutes if you are a beginner).
- Repeat the cycle over and over again for about 15 to 20 minutes. In effect, you will be pushing yourself to increase your intensity every one to two minutes. Your high-intensity challenge phase, therefore, lasts only about four to five minutes in total.

You can run instead of walk or, for that matter, perform any kind of cardiovascular activity and just cycle the intensity to make it an interval training session. HIIT routines vary in composition and time. The above is just an example of how to plan it. Some routines may include exercises that use your own body weight like pushups, squats, burpees and so on. Some may include only cardio, i.e. routines like walking, running or cycling.

If you are a beginner and want to include HIIT, you could start by incorporating it into your daily walk by speed-walking to a point where you are breathless for about 30 seconds every two to three minutes during your walk. This is easily done. Or you could initially start with a 10-minute HIIT routine and then increase it to a total of 20 minutes a day, two to three times a week.

Research has found that you don't necessarily need a continuous stretch of activity to call it 'exercise'. Equal benefits are reaped with several shorter, more intense bouts of activity through the day. If you can't fit in an entire hour at a stretch, then do three 15-minute sessions instead.

So, while the recommendation for accruing 150 minutes of exercise per week still stands as a norm and standard for the general population, if you want to see changes in your fitness levels and physicality, do include two days a week of HIIT and be rewarded.

Personally, I find long duration, lower intensity cardio extremely relaxing so I do that at least thrice a week. This is more meditative and helps me unwind. Of course, walking in the outdoors in Ooty, especially in chilly weather, is invigorating in itself. My HIIT sessions are not more than twice a week for about 20 minutes each.

HIIT is the spark that truly energizes and burns the fat.

Running

While many people have caught the running bug and try to participate in 5- and 10-kilometre runs when there are special events, sometimes endorsed by celebrities, I am not sure how many people are serious runners. Many people I know are terribly excited to participate is such events and thereafter don't pursue it much further. While I do understand that being a part of something is an end in itself for some, getting injured as a result defeats the whole purpose. I am quite amazed when some clients tell me they continue to run during these races (I'm not sure if they technically actually run the entire race) despite being injured. Why would you do that to your body?

If you want to take up running seriously, you need to **train to run.** You need to start to train with weights to strengthen your leg and glute muscles to counter the impact of the running process. When you land on your foot with every step during your run, a single leg experiences the stress of two-and-a-half times your body weight. Visualize the pressure on that leg, knee and ankle. Chances of joint injury are far more when the concerned muscles around that joint are not strengthened adequately. Back, hip, knee and ankle injuries are often the result of poor running technique in addition to poor strength in the lower limb and core muscles.

This is even more important if you take up running later in life. Injuries heal slower and set us back further as we age.

One of the main objectives of training should be **prevention of injury**. Taking up a sport that can potentially lead to injury due to its high impact, without training for it, is sheer recklessness.

MULTIPLE CARDIO ACTIVITIES

It is great to cross-train. This means, to participate in diverse activities in order to challenge your body differently. While this sounds exciting, it requires a certain level of **body intelligence**. By this, I mean that one needs to be acutely aware of how your body moves in response to its position and relationship to the space around you, and the connection between its various parts. A certain level of fitness is also required. By the time you reach 40 years of age, I am hoping you have developed a certain level of body intelligence.

Many cardio classes advertise themselves as 'no injury' and 'low-impact'. While they may be low-impact, it does not mitigate injury. A beginner, however, not familiar with aerobic moves and choreography, for instance, could very well injure themselves even in an extremely low-impact floor aerobic class unless monitored closely.

So while it may sound fun to go to a zumba class on Monday, boot camp on Wednesday and a dance session on Friday, ensure your body is capable and is doing it right in order to prevent injury. In any case, it's important you continue to train with weights to strengthen your muscles so that they protect you from injury through anything you attempt.

Muscle Memory

On the other hand, if you were an athlete in school and have been physically active, the body adapts more easily to alternate physical routines and increasing intensity. The muscles of your body 'remember' how to move and, provided you have been taught to move correctly in the first place, you will find acclimatizing to a variety of fitness routines much easier. The problem arises if you have not been very physically active in your youth. The body adapts to a habitually sedentary lifestyle. It needs to be taught to move properly when you start to adopt fitness later in life, commencing with even learning to walk correctly.

What if you don't like HIIT?

It's perfectly fine if you want to continue to do your low-to-moderate intensity cardio day after day. It will certainly benefit you, but may not *improve* your fitness levels. One problem with cardio routines that last too long is the issue of loss of valuable muscle tissue. If you notice, most long-distance runners, who run miles and miles every day, are very lean or thin. It helps to be of a low body weight when you are doing long-distance running. Perhaps you are of that physique and enjoy it. That's completely your prerogative. But if you want to retain muscle mass, you need to train with weights regularly.

So how many times a week and for how long?

Try and do cardio six days a week. Alternate between longer sessions on alternate day, (walking, cycling, low-intensity cardio class) and include at least two days of HIIT a week to increase metabolism and fitness levels.

Typically, your cardio sessions may look like this:

Days	Cardio Activity
Monday	Walk/Cross trainer/Cardio class, 45–60 minutes
Tuesday	HIIT, 20 minutes
Wednesday	Cycle, 45 minutes
Thursday	Walk/Cross trainer/Cardio class, 45 minutes
Friday	HIIT, 20 minutes
Saturday	Walk, 60 minutes

eleven

Strength and Muscle

Building muscle helps you lose fat!

Now that I've got your attention, let's also talk about all the numerous other benefits of building muscle.

Anyone who hasn't started training to improve muscle mass and strength by now, I implore you to. This is the one thing you can do to improve the quality of your body and your daily living. I've talked at great length (an entire book actually!) about the importance of weight training. In *Gain to Lose*, I describe in detail all you need to know about muscle and fat and how the gain of one means the loss of the other. From personal experience and from watching the women I train, I see that weight training is critical to maintain fat loss. This is especially true as we age.

Weight training is especially important to maintain a firmer, more youthful body.

Here's what happens. As we age, we lose muscle mass. Keep in mind that Indians are already deficient in the muscle mass department. We are inherently endowed with less muscle mass than our Caucasian counterparts.

How Is It Relevant?

Muscle is a critically important tissue when it comes to mobility and functionality. It is also the main utilizer of carbs (glucose) and fat as fuel for its own functioning. It stands to reason, therefore, that the more muscle you have, the more fuel you need and the more likely you are to tap into those fat and glucose stores of energy within your body or from your meals.

Compounding the fact that we already have less muscle mass is that we lose muscle as we age – approximately half a pound a year after the age of 30, and certainly more if you are sedentary, which most people today are.

As we lose muscle, movement and functionality suffers. Difficulties in simple movements like climbing stairs, standing up from low chairs or from sitting on the floor (recall the cross-legged sit-and-stand test in chapter 1), start to manifest. Ask yourself the following questions:

- Do you hold on to the banisters when you climb up and down stairs?
- Do you find it difficult to walk uphill?
- More importantly, do you find it difficult to and feel unstable when you walk downhill?
- Do you need the support of the arms of the chair when you sit down and stand up from a low chair?
- Do you have difficulty doing the cross-legged sit-and-stand test?
- Do you find it difficult to carry your grocery bags or travel luggage?
- Do you have difficulty lifting reasonably heavy objects up from the floor or down from a high shelf?
- Do you end up with 'muscle pulls' and 'sprains' ever so often?

- Do you walk with hunched shoulders or display other signs of poor posture?
- Do you suffer from chronic back pain?

As we lose muscle, our appearance also suffers:

- Do you find that the back of your upper arms have become flabby?
- Has your butt started descending considerably from its original position or has it almost disappeared?
- Do your thighs feel like jelly and rub uncomfortably against each other?
- Does your belly sag even though you may not be overweight?
- Have you started rolling your shoulders forward in a permanently unappealing, slouched position?
- Have you developed a sore back that causes you to walk with a strange gait?

All of the above are the result of poor strength of the muscles and inadequate quantity of muscle mass. For movements to be executed correctly and the body to appear aesthetically pleasing, your muscles need to be adequate in quantity, strong and well-balanced. Muscles exist as pairs in our body, one on either side. A pair of quadriceps muscles in front of the thighs, for instance, extend the knee joint. Our bodies also have opposing or antagonistic muscles that perform the opposing action. So, for example, the quadriceps (or quads, as they are called in fitness parlance), which extend the knee joint, have the hamstrings at the back of the thighs that flex the knee joint. These muscles have to act in synchrony for you to be able to walk, run, squat, climb and sit. If there is an imbalance between these muscles (as there often is), the result is an awkward and difficult execution of movements associated with these muscles, resulting in injury and or pain. Strengthening muscles throughout the body, therefore, should be the prime objective of anyone wanting to lead a pain-free, active life with easy, graceful mobility. Without this strengthening process, muscles often deteriorate and atrophy.

As muscles atrophy or shrink with disuse and fat accumulates in places like the back of the arm, the butt, belly and thighs, they begin to sag. Fat doesn't hold up well to gravity. To appear more 'toned' and firm, you have to build and strengthen the muscles in these areas and burn the fat (with clean eating, cardio and weight training).

Although there is **no such thing as 'spot reduction'** where, for instance, you can selectively burn the fat behind your arms, building overall muscle mass and burning overall fat will address the problem areas. This may take time and fat reduction in the body is genetically determined. Some may initially lose belly fat when they start exercising while others may lose weight in their upper body, face and neck. No matter your genetic propensity, if you continue to exercise regularly, you will eventually address the problem areas.

If there is one thing you can do to maintain a youthful body as you age, it is weight training.

Common Problems and Their Solutions

It can be the most frustrating experience when you bend down to pick up something and end up with a 'sprained' or 'pulled' back. Or imagine playing with your kids (or grandkids) and finding yourself in an uncomfortably twisted position, unable to move.

Here are three common moves that may be part of your day-to-day life. All these moves can be greatly facilitated if you perform the corresponding exercises to build strength in the concerned muscles.

- Bending to pick up a child or heavy object.
- Reaching overhead and lifting something heavy down from a shelf overhead.
- Pushing a heavy piece of furniture or a trolley.

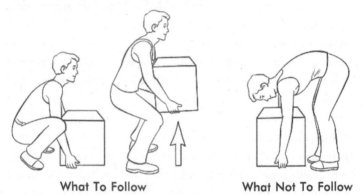

What To Follow   **What Not To Follow**

The exercises for these moves are explained in detail in chapter 14.

The ideal exercise one can do in a gym setting to develop these very muscles is called the **bent-knee dead lift.** This exercise depicts the movement of bending and lifting.

Grasping and lowering an object from above requires the following:

- Great core strength.
- Strength in the shoulders and arms.

Think about getting your cabin baggage from the shelves in an aircraft at the end of your flight. This can prove quite challenging if you don't have the necessary strength in your shoulders, arms and core.

During stopovers on my travels, I invariably manage to indulge in some serious, last-minute duty-free shopping and end up with a fairly heavy cabin bag that I have to manage. These are the times I honestly feel a great deal of gratitude for the serious weight training I put myself through on a regular basis. When the flight lands and everyone springs up to rush off the aircraft (which is something I never quite understand), you can't wait around helplessly for someone to extract your overhead bag. There's no time for that, especially when everyone around you is snarling at anyone stalling in the aisles. You had better be nimble with your luggage!

When attempting to lift something down, stand beneath and slightly away from the shelf above with your feet slightly apart for better balance. Reach up, grasp the object in a stable manner so that the weight is evenly balanced in your hands. Lower without arching the back or leaning backward.

The exercises that strengthen the parts of the body that are involved in this move are:

- The **shoulder press** for the shoulder muscles
- **Bent over rowing** for the upper back muscles
- The **plank** for the core

While pushing a heavy piece of furniture or a heavy trolley, you require strength in the chest muscles, the shoulders and the back of the arms or triceps muscle. In order to push a heavy piece of furniture, place yourself directly behind it in a staggered stance (one foot in front of the other) engage the core, bend forward slightly at the hip joint, place both palms of the side of the furniture and push with the back flat engaging mainly the appropriate chest and shoulder muscles.

Two great exercises to strengthen these very muscles are the **chest press** (or the **pushup**) and the **plank**.

There are several things you may need to do through the day that require some amount of strength and stability. There is the act of pulling your bags off the carousel. Or perhaps carrying a heavy grocery bag, your laptop and your suitcase, or a child along with a heavy bag on the other shoulder. In all these situations, you don't have to worry about ending up with a sprained muscle if you are strong enough or able enough to perform the task.

So there you have it. Three common moves that can be facilitated by strengthening the corresponding muscles. Using weight training to strengthen those muscles will make these moves much easier and prevent injury while performing them. So while weight training has several other health benefits including fat loss, an improved aesthetic (more shapely body), more confidence, higher metabolism, prevention and management of diabetes, osteoporosis and so on, one important benefit is the ability to perform day-to-day tasks with ease.

The Benefits of Building Muscle

- It helps you lose fat.
- It helps prevent (and manage) various metabolic problems including diabetes.
- It prevents and treats osteoporosis.
- It is critical for efficient physical movement.
- Muscle weighs more than fat, a fact that needs to be kept in mind for those looking only at only weight loss on the scale. This can be misleading.
- Muscle is progressively lost with age unless a conscious effort is made to sustain or build it.
- A body with sufficient muscular strength and mass is more efficient, fluid and graceful and is able to handle its own body weight better than a fatty one of the same 'weight' on a scale.
- Building muscle and strength gives you confidence about your own body and its capability. It gives you a certain level of independence that is incomparable.

twelve

Flexibility

How does the flexibility of muscles change as we age? How does this change affect us? Can the flexibility of muscles be improved after deterioration?

These are common questions that arise when we think about flexibility.

When you watch children play, you will notice just how easily flexible they are, twisting, turning and effortlessly sitting cross-legged or on their haunches. As we grow older, we stop doing those things with our bodies. Naturally, our muscles forget how to do them and become less flexible.

Just as the muscle mass and strength deteriorates with age, so does the flexibility or elasticity of muscle. Consciously improving flexibility is important for overall fitness. It could be done by including a serious, prolonged stretch routine to your fitness once or twice a week. Or perhaps you could take up yoga and practise the asanas from a physical fitness perspective to improve flexibility. Yoga, of course, is not limited to the physical poses or asanas alone. It has a whole repertoire of breathing routines and the yogic lifestyle. You may or may not wish to incorporate the entire package. That's entirely up to you, depending on availability of time and so on.

In general, men are inherently less flexible than women. This would also mean that their flexibility deteriorates further with age. This is not to say one cannot improve. Flexibility is such an important part of staying fit and especially preventing injury that even body builders, elite athletes, dancers and those who participate in various sports routinely include serious stretching into their routine.

I love doing yoga sequences twice or thrice a week. It doesn't need to last very long. Fifteen to thirty minutes of practice normally suffice. It helps me pay close attention to my body, and my ability to stretch and balance. It is also a great way to bring an inward focus on the body, enabling me to identify if the entire body is well-balanced and coordinated, if it feels stronger on one side compared to the other, if there are areas of pain or weakness and so on. Awareness of the breath is also crucial in enhancing yogic practice. Without the breath, it could be just about any exercise. The breathing brings about a calm and focused sensation during practice.

I would advise you to start stretching (either incorporate yoga as a modality or include simple stretches that you practice diligently) at least a couple of times a week. It is shocking sometimes when we suddenly realize we are unable to do something as simple as touching our forehead to our knees in a forward seated posture. This is something we were able to do just a little while ago, wasn't it? It's easy to slide when one is not vigilant on a regular basis.

If you are inflexible and start trying to become more flexible late in life it is still not a lost cause. You may not be able to touch your forehead to your knees in the seated forward stretch (illustrated below). But you certainly will improve. Every little increment is meaningful for the body's alignment and movement. Much of the time, the muscular spasm, pain, discomfort, inability to move freely with grace and coordination, can be attributed to the inflexibility of one set of muscles. The opposing muscles may be inordinately strong or even more flexible, causing an imbalance, tightness and awkward movement pattern.

One of the most common areas that become tight and inflexible are the lower back and hamstring muscles at the back of the thighs.

The main muscles of the lower back include parts of the lattissmus dorsi, the thoracolumbar fascia and the erector spinae (there are several smaller ones that I won't include here). So now that I have mentioned some tongue twisters to chew on, let me explain why I did that. These are just a few of the muscles in our body. We have about 650 muscles in total, most with equally laborious names, origins, insertions and functions. It's virtually impossible for anyone to truly comprehend and digest the intricate workings of the human body without being completely awed by it. So much can actually go wrong with it, considering the wheels within wheels, that I am surprised that so little does, despite how we much we neglect our bodies.

We don't just disregard and disrespect our bodies by not exercising or not keeping our weight within a healthy range;

we do so even by over-exercising, not doing the right kind of exercises that our bodies require, and pushing our bodies relentlessly, expecting them to respond the way we want them to. Both ends of the spectrum may harm us. Many of us may be guilty of overuse injury and not addressing the **real needs** of our bodies.

How Does Decreased Flexibility Affect Us?

If you think about it, it's not the speed at which you walk or run that is tested on a daily basis (unless you make it a habit of being late for your work/meeting/bus/train everyday). It's small things like bending down to pick something up or trying to reach into the shelf in your kitchen for that special spice you had stored away. It is the back pain you experience after a day's work seated at your office desk.

In fitness, we most often tend to gravitate towards the activities we enjoy and are good at. So, for instance, if we like running or long-duration, low-intensity exercise, we tend to gravitate towards marathons. If we like music and dance, we might sign up for a Zumba session. If we dislike stretching and have poor flexibility, we likely stay away from yoga. Point is, we have to identify clearly where our weaknesses lie. In all probability, they lie in just those places we are afraid to look, in those areas that we are neglecting. So if you are running miles without paying attention to your flexibility, you are bound to suffer the consequences.

For example, muscular injury is common in runners. (Joint injury is another issue altogether.) It could be a muscle tear, a muscle strain, sprain or just plain overuse. Stretching and strengthening adequately can prevent much of this.

Let me explain **hamstring flexibility**, for instance. The hamstring muscles lie at the back of the thigh, and consist of three separate, long muscles, namely:

- Biceps femoris
- Semitendinosus
- Semimembranosus

These muscles originate from the pelvic bone underneath the gluteus maximus, which is the large muscle of the butt. They run along the back of your thigh bone or the femur, cross at the knee joint and attach to your tibia, which is the shin bone. The primary functions of the hamstring muscle are:

- Knee flexion (bending the knee),
- Hip extension (moving the entire leg backward), and
- External and internal rotation of the legs (turning the leg so the feet move side to side, moving the entire limb from the hip downward).

The hamstring muscles are critical for trunk stability and not just for the movement of the legs. Since they are attached to the pelvic bone, during movements such as walking or running, the hamstring muscles contract and propel you forward by **extending the hip and bringing the femur or thigh bone back in a backward-bending motion**. During the next forward step, the hamstring muscles contract and **bend the knees**. The hamstrings also contract to **stabilize the pelvis** by tilting it slightly backward. The contraction of these muscles counteracts the pulling action of the lower abdominal and back muscles that tilt the pelvis forward.

The following are the most common causes of hamstring inflexibility:

Poor strength in the abdominals and lower back: Hamstring inflexibility is often the result of muscle weakness or instability in another part of the body such as the muscles of the abdomen or lower back. All these muscles are intimately connected. They manage to stabilize the torso by altering the position of the pelvis. The hamstring muscles stabilize the pelvis by providing a counteractive force to the forward pull on the pelvis by the abdominal and lower back muscles. If your lower-abdominal or lower-back muscles are unstable or weak, they cannot provide the force to counteract the backward-bending pull on your pelvis by the hamstring muscles. As a result, the hamstring muscles tighten and shorten as they continue to pull and tilt the pelvis backward.

Wearing high heels all the time: When women wear shoes with high heels they are at greater risk of hamstring inflexibility. Walking in these types of shoes tilts your pelvis forward and causes the knee to be hyperextended. This places an excess amount of strain and tension on the hamstring with each contraction. The continuous contraction and tension causes the hamstring muscles to tighten and become inflexible. If you are hell-bent on those killer heels, then you need to adequately and regularly stretch your hamstrings and pelvic muscles.

Overuse injury and tightness: You may also suffer from hamstring inflexibility as a result of overusing these muscles in sports that require a lot of running or kicking. Not stretching properly before and after a sporting activity can cause stiffness. When you participate in a sport that calls the muscle into action repeatedly (like running) and then don't stretch it enough, it becomes tight and inflexible over time.

Diminished flexibility in the hamstrings increases your chances of injury **since tight muscles are susceptible to spasm, tears**

and strains. When your hamstrings are tight or under tension, they pull the pelvis and lumbar region of the spine away from the sagittal plane, tilting your pelvis backward, flattening the lower back and contributing to lower back pain, muscle spasms and postural problems. Tight hamstrings also deeply compromise your sports performance by limiting the range of movement in your pelvis and hips, thereby altering your form and stride length in sport. Interestingly, tight hamstrings also increase your risk of hip and knee injuries and pain.

To test if you are fairly flexible in the hamstring area, the below-mentioned test will help. If you are able to lift your leg, with the knees fully extended, to about 90 degrees at least (as seen in the illustration below) then you are relatively flexible. Anything less than 90 degrees (that is, the angle between the two legs) can be considered compromised flexibility. With time and improved flexibility, you should be able to gently pull that straightened leg closer to your upper body while keeping the knee fully extended.

Try and maintain at least this level of flexibility.

The **seated forward bend** (seen earlier in the chapter) is a much more advanced test of hamstring and lower back flexibility. In yoga, it's called the paschimottanasana. The name is complicated, but the pose highly beneficial. Many are intimidated by yoga because of the images they see of seemingly impossible positions and phenomenal degrees of flexibility. But all of yoga is not about the Instagram-worthy pictures you are overwhelmed by. It's about gradually building on what you have. My sincere advice, however, would be to find the right teacher – someone who not only understands poses and breathing, but someone who is able to adapt those poses for you. In yoga, besides going through the motions and getting from one pose to another, a degree of mindfulness is required for you to really understand what your body is doing.

> Become more mindful and self-aware as you stretch. Ask yourself questions like:
>
> - Which muscle am I stretching?
> - Where should I 'feel' the stretch?
> - Which counter muscle is contracting to aid this stretch?
> - Am I feeling any pain or discomfort in any area of my body? If so, where?
> - Have I gotten better at this? Has it become easier?

The hamstring muscle and its lack of flexibility is only one of 650 (or more) muscles in the body that can and are often affected by our negligence. So you can well imagine the possibilities for injury, pain, discomfort and bad posture if any one of those muscles is affected. Each muscle has a role to play in our body. Some flex a joint, others extend the joint. Some help us lift;

others aid us in bending sideways or twisting. Most often, groups of muscles function cohesively to bring about a smooth and seemingly effortless movement. Even if one among the group is affected by lack of flexibility (or strength), the movement becomes awkward, painful and unstable.

As already mentioned in the chapter on strength, most skeletal muscles are present in pairs on either side of the body. A pair of hamstrings, one at the back of each leg; a pair of biceps, one in the front of each upper arm, and so on. Most muscles also have opposing muscles, which do the exact opposite job that they perform. So, for instance, the hamstring muscles flex or bend the knee while the quadriceps muscle, located in front of the thigh, extend or straighten the knee. So, as you can see, it is important that all the muscles are addressed when stretching (or strengthening, for that matter). A muscle imbalance occurs when one is stronger or more flexible than its opposing muscle causing the related joint to perform awkwardly. Ultimately, this will lead to pain and poor posture.

Stretching the quadriceps, therefore, should accompany stretching the hamstrings at the back of the thigh.

Can the Flexibility of Muscles Be Improved After Deterioration?

Yes, it can, within reason. You may not be able to touch your forehead to your knee in a seated forward stretch, especially if you are deeply compromised with a lack of flexibility. But every increment in flexibility is a good thing. You will not only begin to see an improvement in your posture and gait, but will also be spared the risk of injury during exercise. I have, however, come across individuals who do improve considerably with regular practice. They always feel better and look better when muscle imbalances are rectified with a proper stretch and strengthening routine. On the flip side, it is also possible to deteriorate rapidly if one doesn't stretch regularly, so it's important to continue to stretch everyday to maintain your flexibility.

Stretching, therefore, is an important part of a fitness routine. I myself find that yoga has become integral to my fitness. I used to (quite honestly) think it was a mere waste of time. It is certainly not. Stretching complements everything else and, most importantly, prevents injury.

Three of the most common causes of injury and pain during training or working out are: overuse, lack of warm-ups and poor flexibility.

Although flexibility seems a trivial aspect of fitness, it is a very important ingredient. Many people think, 'Oh! I can always stretch.' The fact is, you can't! The less flexible you become, the harder it gets and the less inclined you are to attempt it. Over time, everything becomes compromised including your gait and movements. So, flexibility needs a prominent place in your fitness routine, and it only gets better with practice.

- Include stretching every single day. Even 5 to 10 minutes will suffice.
- Never stretch cold muscles or before warming up.
- Dynamic stretching, which is stretching with movement, is a good way to stretch, too, provided it is very controlled and you are not succumbing to momentum.
- Assisted stretches are great if you have the right partner who understands just how much to push you.
- Stretch after your workout.
- Every single person needs to stretch.

thirteen

Move More

Are you sitting down as you read this? How do you feel? How long have you been sitting? Have you taken a break and stepped out? Have you stood up and stretched?

If you haven't, then put this book down, stand up and walk around your room, up and down the stairs or in your garden as briskly as you can for three to five minutes. Then, clasp your hands and stretch them high above your head. Push your clasped hands back as far as possible feeling the stretch in your chest, particularly at the point where your arms meet your chest. Go up on your toes and reach for the ceiling. Take a deep breath and let it out slowly.

THE IMPORTANCE OF MOVEMENT

According to Dr David Levine of Mayo Clinic, 'Sitting is more dangerous than smoking, kills more people than HIV and is more treacherous than parachuting. We are sitting ourselves to death.'

Several studies have shown the importance of 'not sitting' for prolonged periods of time. Moving more through the day is as important, if not more important, than an hour of exercise.

As we age, we do tend to move less. We find ways to remain seated as we work, attend lectures and workshops, sit around watching TV or socialize.

There are some very real problems associated with staying immobile for long periods of time:

- Risk of various cancers like colon, breast and uterus cancers were found to be increased in a study published in the Journal of the National Cancer Institute.
- Risk of heart disease increased in those individuals who sat more than six hours a day. They died earlier than their counterparts who sat for less than three hours a day. Something as simple as not sitting for long periods of time appears to increase longevity. In another study, men who spent six hours or more a day sitting had a 20 per cent higher death rate than those who sat less than three hours a day.
- The risk of obesity goes up several times when you remain seated for prolonged periods of time.

    The risk of diabetes is increased with prolonged sitting in a day. The sensitivity of insulin, the hormone that controls your blood sugar is decreased with continuous sitting, leading to the increased incidence of developing type-2 diabetes. After analysing 18 other studies with 80,000 participants, a study published in the journal *Diabetologia* found that those who sat the most were twice as likely to develop type-2 diabetes.
- Sitting interferes with lipoprotein lipase (LPL), an enzyme that breaks down our fat. LPL activity is directly related to movement, so lying down and sitting still means that levels of LPL drop to an abysmal low leading to the accumulation of fat.

- The risk of depression goes up. Those who sat for more than seven hours a day had a 47 per cent higher chance of developing depression. The very act of moving increases the endorphins to the brain and makes one feel better.

THE SEATED POSITION

The seated position itself is such that it decreases not only the blood flow to the lower limbs but also the neuromuscular stimulation to the leg muscles, causing them to literally go dead.

When continued through life, prolonged sitting causes poor mobility and balance, increasing the likelihood of falling down, which is something we see so often in older people.

The position of sitting, especially in our modern chairs with their 90 degree or more flexion at the hip and knee joints, encourages deep-vein thrombosis or clotting of blood in the veins of the lower limbs as a result of prolonged immobility.

This is regardless of great sitting posture. Even if you have your back aligned perfectly, shoulders dropped, core tightened and so on, it still doesn't help the blood flow to the legs. Good posture may protect your back, but will not circumvent the other negative effects of prolonged sitting.

Your Chair

It was only in the 18th century that the 'chair' made its appearance. Prior to that, we managed with stools and benches, which frankly don't encourage sitting for long due to their lack of a backrest. Nowadays, however, companies vie with each other to make more comfortable chairs than ever before. You have chairs for bad backs, chairs that rotate, slide, swing, massage you, have great quality foam, arm rests and so on, making it very difficult to get off your backside and move once you are seated. The truth is, however good your chair is, it is killing you!

In 1992, Dr Levine asked the question, 'Why do some people not gain weight even when they eat more (even when their exercise is eliminated)?' He then went on to perform an experiment where a group of people were given 1,000 calories/day more than their usual diet and were told not to exercise but to continue with their routine work and they were observed for two months. Some gained weight as expected while others didn't. What was the difference? Those who didn't gain weight moved more through the day. They didn't exercise more, but just moved more. Their bodies inherently understood that they were consuming more than required and, to compensate, they just moved more at work and at home. They may have climbed more stairs, stood instead of staying seated, done more housework and so on.

So how does just moving around help? It results in:

- Increased productivity
- Improved creativity
- More innovation
- Improved memory
- Better mood

Non-Exercise Activity Thermogenesis (NEAT)

This is the calories burnt from activities other than structured exercise, which we commonly disregard. NEAT can be increased by:

- Fidgeting
- Moving more
- Taking the stairs

- Moving your limbs as much as possible
- Standing instead of sitting
- Doing simple things around the house like laundry and cleaning

The Malaise of the Modern World

A metaanalysis (the study of other studies) on detriments of sitting found that higher amounts of time spent sitting was associated with higher risk of dying! And one of the major causes of our sedentary lifestyle is television.

Watching a lot of TV causes depression. This, I believe, is partly due to sitting for long periods of time and, perhaps, partly the result of the kind of channels you watch. But now that you know the harm sitting for long periods can do to you, ask yourself this:

- How many hours of TV do you watch?
- How many hours do you spend on your laptop?

I can tell you that through the writing of this book I've been sitting a lot more than I am used to and it makes me miserable! I use a standing desk sometimes, but when you are researching and reading several articles and trying to comprehend and sort through them while also putting them into some cohesive order into a book, it's hard to keep standing! I go for two walks instead of one to make up for this sedentary behaviour, stretch as much as possible to combat that stiffness in the hips, but it's still not the same as staying active through the day.

So what do you do? Small changes make a big difference:

- Stand up when you watch TV. Stand at least for 50 per cent of the time. I know that sounds crazy but it really works.

- Watch less TV!
- Watch the news on your treadmill/stationary bike.
- Walk around at every commercial break (and, we know there are lots of them!). You are missing nothing if you take a walk down the hall during a commercial break.
- Do squats/calf raises or ab crunches while you wait for milk to boil in your kitchen.
- Get a standing desk. It's a simple contraption that you can actually place on top of your regular desk to raise the surface level. You can then place your laptop or book on it and stand when you work.
- Have you heard of a treadmill desk? It is a treadmill with a tabletop to place your laptop, book etc. on it so you can work as you walk!
- Move every 30 minutes.
- Slip off your shoes and move the feet and toes.
- Stand up and walk around every time you answer the phone.
- Whenever you schedule a meeting with colleagues or employees, why not try a walking meeting?
- Take the stairs whenever you can.
- Exercise at your desk – stretch, do tricep dips or push-ups whenever you can right at your desk.
- Work in your garden.
- Take a short walk after your meal instead of collapsing in front of the TV.
- Walk down to the store instead of taking the car.
- Walk your dog. Getting a dog has been found to be therapeutic in more ways than one.
- We always try and find a parking spot closest to our destination. Consider it a good thing when we don't. We get to walk that distance.

Structured Exercise

The minimum exercise requirement per day as per WHO recommendations is:

> 150 minutes of accumulated exercise/week
> Minimum 30 minutes/day = walking 3.2 km in 30 minutes

Many people do manage to accumulate these numbers, and many work out for much longer than the recommended duration. However, many also believe that an hour or two of 'exercise' entitles them to a sedentary lifestyle for the rest of their day. Prolonged physical inertia is not negated by exercise!

Runners are as susceptible to the setbacks of prolonged sitting as obese people who don't exercise. So, for instance, if you complete your one hour run and then go to your workplace and sit for the next eight hours, you are at as much of a risk of developing the problems previously listed as someone who does not exercise regularly. The hour of exercise does not negate the ill effects of sitting.

This is why sitting is compared to smoking. Exercising for an hour and then smoking a pack a day will not contradict the detrimental effects of smoking, just as an hour of exercise cannot compensate for an otherwise sedentary lifestyle.

Endurance Activities

Any long duration, low-intensity exercise will build endurance. Long walks, treks, long swims and so on fall into this category.

Many people have been misled into believing that one has to exercise at a low intensity for a long time in order to burn fat. This intensity of exercise has been called the 'fat-burning zone'. While it's true that the body taps into fat as fuel when you work out at lower intensities, in order to burn *enough* fat to see a difference you would have to work out for hours on end everyday! How many of us have that kind of time?

There's absolutely nothing wrong with endurance activities. They act as stress relievers besides being a form of exercise. We are talking here about exercise intensities where you are barely breathless and the heart rate is at about 60 per cent of your target heart rate. So, essentially, it's an easy pace that can be sustained for long periods of time.

Most people use this level of intensity for every single cardio workout of theirs. As I mentioned in the chapter on cardio, do include HIIT or higher intensity workouts in order to rev up your metabolism and burn more calories and, therefore, fat. Alternatively, aim to walk faster overall and cover more distance by the end of, say, a month.

Long walks, cycling, treks and so on should most definitely be a part of your life if possible. They help in more ways than one. It's not just about the weight loss after a point, is it? It is about the sheer joy that these kinds of activities bring to one's day. In fact, if done in a group with friends, these can be wonderful opportunities to connect with other people.

So, finally, just move more throughout the day. Find ways to move. Find excuses to move. Enjoy your body and what it can do. Enjoy movement. Explore different kinds of movement like dance, yoga, walking and so on. Let movement become a way of life!

fourteen

Essential Exercises

In this chapter, I will explain a few essential exercises to follow. These exercises are for increasing strength, stability and balance in the body – an aspect of fitness that tends to deteriorate rapidly and alarmingly with age. 'Frailty' is a term we often hear in reference to older people. The cause of this frailty is loss of muscle. The problem with increasing frailty is an increased incidence of accidents and injury. To prevent this very troubling problem and keeping yourself strong through your later years, do go through and learn to do all the exercises illustrated below.

I've divided the exercises into two segments. The first segment covers the essential strength-training exercises, while the second segment deals with exercises that will improve your balance and core strength.

As a side note, arm yourselves with weight-training gloves, a bench, barbells, dumb-bells and a mat.

STRENGTH TRAINING

Strength training becomes incredibly crucial as you grow older, as seen earlier. Here, I have recommended 12 repetitions and

3–5 sets in general, but this will obviously depend on your individual goals.

You need to use a higher weight and lower number of reps (about 6–8) to build muscle and a higher weight and higher reps (10–12) to build strength.

BENT-KNEE DEAD LIFT

This is a great exercise for the lower back, glutes and hamstrings. The exercise mimics the daily action of picking heavy objects off the floor. You can build up to using a really heavy weight for this exercise, as the muscles involved are large and very strong.

Starting position: Stand holding the barbell hanging down in front of your body, close to your thighs. Your palms should face you (called the overhand grip).

Movement: Now start to bend over by pushing the hips backward. Allow the barbell to slide along the surface of the thighs until the hips are as far back as they can go without rounding the upper back. As you lower the weight, your knees will start to bend slightly towards the end of the movement in order to retain a flat back. That's natural. But the essential movement is in the hip hinge. The more flexible you are in your lower back and hamstring area, the lower you will be able to bend at the hip without bending the knees too much.

Now straighten up by extending the hips and knees until you are standing upright again in the starting position.

Breathing: Inhale as you lower the weight; exhale as you lift the weight towards your chest.

Keep the following in mind while performing this exercise:

- Keep the back absolutely flat through the movement.
- The barbell should stay close to the body through the entire move.
- When you straighten up, throw back the shoulders and extend the hip fully by squeezing the glutes.
- Do at least three to four sets of eight to twelve repetitions.
- Keep the head up, eyes level (not looking upward or down to the floor).

THE SQUAT

The squat is a common movement we perform while sitting down to pick up a baby or a heavy box. It strengthens the legs (quadriceps in the front of the thigh, hamstrings at the back of the thigh and the glutes).

Starting Position: Hold the dumb-bells in both arms, palms facing towards your body and your feet are about a hip-width apart. Alternatively, you can hold a barbell across the shoulders.

Movement: Start to sit by pushing the hips backward and then bending the knees. Lower the hips until the thighs are almost parallel to the floor.

Stand up by extending the knees and hips.

The squat is a very powerful movement and builds great strength in the lower body. You can increase the weights you use gradually to quite a heavy weight as the muscles are large and can handle a higher weight.

Breathing: Inhale as you lower your body; exhale as you stand.

Keep the following in mind while doing this exercise:

- Don't allow the knees to travel too far beyond your toes.
- The focus should be on pushing the hips backward, not pushing the knees forward.
- Keep the head up eyes level (not looking upward or down to the floor)

The difference between the bent-knee deadlift and the squat is the extent to which the knees bend. In the deadlift, the knees bend very slightly to lower the weight, which is in front of you. In the squat, the knees have to bend enough for the thighs to reach a position that is parallel to the floor. The deadlift uses mainly the lower back, glutes and hamstring muscles. the squat uses mainly the quads and, to a lesser extent, the hamstrings and glutes. The back is only a stabilizing muscle during the squat.

LUNGE

This exercise is similar to the squat except that you work one leg at a time and also include some amount of balance and core stability as you step forward.

Starting position: Stand with the barbell across the shoulders or holding dumb-bells in your hands.

Movement: Step forward with your right foot and bend the right knee until the right thigh is almost parallel to the floor. The step forward, therefore, has to be a long enough step for you to create a right angle at your right knee joint.

Now step back to your starting position. Repeat the same movement with the left leg.

Breathing: Inhale as you step forward and lunge; exhale as you step back.

Calf Raises

This exercise strengthens and builds the calves, which are rarely addressed.

Starting position: Stand holding the dumb-bells in both hands with your feet hip-width apart.

Movement: Lift the heels and go up on your toes. Lower till the heel almost, but not quite, touches the floor.

Breathing: Exhale as you lift yourself onto your toes and inhale as you lower yourself back down.

Bench Press

The bench press builds and strengthens the chest muscles called the pectoralis muscle.

Starting position: Lie on your back on the bench, knees bent and feet flat on the floor. If your back arches too much in this position, you can even place your feet on the edge of the bench.

Hold the dumb-bells in your arms, palms facing the feet, with elbows bent and at right angles. The arms should be at the level of the shoulders.

Movement: Push the dumb-bells above the chest by extending your elbows. By the end of the movement, the dumb-bells have to be right above your shoulders, with your palms still facing your feet.

Lower by bending the elbows and bring the dumb-bells back to starting position.

Breathing: Exhale as you push the weight upward and inhale as you lower it.

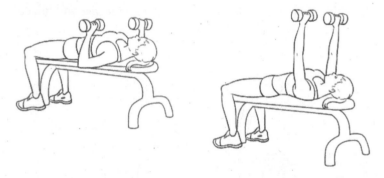

Once you have mastered the bench press and can push a fairly heavy weight, you can start doing push-ups, which use your own body weight.

Push-ups

Starting position: Go down on your mat on your hands and knees. The palms are placed flat on the mat beneath your shoulders but wider than your shoulders. The knees are placed directly under your hips (in the case of a beginner), or slightly behind the hips (in the case of an intermediate) or, if you are an advanced exerciser, you could lift your knees off the mat and stay on your toes.

Intermediate Push-up

Movement: Breathe in and lower the upper body towards the mat by bending the elbows. Lower the chest until it almost, but not quite, touches the floor between your two palms. Exhale as you lift to starting position, extending the elbows fully. Repeat for about 10 to 20 repetitions. This exercise works the chest muscles (or pectoralis), the front of the shoulders and the triceps muscles at the back of the arms, the very same muscles required in pushing that heavy table.

Breathing: Inhale as you lower your body; exhale as you straighten the elbows.

It is possible that your limbs and/or core are too weak for you to be able to perform even the beginner's push-up. In this case, start with the chest press exercise, which uses dumb-bells to build up strength in the very same muscles, then progress to push-ups. Alternatively, you could start with push-ups against the wall and then move down to the floor.

Advanced Push-up

BENT-OVER ROWING

This exercise works on the upper back muscles or the lats; the smaller muscles of the upper back like the rhomboids; and the biceps muscles of the arms.

Starting position: Stand with feet hip-width apart, knees slightly bent, and hip hinged so that the upper body is tilted forward at about 45 degrees. Hold the dumb-bells (or a barbell in both arms) with arms hanging down directly under your shoulders.

Movement: Pull the weights towards the body by bending the elbows until the dumb-bells are brought close to the lower edge of the chest. Extend the elbows and return to starting position.

This action mimics any pulling action that works the front of the arms and the upper back.

Breathing: Exhale as you pull the weight upward by bending the elbows; inhale as you lower them to starting position.

SHOULDER PRESS

This exercise strengthens and builds the shoulder muscles. These muscles are essential for any movement that includes lifting, especially if it is lifting things above your head.

Starting position: Sit on a bench with feet flat on the floor. Hold the dumb-bells in your hands, palms facing forward. The upper arm needs to be at shoulder level and the elbows bent at 90 degrees.

Movement: Straighten the elbows and lift the dumb-bells overhead until the elbows are fully extended and the arms are parallel to each other. Lower to starting position.

Breathing: Exhale as you lift the weight overhead; inhale as you lower it.

BICEP CURLS

This exercise strengthens and builds the biceps muscles in the front of the upper arm. This muscle is required for any pulling or lifting movement like opening a heavy door or lifting a suitcase.

Starting position: Stand with your feet hip-width apart, holding the barbell with the palms facing forward, away from the body. The exercise can also be done using dumb-bells in exactly the same way.

Movement: Curl the arms by bending the elbows until the barbell comes close to the chest level. Lower to starting position.

Breathing: Exhale as you bend the elbows; inhale as you lower weights.

OVERHEAD TRICEPS EXTENSION

This exercise focuses on the triceps muscle at the back of the arm. Although this muscle is used in any pushing movement (like the bench press or push-up, for instance), this exercise isolates the muscle to strengthen and build it.

Starting: Sit at the edge of a bench (it can also be done standing up). Hold a single dumb-bell at one end, behind your head with the elbows bent.

Movement: Straighten the elbow and raise the dumb-bell over your head till the elbow is fully extended. Lower to starting position.

Breathing: Exhale as you lift the arm by extending the elbows; inhale as you bend the elbows.

Keep the following points in mind while doing this exercise:

▸ Ensure that the elbows remain close to the ears during the lifting process. The tendency is to flare the elbows outward.
▸ Don't arch the back if doing the exercise standing up. Doing this exercise in a seated position prevents this problem.

Advanced Bicycle

This exercise is the most effective exercise for the abdominal area. It addresses the rectus abdominis as well as the oblique muscles that form the 'waist'.

Starting position: Lie on your back arms crossed behind the head. Lift both feet off the ground about 6 inches and simultaneously lift the upper body about 6 inches off the ground.

Movement: Bend the right knee and bring it up towards the chest. Simultaneously lift the upper body and twist the torso such that the left elbow touches (or at least moves towards) the bent right knee.

Straighten the knee, untwist the torso. Repeat the movement with the left leg and right elbow.

Repeat continuously, alternating legs in a pedalling motion with the opposite elbows, for about 20 to 30 repetitions. Through the entire set, the legs and shoulders remain lifted off the ground.

Breathing: Exhale every time you crunch your body as your elbows reach for the knees; inhale as you switch sides.

Reverse Curl

Although the rectus abdominis consists of a pair of long muscles running from the lower border of the chest to the pelvic bone, certain exercises like the reverse curl work the lower abdominals (the lower aspect of the rectus) better. I think this exercise is particularly important because it works the lower abs without taxing the back as some other lower ab exercises like the 'scissors' do.

Following pregnancy and childbirth, many women have flabby abdominal muscles, particularly the lower abdomen, which tends to sag. This is an excellent exercise to strengthen that area. It also helps prevent back pain.

Starting position: Lie on your back with your knees bent and feet lifted so the knees are at 90 degrees. Place the hands flat on your mat next to the body.

Movement: By contracting the lower abdominal muscles, lift the legs and hips off the floor, as high as you can, and lower. Do about 20 repetitions and three sets.

The movement has to be smooth and controlled.

Breathing: Exhale as you lift the hips; inhale when you lower them.

Abdominal Crunch

This is the most basic abdominal exercise one does. It works the rectus abdominis. Its action is to curl the upper body towards the lower or lift the lower body towards the torso, as in the reverse curl.

Starting position: Lie on your back on a mat. Keep the knees bent, feet flat on the floor. Interlock your hands behind your head or place them across your chest.

Movement: Lift your upper body, including the head, neck and shoulders off the mat using the strength of your abdominal muscle. Lift as high as you can without straining your neck or any other muscles, then lower till the upper body almost, but not quite touches the floor. Then lift again to complete about 20 to 25 repetitions.

Breathing: Exhale as you lift your torso; inhale as you lower it.

Keep the following in line while doing this exercise:

▸ Keep the neck aligned with the spine by not hyper-extending it. Look straight ahead as you lift and lower.

BALANCE AND CORE

Here are some simple exercises to improve your balance and core strength.

PLANK

This exercise strengthens your core muscles, namely:

▸ The deep pelvic muscles
▸ The abdominals
▸ The deeper and superficial lower back muscles
▸ The deep and superficial muscles of the shoulders

Movement: Lie face down and lift yourself onto your elbows and toes. Hold the abdominal muscles in and tighten the pelvic muscles so the lower back is not overly arched. Hold this position for as long as you can without compromising on form.

Hold for a minimum of one minute. See if you can continue to hold for about three minutes or more. Breathe normally as you hold.

SIDE PLANK

This is similar to the plank but works the muscles at the sides of the abdomen or the waist – the obliques. It also works the shoulders as they hold you in position.

Movement: Lie on your side on a mat. Raise yourself up on to your elbow and align your entire body in a straight line with only the side of the lower foot and the elbow touching the ground. The feet should be stacked one on top of the other.

To make it a little easier, you can start with planting the upper foot on the floor in front of the lower one.

Hold for at least a minute and repeat on the other side. Breathe normally as you hold.

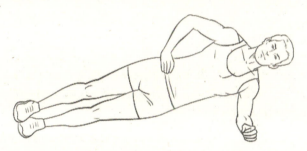

QUADRUPED ARM-LEG RAISE

This exercise works the core, shoulders, upper back, lower back and the glutes. It also calls into play your balance and core strength. The exercise looks simple enough but is very effective in strengthening areas you otherwise do not address.

Starting position: Start on your mat on your hands and knees.

Movement: Lift the right leg straight up behind you and simultaneously lift the left hand in front of you up to the level of your left ear.

Hold this position for 40 to 60 seconds and repeat on the other side. Breathe normally as you hold the position.

Lying Back Extensions

As we age, a very common problem we face is lower back pain. One of the reasons for this is the poor strength in the muscles of the posterior chain or the back.

Starting position: Lie face down on your mat with arms extended overhead.

Movement: Lift the upper and lower body simultaneously off the mat. Hold for a few seconds and release. Do 10 to 15 repetitions per set and do about three sets. Avoid hyperextending the neck by looking up. Instead, keep your neck aligned to the spine.

Breathing: Exhale as you lift the upper body; inhale when you lower it.

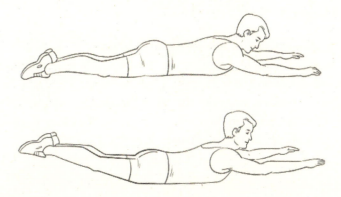

T-STAND TO KNEE-UP

This exercise improves your balance and core strength. As you move from one unbalanced position to another, your core muscles come into play to keep you upright. When you are a beginner, please stay close to a sofa or stand on a soft carpet in case you lose your balance while doing the exercise.

Movement: Stand with feet hip-width apart. Lift the right leg by bending the knee. Take the same leg backward as you fold over, forming a 'T' by stretching the arms alongside your head and ears. Hold for a few seconds, then bring the same leg to the front for a knee-up.

Repeat this move 6 to 10 times. Repeat on the other side.

ONE-LEGGED STAND

This is an exercise to improve your balance.

Stand with feet hip-width apart. Bend the right knee and place the right foot on the inner or front aspect of the left thigh. Lift the arms overhead and place the palms together. Focus your gaze on a specific point in front of you to maintain balance. Hold the position for at least a minute.

As I mentioned before, there are hundreds of exercises we can do to address every part of the body. I have pared it down to the bare essentials. If you do the above exercises and repeat them twice or thrice a week until you are very sure of the exercises, the way to do them and, more importantly, the way not to do them, then you are ready to start varying them to challenge the body and prevent boredom.

Don't start including a large number of exercises in your routine when you are a beginner. The exercises by themselves may be great but may not be ideal for you considering your fitness level. Including many different exercises could, of course, break the monotony of working out, but you need to build a strong foundation of fitness before trying more challenging moves. You can include different movements using different muscles to challenge yourself during workouts when you are a more advanced exerciser.

I would also advise you to increase the weights you use to do the strength training part of the exercises until you are able to lift a respectable amount of weight, which in turn will indicate that you are strong. If you are struggling with one- to two-kilo dumb-bells, it's an indication of inadequate strength. Aim to build up to a minimum of about four- to six-kilo dumb-bells. A higher weight may be used for exercises using larger muscles of the chest, back and legs and a lower weight for the smaller muscles of the arms. Don't be afraid to gradually increase the weight of the dumb-bells or barbell you use.

Finally, you must remember that training to build strength and balance is not just important (especially as we age) but also very empowering. They make you feel so much more confident about your body and your ability to perform various daily tasks. Most importantly, they help to prevent ailments associated with this period of your life, such as osteoporosis, muscle weakness and atrophy in both men and women.

A BASIC STRENGTH TRAINING ROUTINE

This is a very basic routine that can be used by any beginner. Once you have advanced, you can do more elaborate routines, splitting up the body parts and including 1–2 body parts per day with more exercises per body part and thereby including weight training every day of the week. There are also many advanced training techniques like super setting, circuit training, drop sets, staggered sets, negative reps and so on that can be built into your routine to make it more challenging.

Days	Body Part	Exercise	Sets	Reps
Mondays and Thursday	Lower body	Deadlift	3–4	10–12
		Squat	3–4	10–12
		Lunge	3–4	10–12
		Calf raises	3–4	10–12
	Upper body	Bench press	3–4	10–12
		Bent over rowing	3–4	10–12
		Shoulder press	3–4	10–12
		Bicep curls	3–4	10–12
		Overhead tricep extensions	3–4	10–12
	Abs and core	Advanced bicycle	3–4	20–30
		Plank	3	10–30
		Abdominal crunch	3	10–30
		Reverse crunch	3	10–30
		Side plank	1–3 min	10–15
		Quadruped arm-leg raise	1–3 min	
		Lying back extensions	1–3 min	
		T-stand	3	
		One-legged stand	1–3 min	

fifteen

The Importance of Posture

Have you ever met someone who has a youthful face, is fairly slim, but who somehow looks older?

The way we carry ourselves says a lot about the condition of our physical body and, very often, about our mental state as well. Don't you feel like drawing your shoulders in and curling up into a ball when you are feeling down? Slouching, for instance, is not just an indication of lethargy or poor posture due to inadequate back strength, but could also be an indication of depression, low self-esteem or sadness. 'Stand up straight, don't slouch,' is something we were told constantly in our childhood. By standing up straight, you centre your weight over your feet. This also helps you maintain correct form while exercising, which results in fewer injuries and greater gains. It also makes you look and feel better.

Poor posture may be a result of bad habits developed in childhood. Continuing the poor posture could lead to physical problems, further preventing good posture, like:

- **Poor flexibility:** Inflexible muscles decrease your range of motion (how far a joint can move in any direction). For example, overly tight, shortened hip muscles (called hip

flexors) tug your upper body forward and affect your posture, while overly tight chest muscles can cause your shoulders to roll forward, making you appear hunched.
- **Poor strength and muscle imbalance:** Muscle strength affects balance in a number of ways. All muscles in the body are present in pairs, one on either side of the body. Most muscles also have 'antagonistic' muscles, which perform the opposite action. For example, as mentioned earlier, the pair of quadriceps muscles (the quads) in the front of the thighs extend the knees and straighten the leg. The antagonistic muscles to the quads are the hamstring muscles situated at the back of the thigh. The hamstrings flex the knee and bend the leg. A muscle imbalance where there is far greater strength in the quads will result in poor posture, mobility, exercise form and increase the propensity for injury.

What Good Posture Looks Like When Standing

The Front View of Your Body

- Your chin should be parallel to the floor.
- Your head should not be tilted to one side or the other.
- Your shoulders should be even (not one higher than the other) and parallel to the floor.
- Your spine should be 'neutral' (neither overly arched to overemphasize the curve in the lower back nor completely flattened).
- Your arms should hang at your sides with elbows pointing backwards and elbows and arms should be even.
- Your abdominal muscles should be engaged.
- Your hips should be even. One side should not be lower than the other.

- Your knees should be level and should be pointing straight ahead.
- Your body weight should be evenly distributed on both feet.

The Lateral or Side-view of Your Body

- Your head should be right above your neck, not thrust forward.
- Shoulders should lie just beneath the ears and not be rolled forward.
- Your spine should curve forward just beyond the level of your chest and be slightly backwards at the level of the hips.
- The hip should be directly below and in line with the shoulders and ears.
- Your knees and ankles should be vertically in line with your shoulders and ears.

What Good Posture Looks Like When Seated

Many of us spend a lot of time sitting, so your chair becomes very important. The ergonomics of our chair, therefore, are important for comfort. Poorly designed chairs can cause back pain and poor posture. When sitting down, keep your chin parallel to the floor, your shoulders and hips vertically one below the other, and your knees and feet pointing straight ahead. This is easier said than done. Most people slump over a computer or slouch in their chairs. It takes a very conscious effort not to.

In the chapter called 'move more' I have explained the drawbacks of sitting for long periods of time. Do read that chapter to understand just how detrimental sitting is for long periods of time. Try and move every half an hour to avoid the complications resulting from prolonged sitting.

Muscles That Affect Posture

Core Muscles: The **core muscles** of the back, sides, pelvis, shoulders and buttocks form a sturdy central link between the torso and limbs. Weak core muscles encourage slouching, in which the body tips forward or sideways and is thus off balance. Strong lower leg muscles and core help keep you stable while standing.

The core muscles include:

- The muscles deep within your pelvis.
- The muscles deep in your hip joint.
- The muscles deep within your shoulders.

Postural and phasic muscles: **Postural muscles** are the muscles that help keep you in an upright position. These are:

- The back muscles surrounding the spine called the erector spinae.
- The hip flexors that help lift the leg at the hip joint.
- The calf muscles.
- Chest muscles or pectoralis.
- Neck muscles or the upper trapezius.

These muscles tend to become tight with underuse or overuse. How many of you experience tight neck muscles or back pain when you are stressed or have been standing for long periods of time? Without you even realizing it, you use all the postural muscles while standing, including your back and neck muscles. If these areas are weak, they tend to get strained with prolonged standing.

Phasic muscles, on the other hand, include the deltoids or the superficial shoulder muscles, the glutes or buttock muscles, abdominals and triceps at the back of the upper arm. These muscles are responsible for movement. They tend to become weak and flabby with underuse, which is the opposite of the tension or tightness experienced with the postural muscles.

In order to check your posture and improve it, stand with your back to a wall. Place your heels against the wall, and then step slightly away from the wall (about the length of your foot). Now lean back until your buttocks and back touch the wall. Push your head back, until the back of your head also touches the wall. Most people will have to tilt their chin up in order to get the backs of their heads to touch the wall. That is not the kind of posture you want. If you cannot get the back of your head to touch the wall without tilting it, push it back as far as it will go by pressing on your chin while keeping the chin parallel to the floor. Hold it there for 20 seconds. In time, this will improve your alignment enough so your head will reach the wall.

SPECIFIC POSTURAL EXERCISES

Alignment in movement

A balance ball, or Swiss ball as it is called, is very useful to improve alignment while you strengthen the deep muscles of the pelvis and hips. Sit down on the balance ball with your knees at a 90-degree angle and feet flat on the floor about hip-width apart.

Sitting in your best strong posture and keeping your knees, torso and head still, use your pelvis to move the ball in circles. First, try three circles clockwise, then anticlockwise. The movement has to be slow and steady. It looks easy but it isn't that simple. You may find that it is easier to move in one direction than in the other. This movement engages muscles deep in the pelvis and hips, muscles that assist posture and that are rarely appropriately used. Practise this move till you are able to do it right in both directions.

Resistance band exercise

The resistance band is a useful and simple piece of equipment. It is a thick elastic band about two meters in length that is available in various degrees of resistance depending on if you are a beginner, intermediate or advanced exerciser. As a beginner, choose a beginner's band with the least resistance. Increase the resistance or intensity as you advance.

This exercise works the deep muscles of the shoulders. These are the muscles that keep the shoulders well aligned, preventing them from rolling forward.

Hold a resistance band in both hands with your palms facing backward. Raise your arms to shoulder level so that your palms now face the floor. Maintain tension in the resistance band right at the start of the exercise. Pull the band outward, widening the arms, squeezing your shoulder blades as you open up your chest. Release to starting position and repeat the movement very slowly five to ten times. Rest and repeat for three sets.

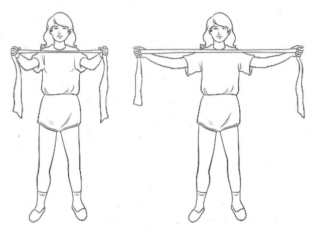

Abduction and Adduction to Strengthen the Deep Shoulder Muscles

Cat Stretch

This exercise releases the spine and makes it more mobile and flexible.

Go down on your hands and knees on a mat. As you breathe in (inhale) lift your head and tail (your hips) as you arch your back. Exhale and reverse the movement by tucking in your head and your tail, squeezing your pelvic muscles. Repeat this movement 5 to 10 times along with the breathing.

Downward Dog

This is an exercise to lengthen the spine and improve flexibility of the lower back and hamstrings.

From the hands and knees position on your mat, push your knees off the mat so that only your feet and hands are on the mat; lift your hips high, keeping the back flat. Allow your head to drop between your shoulders in a loose and comfortable way. Try and touch the heels to the floor in this 'inverted V' position. Hold the position for as long as you comfortably can.

This is a wonderful pose. With practice, it gets easier and can even be very relaxing.

Plank

Lie face down and lift yourself on to your elbows and toes. Hold the abdominal muscles in and tighten the pelvic muscles so the lower back is not overly arched. Hold this position for as long as you can without compromising on form. Hold for a minimum of a minute. See if you can continue to hold for about three minutes or more. This exercise is great for strengthening your core.

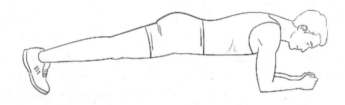

Quadruped arm-leg raise

This exercise works the core, shoulders, upper back, lower back and the glutes. It also calls into play your balance. The exercise looks simple enough, but is very effective in strengthening areas you otherwise do not address.

Start on your hands and knees on the mat.

Lift the right leg straight up behind you and simultaneously lift the left hand in front of you up to the level of your left ear.

Hold this position for 40 to 60 seconds (or as long as you can) and repeat on the other side.

Prone boat

This exercise strengthens the entire back.

Lie on your stomach on a mat. Lift your head, shoulders and your legs off the mat by tightening your entire back and glutes. Keep your neck aligned to the rest of your spine. Hold the position for as long as you can. Relax and repeat two to three times. Make sure you don't lift your head too far upward or backward as this might strain the neck.

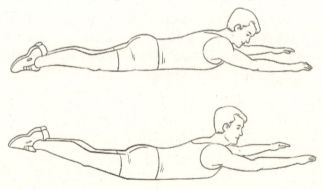

All the above exercises will help align the spine and strengthen and stretch the appropriate muscles responsible for maintaining good posture. Do them regularly at least two to three times a week. It will only take you about 15 minutes to complete the routine.

However there are two more important facets to posture:

- **Inner well-being:** An important aspect of posture is your inner well-being. Standing up tall is an expression of how you feel within, or how you feel about yourself. Pay close attention to your inner well-being in order to stand tall in the real sense of the word. When you're depressed, tired, frustrated or anxious, your body language will express it as such. It also works the other way round. Standing up tall improves self-confidence.
- **Mindfulness:** Being aware of your posture is the most important aspect of good posture. If you are unaccustomed to standing and sitting tall, you tend to retract to old habits pretty quickly even if you diligently exercise the relevant muscles. It takes a conscious effort to keep the shoulders relaxed yet retracted, chest open and head held high. What an effort, you may think. Is it worth it? Of course, it is! It becomes more comfortable and natural to hold your body this way after a while. Standing tall is not just physically more attractive, but it makes you look and feel better and more self-assured.

sixteen

Improving Balance as You Age

Our physical balance tends to deteriorate as we age. This could be problematic as it often leads to falls and injury.

Balance is a critical aspect of fitness. It is the ability to remain stable irrespective of the position (whether sitting, standing, kneeling etc.) or movement (walking, running, exercising etc.) of the body. Balance depends on biological systems within our bodies that enable us to understand unconsciously exactly where our bodies are in relation to the space around us and the ability to maintain that desired position. Normal balance depends on:

- Information to the brain from the inner ear
- Sight
- Touch
- Muscle movement or contraction

Around one in three people over the age of 65 experience a fall every year, according to the World Health Organization. Falls result in not just serious (sometimes life threatening) physical injury, but also in loss of confidence and restriction of physical activity. Once you experience a fall, the fear of falling becomes imprinted on the brain and a loss of confidence leads to restriction of physical activity, which then leads to a greater risk of falling. This turns into a self-perpetuating negative feedback loop.

According to a study conducted in France, older women who followed a two-year exercise programme to improve balance cut their risk of being injured in a fall by about 20 per cent. The lead author of this study, Fabienne El-Khoury of the Pierre Louis Institute for Epidemiology and Public Health in Paris, said that women who did balance exercises performed much better on balance tests.

CAUSES OF LOSS OF BALANCE AND FALLS

Loss of vision: The eyes observe where the body is in space and also register the directions of motion. Our eyesight starts to deteriorate after the age of 40. Even if you have 20/20 vision, get your eyes checked regularly after the age of 40. It is not just a decreased sense of balance that can lead to falls, but also the folded edge of a mat or edge of a table that you missed seeing that can be a health hazard.

At the lobby of a hotel I stayed in recently, the flooring tiles were so bizarre that one couldn't quite fathom if they were steps or if the floor was flat. I was surprised this visual deception wasn't causing more accidents, or perhaps it was and I didn't know about it. In any case, I walked around gingerly the entire time, wondering how such design catastrophes were allowed and admonishing myself that perhaps I needed glasses. I see this quite often though – badly built staircases with barely any space to place your toes, leave alone your entire foot; lighting so deceptive you can easily miss the floor or a step; dangerously placed floor mats at the top of a staircase and so on. With decreased vision, these are all disasters waiting to happen.

Loss of the sense of touch: The pressure receptors on the skin, such as those located on the feet, sense contact with the ground. Loss of sensation, as a result of any number of neuropathies including diabetic neuropathy, reduces the sensitivity to touch and pressure. Not only does this prevent an accurate assessment of terrain, but it can also cause injury from ill-fitting shoes.

Muscle and joint sensory receptors: Sensors within the joints report which parts of the body are in motion. These sensory receptors may also be compromised in various neurological medical conditions like Parkinson's or metabolic conditions like diabetes.

Loss of strength, especially in the lower body: When the muscles of the lower body become weak or atrophic, any position that calls upon their strength to keep you stable (for instance, balancing on one leg, reaching up on your toes, squatting or bending) can cause you to lose balance and fall over.

Ear problems: The inner ears (also called the labyrinth) monitor the directions of motion, such as turning and forward, lateral or vertical movement. Damage, infection or inflammation in the ears can compromise balance. Even a bad cold or sinusitis can potentiate a loss of balance. This is why you need to be extra cautious while exercising when you have an upper respiratory tract infection. Loss of balance can potentiate a fall.

Age-related changes in the white matter of the brain: The brain and the spinal cord process information from the other systems and make coordinated sense out of it all. Damage to the brain or deterioration of the brain make this assessment inaccurate, leading to misjudgment and falls.

PRACTICAL SOLUTIONS TO PREVENT FALLS

These are a few paths you can take to make sure that ageing remains injury-free as far as possible. These are:

- Medical solutions
- Exercise solutions
- Safety

MEDICAL SOLUTIONS

- Do see an **ENT** professional to rule out any ear problems.
- If you are much older and balance issues seem to have suddenly amplified, do see a **neurologist.** A brain MRI may be required to rule out degeneration of white matter.
- **Get your eyesight** checked. Being short-sighted will impair depth perception and cause all kinds of accidents like missing a step, tripping over a low stool and so on.
- **Check your medications.** Some medications like sedatives, anxiety pills, antidepressants, even cold medication and antihistamines could make you drowsy or impair balance. The drowsiness may linger even if the pills are taken at night. This can make you unstable and increase the chances of falls. Reactions to many drugs and antibiotics can cause dizziness. It is critical that you be fully cognizant of the medications you are taking and inform your trainer of them if you are training at a gym.
- **Get enough sleep.** Sleep deprivation will make you drowsy and lacking in alertness during the day. If you suffer from insomnia, do speak to your physician.

Exercise Solutions

Single Leg Stance Without Movement

From a standing position, lift one leg off the floor. Place the lifted foot as high as you can on the thigh of the other leg. Hold this position for as long as possible. Repeat on the other side. You can hold on to the edge of a countertop for support initially and then as you get more comfortable, take your hand away from the counter and lift both arms overhead, touching the palms together. The key is to focus the eyes on a distant object at eye level or at the floor in front of you. Keeping the gaze steady improves balance. This is a pose commonly taught in yoga and is called tree pose or *vrksasana*. (See diagram on page 178.)

Also try the position with your eyes closed (please stay on a carpeted surface and close to a sofa for support if required). You will find that the time you can hold a one-legged position with your eyes closed is horrifyingly short, perhaps less than 30 seconds.

Single Leg Stance With Movement

Stand on one leg (you could initially hold on to a countertop for support). With the outstretched toe of the other leg, tap on the floor to the front, side and back – i.e., 12, 3 and 6 o'clock positions. Repeat 10 to 15 times, then switch sides and repeat with the other leg. You should be able to do this exercise without support as time goes by.

As per the illustration on the right, lift one leg off the floor and on one leg turn slightly to the left, then right, moving only at the hip. Repeat 5 to 10 times with each leg.

T-stand

Stand on one leg. Bend the upper body forward until it is almost parallel to the floor and at 90 degrees with your standing leg. Raise the lifted leg behind you until it is almost parallel to the floor and at 90 degrees with the standing leg. This forms a 'T' with your lifted leg, your arms and the standing leg. Hold this position for as long as you can. Switch legs and repeat on the other side. (See diagram on page 177.)

Chair Sits

Stand in front of a low chair with your back to it. Step forward about a foot in front of the chair. Now sit back on the chair without using support and then stand up again. This movement mimics the 'squat'. You require leg strength, core strength and balance to be able to do the sit-and-stand without support. Repeat this movement about 5 to 10 times. When you begin, you may use support, but gradually try and do it without support.

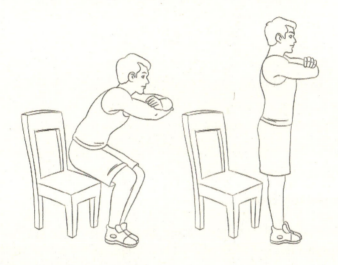

Quadruped Arm-leg Raise

Go down on your knees and hands on a mat. Lift you right hand out in front of you at the level of your head and simultaneously lift your left leg behind you to the level of your hips, holding both arm and leg parallel to the floor. Hold this position for as long as you can, then switch sides. (See diagram on page 175.)

Squats On a Bosu Ball

A Bosu ball – a fitness tool that looks like half a ball – can be used to improve balance.

Place the ball with the curved side on the floor and stand on the flat end. Squat 10 to 15 times keeping your arms stretched in front of you or crossed against your chest and maintaining balance as you squat. This is an advanced exercise and requires practise.

Single Leg Dead Lift

Hold dumbbells in both hands. Balancing on your left foot, engage the abs and bend forward, hinging at the hips while reaching toward the ground with both hands (and the dumbbells). Raise your right leg straight out behind you for counterbalance. Extend the hip as you return to the starting position. Keep your knee relaxed and back flat throughout the movement. Switch legs and repeat.

If holding weights in both hands proves difficult at first, you could start with holding one dumbbell in your left hand (if you are standing on your left leg) and hold on to a support with your right hand as you bend forward.

V-sit

Lie on your back on a mat. Lift both legs to a 45-degree angle, keeping the knees extended. Now lift the upper body to a 45-degree angle keeping the back flat. You are now in a 'V' position. You can reach your arms forward towards the toes and even hold on to the big toe. This is an advanced exercise that engages your core and challenges your balance.

Cross-legged Sit and Stand

This is a simple way to ascertain your balance, coordination and core strength. This test has even been used to determine longevity as explained in chapter 2.

Stand with feet hip-width apart. Now cross your feet. Hold your arms at chest level. Sit on the floor, keeping your feet crossed. Do this without support. From this cross-legged seated position, stand up without support. This looks deceptively easy, but it is not.

Repeat 5 to 10 times with right leg crossed over your left and 5 to 10 times with the left leg crossed over your right. (See diagram on page 31.)

Tai Chi and Yoga

Tai Chi, an exercise form based on martial arts, is excellent for balance as it calls for a constant shift in body weight while balancing on one leg or the other. Yoga uses different body positions and sustained holds as well as sequences of poses that call for balance and stability and so can be used to improve static balance and flexibility. Both Tai Chi and yoga are excellent for balance.

SAFETY

Often, we lose our balance accidentally. Being constantly aware of your surroundings can prevent such mishaps. But, despite your best efforts, if you do trip or fall, being fitter and stronger (with regular exercise) always reduces the extent of injury as quick reflexes will help break your fall while strong muscles will help take the impact of a fall.

- Beware of mats and carpets with folded edges.
- Having kids or pets at home would mean toys and other small items strewn around. It's easy to trip over or slip on these.
- Wear the right kind of footwear. The soles of some shoes are extraordinarily smooth, which can lead to slips and falls.
- Be conscious of slippery floors, uneven flooring and stairs.
- Use anti-skid tiles in bathing areas and where floors tend to get wet.
- Low tables, open doors of low cabinets and even footstools can be safety hazards.

When you're preoccupied with texting on your phone, it is easy to miss something as obvious as a step or a carpet. Being aware of your surroundings, especially in a gym or the kitchen, for instance, is crucial to prevent falls and injury.

PART III

UNDERSTANDING YOUR MIND AFTER 40 AND TAKING CARE OF IT

seventeen

Stress

Stress is a significant aspect that affects our inner selves, our weight and overall well-being. In my practice I always question the patient or client (depending on if I am wearing my 'doctor' hat or 'fitness and lifestyle consultant' hat) about their stress, sleep and relationships. They are all extremely relevant to health. The amount of *perceived stress* can also determine how an individual experiences pain, how well they recover from disease, and their overall attitude to illness and well-being. Or if they have come to me as a client to lose weight or get fitter, how they apply themselves to the workout, how consistent they are and how successful they are at achieving their goals.

Pioneering Hungarian-Canadian endocrinologist Hans Selye used the term 'stress' to represent the effects of anything that seriously threatens the internal homeostasis of our body.

In human life, stress is a given. How we deal with it, though, differs from one individual to the next. Stress plays an important role in wellness but is such a common and misused word these days that pretty much everything is labelled as being 'stressful'. Each of us reacts to stressors differently. The same situation may lead one person to function better while another may fall apart.

Stress evolves with age. What was stressful in our twenties and thirties (our in-laws, early career, young children, finance etc.) may not be the same things that bother us as we age. Today, it may be ageing parents or in-laws, loss of a significant other, a floundering marriage, empty nest syndrome when the children have moved away leaving you suddenly lost and alone, retirement or ill health. There is always something to contend with right through our lives. Learning how to cope is more important than trying to eliminate stressors altogether, as that is not quite possible.

The Importance of Stress in Leading a Meaningful Life

I believe that some degree of 'stress' or 'striving' is actually good and even necessary for human growth. It brings about meaning and the desire to improve, live and experience life. What I mean by this is that while we all have various problems or stressors to contend with, it is often these very stressors that give our life meaning! The ability to overcome and deal with the stressors, whatever they may be, and the ability to come out on top are somehow 'meaningful' enough to make that very stressor important for our growth. This ability to survive and even thrive is an important aspect of human existence. Without this 'stress' (as we like to call it today), life would be colourless, placid and even boring. What comes to my mind is a pertinent quote by Nietzche, 'That which does not kill me, makes me stronger.'

We must start to understand the importance of stress/setbacks in our lives, especially as we grow older, and use them to our advantage as stepping-stones to resilience. We must embrace it as part of the uniquely human journey.

There are two kinds of stress:

- Acute stress
- Chronic stress

Acute stress could be the result of sudden bad news like the loss of a loved one or a job, a divorce and other situations that bring or threaten to bring about a drastic change in our lives. For instance, changing homes is considered to be on top of the list of stressors. Each of these events will produce different levels of stress. Most, however, are limited in duration when managed well. The symptoms produced by acute stress are most often self-limiting. This means that when what you believe is stressful passes, the symptoms and the physiological response in the body dissipate. If acute stress is overlooked, it can result in chronic stress.

On rare occasions, acute stress may be so devastating that it could result in a severe bodily reaction. Taken to the very extreme, severe emotional stress may even cause heart failure. This is called the Broken Heart Syndrome or Takotsubo Cardiomyopathy. (I've discussed this in greater detail in the appendix.)

Chronic stress is often the result of acute stressors not being addressed in a timely manner. For instance, grief over the loss of a loved one is a definite cause of stress. The grieving process continues for several days, if not weeks. Over time, however, we come to terms with it, albeit with difficulty. Sometimes one may continue to grieve, feel guilt, anger, helplessness and so on for an extended period of time, which could lead to the symptoms of chronic stress. If the loss of your job, which is an acute stressor, results in you becoming resentful and angry followed by not being able to find another suitable job, and this is compounded by related problems at home due to a financial setback, it could once again become a source of chronic stress.

Importantly, chronic stress can also result from small, innocuous things like taking care of your home, your children and parents, while also trying to get to work on time every day. It could result from a problematic relationship or financial complications.

These may not seem 'stressful' in themselves, but compounded and depending on how you deal with them, they could be genuine sources of great stress.

Recognizing Stress

This is the very first step in dealing with stress. You can't change something you don't even recognize or acknowledge. If your work or career is your source of stress, that needs to be attended to. If a relationship is tumultuous, then that needs addressing too. Once you are able to identify your stressor, there are many ways of addressing the problem.

Real stress or perceived stress?

Ask yourself if the thing you find stressful is truly something you need to feel anxious about and needs to be viewed as a true source of stress or if it is **your perspective of it** that is causing you stress.

So, for instance, making a presentation to a large audience can be unnerving and viewed as stressful. A myriad possibilities run through your mind – you may forget your lines or you may lose your voice. If you start to imagine all the conceivable ways in which you could make a fool of yourself on stage, then it becomes stressful! How you perceive something and all the thoughts that rattle around in your mind are usually the real cause of the stress.

For me, travel used to be a great source of stress. Considering I travel as much as I do, that was not the best situation. I would mostly be stressed about what I thought I might forget – my phone, my keys, the ticket, my passport and so on. The anxiety would set in the night before and I would invariably wake up with a headache on the day I was meant to travel. Once I started telling myself that there was really nothing I could 'forget' that I couldn't replace or retrieve and there was honestly no need for panic, I started to let go of the stress. When situations arise, as they sometimes do (like the time when I was held up at immigration one time when I hadn't printed out the details of my hotel stay, something they insisted on), I have conditioned myself to deal with them to the best of my ability, see the humour in it all and move on.

Contrary to general belief that all forms of stress are harmful, some forms of stress do help us. Having a deadline, for instance, spurs some of us into action (though it may make others freeze, of course). This is **good stress or eustress**. You need to understand if the stress you feel is making you more productive by driving you to complete tasks, meet your deadlines, be productive and result in progress. This kind of stress is useful and even beneficial. It can keep us motivated. Without some degree of eustress or pressure, we could become complacent.

Distress, on the other hand, is the form of stress that engulfs us in a strangle-hold, preventing further productive action. When the body is exposed to physiological responses to stress over long periods of time it becomes depleted, the immune system breaks down and there is a tendency to develop long-term side-effects like depression, anxiety, memory problems, weight gain or weight loss and various gastrointestinal symptoms like gastritis or acidity.

Most of the time, the stress is not quite so dramatic that it needs to be addressed immediately. Much of what we experience is muted in intensity and present over a period of time. These are life events or situations which cause a low degree of discomfort, apprehension, anger, resentment and many such negative emotions. When these are left unchecked and unattended to, they can multiply in intensity to become much larger and cause great bodily damage.

Ask yourself the following questions:

- Are you able to identify your most common stressors? Write down a list of the things that cause you the most stress.
- How do you react to them? Panic? Anger? Sadness? Isolation? Resentment? Or do they provide better motivation? Focus? Increased productivity? Excellence?
- How often do you experience stressful situations and feel stressed in a day and/or in a week?

Identifying your source of stress is the first step in dealing with it. Then identify how you normally react to what you perceive as stressful. These patterns of behaviour are habitual. These are probably the things we are accustomed to doing when we feel stressed and anxious.

- Do you often feel a sense of lack of control and anxiety?
- Do you feel sad, angry, depressed or resentful much of the time?
- Do you have difficulty sleeping? How many hours of good quality sleep do you get?
- Do you experience a loss of appetite or have difficulty in controlling what you eat?
- Do you suffer from acidity, gastritis or headaches?
- Do you suffer from palpitations, breathlessness or chest pain?

All of the above may be symptoms of chronic stress. Let's face it, no one is spared the demands of a stressful life. With age and maturity, you should learn to deal with situations better. Stress can cause a variety of symptoms as mentioned above and some may mimic an organic disease so closely that you may go through a gamut of tests only to be finally told, 'It must be stress.'

Response to Stress

Your response to stress and how you deal with it can in itself prove to be detrimental to health and well-being. Some may deal with stressors by overeating or substance abuse; others might not be able to get enough sleep. This manifests more with age. Overeating or insomnia (which may be your response to a stress), may not be quite as evidently injurious when one is younger. The body is young and manages to cope with the abuse or the effects of stress far better than it does when we get older. Obesity, hypertension, heart disease and depression have all been related to leading high stress lives and become realities with age.

Yet others may handle stress better. Is there a better way to handle stress? Surely there is. While, clearly, one cannot eliminate stress completely, it is possible to recognize and manage it effectively at least, for the most part.

The body responds to acute stress by the **fight-or-flight response** kicking in. American physiologist Walter Bradford Cannon first described the fight-or-flight response, also called the 'acute stress response', in the 1920s as a theory of how animals react to threats with a response from their sympathetic nervous system. This response was later recognized as the first stage of a general adaptation syndrome for humans as well when they were faced with stressful situations.

Imagine you are taking a stroll in the woods and you suddenly come across a lion. Picture your first response. You probably freeze, your heart races, your breathing becomes shallow and rapid, palms get sweaty and there is a terrible feeling of dread and fear within you. You may then proceed to stay and fight (good luck with that!) or take flight.

Today, while the above scenario is highly unlikely for most of us, the equivalent of that would be perhaps being called into your boss's cabin, being attacked by a thief, the act of giving a public speech and so on. The immediate response of the racing heart, sweaty palms and a queasy stomach subside once you realize there's nothing really to worry about or once the stressful event has passed.

If, however, you experience the stress response in small doses over a long period of time, the body starts to react differently by becoming physically and mentally ill, leading to chronic stress.

Memory recall as a cause of stress

You have probably come across the term Post-traumatic Stress Disorder or PTSD in reference to soldiers who have fought in wars. You don't necessarily have to go to war to experience it, however. You could relive a traumatic event in your own life, leading you to experience PTSD. Sexual assault, accidents, physical attacks, the loss of a loved one can all lead to forms of PTSD. You may repeatedly relive a stressful event like a robbery, for instance, or the grief of a loss, creating a stress response for yourself that may not be representative of what is actually happening in real time, but is very real in your mind. This could then lead to chronic stress, anxiety, depression or even panic attacks. The event which was originally stressful is replayed in an endless loop in the mind, causing the very same stress response and subsequent health problems.

The cortisol response

The hormone cortisol is responsible for the fight-or-flight response during acute stress. Cortisol is a steroid hormone produced by the two adrenal glands located one on top of each kidney. In addition to stress, it is also released in response to events and circumstances such as waking up in the morning and exercising. The physiological symptoms you experience (a racing heart, shallow, rapid breathing etc.) are the result of the action of cortisol on the brain. Cortisol also has far-reaching, systemic effects.

When chronically elevated, cortisol can have terribly damaging effects on weight, immune function and chronic disease risk.

The release of this hormone in response to a stressful event leads to a cascade of other biochemical and hormonal reactions in the body. Ideally, this cascade is terminated after a while, once the stressful event passes, by what is called a **hormonally-driven negative feedback loop.**

The following is how the stress response operates as its intended survival mechanism:

- When an individual is faced with a stressor, a complex hormonal cascade ensues and the adrenals secrete cortisol.
- Two hormones — adrenalin or epinephrine and cortisol — are responsible for the immediate physiological response to stress.
- Adrenalin is the first responder and prepares the body for a fight-or-flight response mainly by stimulating the **sympathetic nervous system**, which causes all the symptoms described (racing heart, sweaty palms and so on).
- Cortisol is secreted a little later than adrenalin and persists when the perceived stress is longer in duration.

- Cortisol prevents glucose from being stored in the liver, releasing it instead into the bloodstream, in order to provide an immediate source of energy to large muscles (in case you need to run!).
- Cortisol simultaneously inhibits the production of the hormone insulin in order to prevent the glucose from being stored, favouring, instead, its immediate use.
- Cortisol narrows the arteries while another hormone, epinephrine, increases heart rate, both of which force the heart to pump harder and faster and also elevate the blood pressure.

The above cascade makes the body ready to respond to the stressful event. Once the stressor is reduced, or, if you use a stress-relieving technique you are adept at (like deep breathing, relaxation, meditation, exercise and so on), these stress hormones return to normal and the body's internal milieu is restored.

Often, however, we are faced with (what we perceive as) a continuous stream of stressful situations provoking the 'stress response' or the 'cortisol response', which means that the body is relentlessly bathed in the stress hormones with the resulting consequences. As already mentioned, **this could be in response to real stress or something you perceive as stress**. Either way, the physiological response is the same. The body cannot differentiate between a real stressor and an imagined one. The continuous exposure to cortisol and the subsequent reactions are detrimental for the body.

Causes of Stress

Trying to Succeed in Multiple Domains

This is one of the main causes of stress today. Actually, it would be more accurate to say that the stressor is the fact that we **expect**

ourselves to succeed in multiple domains. We put enormous pressure on ourselves. It's like a juggler trying to keep all the balls in the air. The triggers are much the same for both men and women, with just slight variations.

Children: Children can be demanding. Being responsible for children and their lives right up to the end of yours can be a terrifyingly stressful concept.

Partners: A life partner can be a source of anxiety or gratification, depending on the relationship.

Taking care of aging parents: Many of us have the added responsibility of taking care of aging parents or in-laws in addition to our own families. This is also an enormous responsibility and could be a source of stress.

Household responsibilities: Taking care of the mundane and day-to-day activities at home may be your responsibility. Paying the bills, seeing to repairs, maintaining the home and so on is both time-consuming and can be drudgery and, sometimes, a cause of great stress.

Food: Most women are the **nutritional gatekeepers** of the family unit, and providing appropriate food for the family is a great responsibility. It includes the shopping, decision-making about what food is to be prepared and cooking it or getting it cooked and catering to the different palates of different family members (for instance, elders may need a special diet at home). All of this is a colossal effort that is often undervalued. Sometimes I see women who toil endlessly with no appreciation from the family. More than the work itself, it is the lack of acknowledgement that may be the primary source of stress.

Work: Working outside the home, especially when it is in addition to the above responsibilities, can be a source of stress.

Many women enjoy the opportunity to work and have a career of their own. So while this may be difficult to manage, it is sometimes a choice several women opt for. At other times it may be a necessity, perhaps financial. Either way, working outside the house, balancing time spent with the family, negotiating leave, money, effort and, most importantly, the pressure we place on ourselves in such situations can be immensely draining. Moreover, if you don't enjoy what you do and especially if it is not adequately rewarding financially or in any other way, it can become tedious. Not all women choose to work outside the home, however. Some prefer to be stay-at-home moms.

For most men, working, supporting the family and being successful career-wise is something they actively pursue. I say most men because today we are seeing paradigm shifts, of course. When work becomes a source of stress – perhaps because of an unpleasant boss, poor remuneration or just a failure to 'succeed' in their given career – it can severely affect one's psyche. Depression, alcoholism, substance abuse or any number of unhealthy coping strategies can result from the stress of work. Even if the money is good, just living the high life can be a source of stress. This is more apparent when one is dependent on the opinion of others or is trying to live up to someone else's ideal.

Self: How can taking care of and making time for yourself be stressful? Upkeep of oneself with the necessary clothes, accessories, visits to the beauty parlour, etc. takes a lot of effort and energy. While self-care is important and should be pleasurable, it can be something that some obsess about. Scheduling in exercise, meditation, travel, holidays and social events, all of it can either be great stress-busters or stressful in themselves.

Succeeding in multiple domains such as home, work and caregiving can be that much less stressful if you get the right kind of help and cooperation from those around you. If you have parents or in-laws who take care of your kids when you are at work or have help to get dinner prepared every day, it's that much less stressful. This is not only because the physical workload is diminished, but also because the responsibility is collective and there is a sense of belonging and caring that we humans so require for our well-being.

- **Body image:** Having a poor body image is a great source of stress! Body image is our perception of our physical selves including our physical appearance and sexual attractiveness. This may be a distorted, overly critical view resulting from **poor self-esteem or social expectations.**
- **Clutter:** Many of us hoard things that we may never use in this lifetime. Why do we do that? Perhaps somewhere at the back of our minds we think, 'Maybe one day I will lose 10 pounds and get into that dress/suit' or 'One day all these tools will come in handy'? In the meantime, the clutter accumulates, gathering dust. Amassing clutter adds to stress.

This is only **physical clutter**, however. What about **emotional clutter**? What about the recurrent thoughts that work their way into our minds at any given time? How about the various contradicting and conflicting feelings, the resentment, anger, fear and all the emotions that clutter our minds to hinder productive thinking and living?

Then there is our **digital clutter** – the innumerable emails, Facebook/Twitter/Instagram posts, constant newsfeeds, myriad articles we collect and never read, and messages we are yet to respond to.

All of this adds to stress. **Freeing ourselves of our clutter on a regular basis has huge benefits like freeing up both physical and emotional space.**

Long-term Effects of Elevated Cortisol/Stress

Belly Fat

The main function of cortisol is to inhibit insulin so that there is plenty of glucose available for the muscles in times of stress. (Evolutionarily, this was probably because then we could run away from a threatening beast!) Over time, when this happens once too often, the body becomes **insulin resistant** and the blood glucose levels remain elevated, potentiating the onset of type 2 diabetes.

Cortisol also leads to the **accumulation of fat.** One of its functions is the storage of fat, especially deep in the abdomen – this, as we know, is the highly detrimental belly fat as explained in the chapter on belly fat.

Another way in which cortisol leads to weight gain is by directly influencing the **appetite** centers in the brain (in the hypothalamus). Our appetite is stimulated creating craving and false hunger signals, which cause us to overeat.

> How many of you eat indiscriminately when stressed? How many reach for those particularly favourite foods like crisps, pizza, chocolate or ice cream when you are feeling anxious, stressed or sad? There is a reason for this. It's not just your lack of 'willpower' as you may believe, but the effect of cortisol on your brain. The solution, therefore, is not to try to use willpower to resist cravings, but to learn how to reduce cortisol by managing stress effectively.

An Immune System That Is Shot to Hell

Chronically elevated cortisol levels can lead to a reduction in immunity. This, in turn, makes you susceptible to myriad illnesses, colds, coughs and even the development of strange allergies. When you are overworked or sleep-deprived it is interpreted as 'stress' by the body, leading to reduced immunity and the tendency to fall ill. Severe stress can even lead to very serious consequences like **premature menopause, post-traumatic stress disorder, heart disease and diabetes.**

Problems With the Gastrointestinal System

Prolonged or chronic stress leads to indigestion and gastritis. Stress causes the mucosal lining of the gut to become inflamed and irritated. In the long term this can lead to **stress ulcers**. Some develop **irritable bowel syndrome or colitis** in response to chronic stress.

The gastrointestinal system also responds to acute stress – surely you've experienced the horrifying feeling of an unstable gurgling tummy when waiting for an interview, anticipating results or expecting important news? The funny feeling named 'butterflies in the tummy' is caused by a reduced blood supply and altered nervous stimulation to the gut during the fight-or-flight or stress response when the blood is redirected to the larger muscles.

Stress to the Heart and Blood Vessels

As we have already seen, during stressful times, the blood vessels are constricted, increasing blood pressure to enhance the delivery of oxygenated blood to the working muscles. This is advantageous during actual 'flight', but the trouble is that most often there is no such physical 'flight' involved. Either the stress is chronic, or we never manage to overcome the stressor. Over time, with prolonged exposure to such a physiological response, there is **inflammation in the walls of the blood vessels** and a build-up of **plaque**. The plaque, along with an elevated blood pressure, makes for the perfect scenario for a **heart attack**.

Stress-related Memory Loss

Extreme stress can cause loss of memory. We've heard of stress-related 'selective amnesia' where individuals block out stressful events in the past in order not to relive the pain. A low degree of stress over a long period of time can also lead to the malfunctioning of the hippocampus, an area in the brain responsible for memory. Stress, in addition to lowered estrogen levels during menopause, can cause serious episodes of forgetfulness leading to further anxiety and stress. Who hasn't experienced the 'where did I leave my keys' syndrome? This happens most often when we are trying to multitask, something we frequently do. We forget minor details like keys because our brains are overloaded with information and tasks and choose to 'forget' seemingly unimportant things like keys. We all know how stressful and annoying that can be!

Depression

Stress is also connected to depression. Even low levels of unaddressed stress can lead to symptoms of depression. Chronic unaddressed stress can lead to reduced levels of serotonin, dopamine and other neurotransmitters in the brain that are responsible for our mood.

Substance Abuse and Addictions

Depending on your coping mechanism, you may turn to alcohol, tobacco, gambling, prescription drugs, sex or any number of addictions to deal with stress. All of these compound the problem and further impair health.

Diminished Libido

One of the most common side effects of stress is a reduced sex drive. If marital stress is a problem, the animosity is sufficient to dampen any amorous expressions. Anxiety, depression, sadness are not compatible with libido. In addition, the effects of stress on the brain leading to the reduction of important neurotransmitters may be responsible for decreased libido.

Social Withdrawal and Isolation

One common response to stress is social withdrawal and isolation. Unable to handle the emotional pain, some people tend to abandon social connections. This is, perhaps, one of the most detrimental things to do. Staying connected with loved ones can be a huge help in finding a way to get out of a stressful situation. Closeness with other people, meaningful relationships, conversations, counsel, affection and caring are important ways to overcome stressful times.

MITIGATING STRESS

Men and women react to stress differently. Typically, men close down or repress their feelings, turn to alcohol, try to create a relaxing diversion like playing a sport, and compartmentalize in an attempt to escape or shut out the stressor. Women, on the other hand, tend to reach out to others, get emotional, talk about their stressors, and connect on a personal level. The reason for this is physiological. During the immediate stress response, the hormones cortisol and epinephrine are released in both men and women. These hormones produce the typical and immediate 'stress response'. A third hormone, oxytocin, comes into play a little later to reduce the effects of adrenalin and cortisol, and mitigate the effects of stress. Oxytocin is the hormone responsible for connectivity and closeness. However, men secrete far less of this hormone than women. In a study published in the July 2000 issue of the journal *Psychological Review*, researcher Shelly E. Taylor said that women **tend and befriend** (that is, reach out and take care of others) during stressful times more than **take flight or fight.** The reason for this is the hormone oxytocin. So while we may think that reaction to stress often programmed in us or is stereotypical in how the different genders deal with it, there seems to be a hormonal reason for it as well.

I have explained below a few ways to mitigate stress.

Connecting With People

Connecting with people one is close to has been found to be a great stress-reliever. Sharing your thoughts, fears, responsibilities and joys tends to mitigate stress. Having deep relationships in your life is, therefore, important, not just to bring joy but also to relieve and manage stress.

As mentioned earlier, a hormone that plays a key role in stress relief is oxytocin, also called the **'cuddle hormone'** with good reason. The hormone is released in large quantities in women during labour and the delivery of a child. It is also required for milk letdown post-delivery. Oxytocin has very powerful effects on the brain. It helps in the initiation of maternal behaviour that leads to the bonding of the mother with the baby soon after it is born. Research has found, for instance, that a female deprived of oxytocin during labour and delivery will have a compromised maternal instinct towards her offspring.

Oxytocin is the 'lovemaking' hormone and is released during sexual orgasm. It creates the bonding between couples. It has been found that people who touch and hug more have higher levels of oxytocin and thus an enhanced sense of connection.

It is also the hormone released during physical contact (other than sexual contact). Social psychologist Dr Shelley E. Taylor of the Social Neuroscience Lab, University of California, coined the term 'tend and befriend', which is the opposite of the 'fight and flight' response, which appears to arise from the release of oxytocin. So, gestures and actions such as holding hands, touching, hugging, etc. all release oxytocin, creating a bond and 'affection' between the people involved. When you get together with your friends for a coffee and chat, oxytocin is released, leading to a 'feel-good' after-effect. Being with people you love, friends and family raises the level of oxytocin and well-being.

Humans need companionship and connectedness. No doubt some enjoy it and seek it out more than others, but we all need the warmth of human connections. Staying connected and maintaining meaningful relationships both require time, effort and energy. All of these are in short supply these days. Given the various benefits of positive human relationships, it makes sense for us to nurture them to the best of our ability.

Exercise

Exercise is one of the greatest stress busters ever known. It has been well-researched and documented to be very useful for short- and long-term stress relief. I am sure you have often noticed that going out for a walk 'clears your mind' when you are anxious.

- Exercise creates a sense of euphoria due to the release of endorphins in the brain.
- The repetitive motion during exercise diverts the mind (and the thought process) from the stressor to the act of the physical movement itself.
- The fact that you are sometimes breathless or may be in the midst of a group class with music playing and other people around you also works as a welcome diversion.
- Brain-derived neurotrophic factor or BDNF, a protein necessary for survival of neurons, is increased with exercise. BDNF can be viewed as brain fertilizer! A lowered level of BDNF is associated with depression.
- Exercise helps by normalizing sleep. Good quality sleep is known to be neuro-protective or protective of the nerve cells and neural network in the brain.
- A heightened response to stress is moderated by exercise, a biological 'toughening up' of the brain so stress has less of a central impact.

Meditation

Meditation is also a great way to mitigate stress. Learning to meditate is probably one of the best things you can do to physically alter your brain cells. There are different kinds of meditation and you have to find what works for you. Even 10 minutes a day sets the stage for a calmer experience.

I am one of those people who is not comfortable with chanting, incense, mantras or even guided meditation. I had to find a way to meditate by myself. A way around all the challenges my own brain set up! Having done that, I can say it is truly beneficial to calm and soothe the mind.

Asking for Help

Many people find it hard to truly reach out for help when it is required, not to mention the still-existing social taboo related to consulting a therapist. Asking for help may be as simple as talking to someone to unburden yourself, or quite literally asking for help to find a solution to your problem as you see it. You could reach out to a trusted family member or friend. We usually ask for help from people close to us, or someone we are truly comfortable with. This means we need to have already established enduring relationships with a few people for us to be able to connect with when required. This is also a reason why it is important to sustain and nurture relationships. Or you could seek out a therapist. Remember that depression or stress that is impairing your mind or body to function normally needs to be treated just like a physical ailment.

Prioritize Time

You cannot possibly be at everyone's disposal at all times. You need to prioritize when you are available at work, at home, for the family, for friends and, most importantly, for yourself! This takes effort and some amount of tact or diplomacy. A large part of stress comes from being unable to meet the demands of those around you. Finding quality time for yourself is important to unwind and discover ways to recharge your energy.

Find the Humour in Things

Humour is a great way of dealing with stress. Witty conversation and laughter can ease stress. A study that looked at patients with pain from fibromyalgia (which is a chronic disease characterized by painful, sore muscles and joints, the cause of which is most often unknown with treatment varying from painkillers to cognitive behavioral therapy or CBT) found that the tendency to use humour was associated with lower levels of psychological distress. Laughter produces a release of endorphins, relieves stress and muscular tension, creates total body relaxation, boosts the immune system and even improves your blood flow to the heart and condition of the blood vessels. The old adage, 'Laughter is the best medicine' is very real as the benefits of laughter reach far beyond just momentary enjoyment.

Negative styles of humour, with belittling or condescending jokes have the opposite effect, elevating stress levels and negativity.

Change Your Perspective

It finally comes down to changing your perspective of the stressful situation. This requires a lot of insight, maturity and, most importantly, practise. Some people have an inherent capacity to look at things differently, stay optimistic and be resilient. Others have to work at it. Changing your perspective means not looking at situations as a source of 'stress and anxiety' but embracing difficulties and setbacks with élan and learning to grow from them. Counselling, especially cognitive behavioral therapy or CBT, and psychotherapy can help to some extent. Putting in the 'work' that will bring about this change, however, is entirely your responsibility.

While stress is inevitable in our lives, learning to manage it is optional. We can learn to deal with stress using the various methods mentioned or we will have to deal with the problems caused by chronic stress. This is a choice we have to make. It may seem easier to deal with stress by medicating ourselves or drinking alcohol. Although anti-anxiety drugs do have a real (short-term) role in managing stress, anxiety and panic attacks, they are not a permanent solution. They can in themselves lead to problems of habituation and addiction. Understanding the reasons behind the stress in our lives and dealing with them in the appropriate manner using the right tools will keep us healthier, calmer and happier.

As we grow older, we also need to recognize the reality that stress and adversity is a given. The adverse effects of it, however, are a choice. When the body is constantly bathed in stress hormones, the detrimental effects are bound to surface, especially as we age. One of the ways to put things in perspective is to understand and differentiate what is under our control and what isn't. Known as the **dichotomy of control**, this concept enables us to have more clarity about what is within our control and how our efforts may change a given situation versus what is not within our control and the futility of stressing about it. For example, how you lead your life, whether you seek approval or validation from others, how hard you work, how much you use and are influenced by social media, what you do to unwind and your own search for meaning in life is within your control. These are aspects of our lives that we often revisit as we grow older. On the other hand, the lives and choices of your children are not within your control, especially as they get older and grow more independent. Getting bent out of shape about their life choices is not beneficial to you in any way.

With age should come maturity and wisdom to make the above differentiation and minimize how we **react to stress** with the understanding that adversity is an integral part of life and we, in fact, need to **embrace it fully to lead fuller, more meaningful lives.**

eighteen

Sleep

I love my sleep. During the time I spent in medical college, I frequently suffered from insomnia. The terribly disturbing anatomy dissections on dead bodies in my very first year, the enormous workload, the environment and heat of Madras, where I was studying, may have had something to do with it. Perhaps as a result of having suffered from insomnia for many years, I now have a tremendous respect for my sleep.

Sleep has been found to be one of the most important aspects of well-being. It's a common myth that you can get by with little sleep. The importance of good sleep goes way beyond just banishing your under-eye circles or acquiring that daisy fresh skin! Too much and too little sleep can go as far as affecting your lifespan.

It's almost fashionable these days to talk about how you manage on 'so little sleep'. This is both silly and damaging to health and well-being. If you've been around someone who is sleep-deprived and irritable, you know how disturbing that can be.

Sleep is required for repair and regeneration of the body and for cognitive processes like memory and thermoregulation. Good quality sleep, therefore, should be very much a part of a healthy lifestyle. Deep sleep that occurs during the slow wave sleep and REM (rapid eye movement) sleep is critical for memory and brain function. This is the time short-term memory is converted and stored away as long-term memory clearing space in your brain to acquire more new information when you wake. This is called **memory consolidation.**

As people age, they find it harder to fall asleep and have trouble staying asleep. They may also have fragmented sleep and a decline in REM sleep, which is essential. These symptoms of abnormal sleep patterns seem to be part of the ageing process, though it is unclear exactly why it happens.

During peri-menopause and menopause, symptoms like hot flushes, pain or even depression can keep you awake. About 40 per cent of women complain of lack of sleep during these years. Insomnia is very much a part of the menopausal list of problems. In men, similar changes occur with far less intensity as they grow older and go through andropause, with depression and anxiety leading to sleepless nights. On the other hand, a fast-paced high-stress life, a high-level job, travel or financial responsibilities may be the cause of great angst leading to insomnia.

When training to be a doctor, you tend to also train to sleep less. It's part of the job profile to be able to function at your optimum even when woken up in the middle of the night, to operate for instance. I know that we train to do this and are good at it, but I am quite sure that it has taken a toll on our health and well-being. I consciously try and 'catch up' on sleep, but as you will see later in the chapter, one can never truly pay off a sleep debt.

Ask yourself:

- How many hours do you typically sleep?
- Do you feel rested in the morning?

- Do you sleep soundly or are you restless through the night?
- Do you need help getting to sleep? Do you use sedatives?

An ideal amount of sleep would be about six-to-eight hours of good quality sleep every night. The amount of sleep required can vary for individuals, however. Those on night shifts or who work very long, irregular hours, like healthcare workers, caregivers, airline crew, shift workers or new mothers, are likely to have poor, erratic sleep patterns. These kinds of lifestyles have been found to have several worrying health consequences, especially with age.

STAGES OF SLEEP

There are two basic stages of sleep: rapid eye movement (REM) sleep and non-REM sleep (which has three different stages). Each stage is characterized by specific brain waves and neuronal activity. Your brain will cycle through all stages of non-REM and REM sleep several times during a typical night, with increasingly longer, deeper REM periods occurring toward the early hours of the morning.

Stage 1 non-REM sleep is the period when you just fall asleep from wakefulness. During this short period that lasts several minutes of relatively light sleep, your heartbeat, breathing and eye movements slow down. Your brain waves begin to slow from their daytime wakefulness patterns. Your muscles relax with occasional slight twitches.

Stage 2 non-REM sleep is a period of light sleep just before you enter deeper sleep. Your heartbeat and breathing slow further, and muscles relax even more. Your body temperature drops and eye movements stop. Brain wave activity slows down but is marked by brief bursts of electrical activity. You spend most of your repeated sleep cycles in this Stage 2 sleep rather than in the other stages of sleep.

Stage 3 non-REM sleep is the period of deep sleep that you need to feel refreshed in the morning. It occurs in longer periods during the first half of the night. Your heartbeat and breathing slow to their lowest levels during this stage of sleep. Your muscles are completely relaxed and it may be difficult to awaken you. Brain waves become even slower.

This is when the mind slips into **REM sleep**. Your first REM cycle will occur about 90 minutes after falling asleep. Your eyes move rapidly from side to side behind closed eyelids. Brain wave activity becomes mixed and almost like that seen during wakefulness. Your breathing becomes rapid and irregular, and your heart rate and blood pressure increase to near waking levels. **Most of your dreaming occurs during REM sleep**, although some can also occur in non-REM sleep. Your arm and leg muscles become temporarily paralyzed, which prevents you from acting out your dreams. As you age, you sleep less of your time in REM sleep.

Sleep depends on two systems in the body:

- The homeostatic system, or the internal biochemical system that generates the need to sleep after a length of wakefulness. The longer you stay awake, the more you feel the need to sleep.
- The circadian rhythm, or the body's internal clock that is controlled by a circadian pacemaker that is present in the brain and syncs our system with day and night. Sleeping at night and staying awake during daytime is a light-related rhythm that is affected by light and darkness.

The two processes work together to create a balanced sleep-wake cycle. Thus, when these systems are disrupted due to long work hours or wakefulness at night, several things can go awry within the body. A few days of poor sleep may not affect you in the long-term, but constant sleep deprivation most certainly will. As mentioned already, for some people, problems with sleep patterns appear as we age. Hormones, medical problems, obesity, medication and stress may all contribute in varying degrees to poor sleep.

There are several different types of sleep problems. You may:

- Take a long time to fall asleep (stressful negative thoughts, anxiety, not tired enough).
- Wake up several times in the night (perhaps due to hot flushes, wrong temperature in the room, too much food and indigestion).
- Wake up early and be unable to get back to sleep.
- Wake up tired (poor quality sleep).
- Feel very sleepy during the day (due to lack of good quality sleep).

Causes of Poor Sleep

There can be several reasons why you are sleeping poorly:

- **Too much stress:** Worrying about various things in your day or life can prevent you from good sleep.
- **Poor sleep hygiene:** There are several things like your phone, iPad, TV or even the temperature of your room that could prevent you from having a good quality sleep.
- **Obesity:** Being severely overweight can cause sleep apnea (where you don't breathe for a few seconds at a time when

you are asleep). This causes you to wake up several times in the night and leaves you exhausted in the morning.
- **Medical problems:** Several medical problems may cause poor sleep including arthritic pain, heart disease or indigestion.

PROBLEMS RESULTING FROM SLEEP DEPRIVATION

- **Type 2 diabetes:** Type 2 diabetes is associated with lifestyle and genetic factors. Disruption of the circadian clockwork leading to poor sleep might play a role in the development of metabolic disorders like type 2 diabetes. Chronic jet lag or working erratic shifts has a deep impact on metabolic health. Such individuals have a greater propensity for insulin resistance leading to type 2 diabetes.
- **Obesity:** Sleep deprivation leads to abnormal and erratic eating habits. The body is unable to distinguish hunger from sleep deprivation and fatigue. The tendency to overeat, eat at night and indulge in sugary carb-loaded foods is greater when one is sleep-deprived. Sleep helps maintain a healthy balance of the hormones that make you feel hungry (ghrelin) or full (leptin). When you don't get enough sleep, your ghrelin levels are increased and the level of leptin goes down. This creates feelings of hunger and food-seeking behaviour. It's a catch-22 situation. Sleep deprivation leads to overeating and the associated fatigue can prevent exercise and/or movement leading to obesity. Obesity, in turn, can cause problems like sleep apnea and further sleep deprivation.
- **Hypertension, stroke and heart disease:** These are more common following chronic sleep deprivation. This is the result of cortisol, the stress hormone that is released when you are constantly sleep-deprived.

- **Memory and attention problems:** The brain is highly sensitive to sleep deprivation. When it is not adequately rested, attention and working memory are compromised. The incidence of accidents, poor performance and short-term memory lapses are more common following sleep deprivation.
- **Depression, suicide and risk-taking behaviour:** These are increased with sleep deprivation. People who suffered from lack of sleep were found to be more reckless.
- **Social dysfunction:** Sleep deprivation causes mood swings, low moods and poor social skills. This, when combined with menopausal symptoms, may not pan out very well for you.

IMPROVING YOUR SLEEP

Improve Emotional Well-being

It is critically important to understand that emotional well-being is at the heart of good quality sleep. Interventions designed to increase levels of psychological or subjective well-being, such as daily gratitude exercises or benefit-finding, have the added benefit of reducing the experience of insomnia. Life satisfaction, feeling of 'agency' or meaning and purpose in life appear to coincide with better quality sleep. Therefore, right at the onset, while trying to sort out sleep problems, it is worthwhile to explore other aspects of wellness.

Let Go of Unhelpful Thoughts and Expectations

While having a purpose/meaning in life and improving life satisfaction should be a priority, remember that it is an ongoing project. Worrying endlessly into the night about incomplete tasks and goals is not a helpful strategy and turns out to be a surefire way of hindering sleep. What is not done today may be followed up tomorrow. The night time of quiet and solitude may be fertile ground for endless worrisome thoughts. Learning to 'let go' temporarily is helpful and can be a learnt skill.

Practise Sleep Hygiene

- Follow a regular sleep schedule. Go to sleep and wake up at the same time each day, even on weekends or when you are on holiday. This is especially true if you are a poor sleeper.
- Avoid napping during the day. Naps may keep you awake at night.
- Develop a bedtime routine. Take time to relax before bedtime each night. Read a book, listen to soothing music or soak in a warm bath.
- Try not to watch television or use your computer, cell phone or tablet in the bedroom. The light from these devices makes it difficult for you to fall asleep. Alarming or unsettling shows or movies, like horror movies, may also keep you awake.
- Keep your bedroom at a comfortable temperature, not too hot or too cold, and as quiet as possible.
- Use heavy duty drapes or blinds to keep out unnecessary light from outside.
- Exercise at regular times each day but not within three hours of your bedtime. Exercise is a stimulant and you may have difficulty falling asleep if you exercise too close to bedtime.
- Avoid eating large meals close to bedtime, they can keep you awake.

- Stay away from coffee late in the day. Caffeine (found in coffee, tea, soda and chocolate) can make you too wired to sleep.
- Maintain a sleep diary to record how many hours you sleep and how rested you feel. These days you have devices that do this for you like your Fitbit. I am a bit skeptical of sleeping with devices but if a device helps you understand your sleep patterns better, by all means use it.

Exercise Regularly

Regular exercise, preferably earlier in the day, helps you sleep better. The various benefits of exercise such as weight loss, better mood and lowered stress, aid good sleep. Exercising too strenuously and late in the day can actually prevent sleep by keeping you wired. A moderate-paced walk is fine, but a heart-pumping run may not be.

Manage Stress

Any number of psychological stressors may keep you awake at night. Ruminating on the stressors of the day will lower your ability to fall and stay asleep. Learn to manage your stress better.

Rule Out Other Medical Disorders

Other disorders that may be impairing sleep are sleep apnea, heart problems, heartburn and indigestion, painful conditions like arthritis or fibromyalgia, kidney disease, thyroid disease or a breathing disorder.

Learn a Meditation Technique

A simple 10-minute meditation technique can help you fall asleep. Learning to meditate is not the same as just relaxing or sleeping. It is the ability to observe the spontaneous wandering of the mind without getting too involved or judging the thoughts themselves. This can also be learnt with time and practice. During meditation, special waves called **alpha** and **theta waves** are increased in the brain. Theta waves indicate deep relaxation and are seen in highly experienced meditators. They arise from the frontal (behind the forehead) part and the mid-brain and when the brain is in a state of 'relaxed attention' that monitors our inner experiences.

Alpha waves are those that arise from the posterior part (or back) of the brain and indicate 'wakeful rest', meaning that the brain is withdrawn from any kind of intentional, goal-oriented task but is observing its own thought processes. What you learn in meditation is **non-directive relaxation** of the mind where thoughts are allowed to flow with no judgment or attachment but only observation.

Meditation is a powerful tool to improve sleep, relieve depression and anxiety, improve attention and concentration and overall sense of well-being.

Learn Progressive Muscle Relaxation

Consciously relaxing your muscles helps you sleep. Lie down or make yourself comfortable. Starting with your feet, tense the muscles as tightly as you can. Hold for a count of 10, and then relax. Continue to do this for every muscle group in your body, working your way up to the top of your head.

Avoid Alcohol

While ingestion of alcohol may make you sleepy, rebound awakening and insomnia are common after-effects of alcohol intake.

Try Soothing Teas

Drinking teas like chamomile tea at bedtime can help you relax.

Try Melatonin

Melatonin is a naturally occurring hormone that is released from the suprachiasmatic nucleus or SCN in the brain. It is released at night and is triggered by darkness and its levels remain elevated throughout the night until suppressed by the light of morning. Although melatonin tablets as a supplement do not appear to be particularly effective for treating most sleep disorders, they can help sleep problems caused by jet lag and shift work. Simple exposure to light at the right time, however, is just as effective.

Consider CBT

Cognitive Behavioural Therapy (CBT) has been found to be highly effective for those who find disturbing thoughts and emotions robbing them of sleep. This is a form of psychotherapy that seeks to alter thought and behavioural patterns. A study at Harvard Medical School found CBT to be more effective than sleeping pills for treating insomnia.

CAN YOU MAKE UP FOR YOUR SLEEP DEBT?

Apparently not, according to research. Some people take afternoon naps as a way of dealing with the fatigue of sleep deprivation. Naps may provide a short-term boost in alertness and performance. Napping, however, does not provide all of the other benefits of prolonged night-time sleep. **Thus, you can't really make up for lost sleep.** Some may sleep more on their days off to make up for a busy week. Although extra sleep on days off might help you feel better, it can upset your body's sleep–wake rhythm. Someone who manages to nap or get a good night's sleep after pulling all-nighters may recover temporarily for a few hours following the nap. The longer they continue to then stay awake, the more the sleep debt is likely to catch up with them, causing foggy brain, trouble remembering and poor reaction time. It may, therefore, require several nights of extended sleep to pay off your sleep debt.

Using Sedatives to Sleep

It's easy to pop a pill to fall asleep. That may be your solution to the struggles you face with sleep. Sedatives need to be prescribed by your physician. They should not be taken as and when you think you need them.

Short-term insomnia may be treated quite effectively with sleeping pills. But it's important to know that they do have side effects and may cause dependency and addictions for some people. You can build up a tolerance for the dosage of the drug and, with time, may require a higher dosage to produce the same effect.

Researchers at St Luke's Hospital's Sleep Medicine and Research Center in St Louis, Missouri, studied the effects of sleep medication on the quality of sleep, especially the effect of medications of memory consolidation. As explained earlier in the chapter, this is the process by which sleep enhances our ability to store away short-term memories we have perhaps experienced during the day into long-term memory, clearing the cache, so to speak, for new stuff. Sleep that is induced with sleeping pills has been found to be less restorative than natural sleep.

Natural supplements like the roots of the valerian plant and kava, a type of pepper plant, have been used to aid sleep. The term 'natural' is often used alongside 'safe' but these substances can interact with other drugs you are taking and result in liver damage and other ailments. It's best to consult a doctor before you try natural products.

Drawbacks of Using Sedatives to Sleep

- **Affects memory:** Using medication to sleep affects our ability to remember things. This, in addition to the menopausal and peri-menopausal memory setbacks, can be quite catastrophic.
- **Creates dependence and addiction:** If no attempt is made to deal with the real problem for insomnia (this could be stress, anxiety or a medical condition), it is easy to become dependent on popping a pill at night to help you sleep.
- **Creates tolerance:** Drug tolerance can occur whereby the same dosage does not work for you anymore and you may need to gradually keep increasing the dose for it to be effective. This, in turn, will increase the side effects of the drug itself.
- **Side effects:** Sleeping pills can create early morning drowsiness depending on dosage, as well as clumsiness, loss of balance, blurred vision, constipation, nausea and dry mouth.
- **Rebound insomnia:** Your insomnia can become worse once you stop the medication.
- **Drug interactions:** Prescription pain killers, other sedatives and alcohol interact with sleep medication.

- **Withdrawal symptoms:** There is a real fear of withdrawal symptoms like nausea, sweating and tremors if you abruptly stop taking sleeping pills.
- **Allergic reaction to the drug itself:** Memory lapses, hallucinations, swelling, itching can occur.
- **Complex sleep-related behaviours:** Reactions like sleepwalking, sleepdriving even sleepeating (with no recollection of having eaten!) can occur when on the medication.

This doesn't mean medication should never be prescribed. There is a place for it in the short-term to cure intractable insomnia. It may be used as a crutch, so to speak, to temporarily tide you over an acute phase of insomnia. This is similar to using a crutch when you break your leg. For the leg to heal effectively, however, you need the help of physiotherapy, stretching and strengthening. Similarly, as you get your sleep using an assisting drug, start to implement other ways of inducing natural sleep such as learning meditation, starting CBT, exercising, practising sleep hygiene and so on to wean yourself off the drugs and get into a rhythm of natural sleep.

Recognize and accept that sleep patterns may change with age. Identify other causes of poor sleep like a medical problem or anxiety. Find natural, effective ways of improving sleep like exercise, meditation and progressive muscle relaxation before heading off to the chemist for sedatives. Don't underestimate the power of good sleep. It should be top priority for you to be able to function to your optimum, stay well, have good relationships and have a positive life experience.

nineteen

Relationships and Quality of Life

Positive social connections that promote social integration and social support have been linked to positive health behaviours and emotional states like feelings of belonging and purpose. In his book, *Loneliness: Human Nature and the Need for Social Connection*, Dr John Cacioppo, a highly renowned social neuroscientist from University of Chicago, delves deeply into the subject of human bonds and connections. In it, he says that loneliness is quite literally damaging to the heart.

As we grow older, the need for deeper connectedness with other human beings increases. Loneliness does not mean aloneness. One can be amidst a sea of humanity and still be extremely lonely and, at the other end of the spectrum, be physically alone but not feel lonely. The effects of loneliness are as bad for the heart as other well-known risk factors such as obesity or a poor socioeconomic status, leading to a higher risk of premature death.

Good relationships are paramount to an enhanced life experience. There's just no denying the truth in that. Human beings are meant to be sociable and connected to one another. The degree of connectedness depends on many things, including how much time and effort we allow for relationships, individual personalities (introverted versus extroverted people), the kind of society we live in (societies like ours, where people are more inclined to connect than in others) and the perceived need for connections.

Relationships can be a source of great stress or provide respite from it. Not all relationships turn out well, and some can be downright painful. You may need to walk away from some for your own well-being. Each relationship, however, has lessons to teach us (above all, about ourselves) that help us grow. Having someone (or a few select people) you can count on and connect with deeply and who are truly 'on your team' goes a long way in mitigating much of the day-to-day stress we all encounter. An absence of this kind of support can be a source of deep loneliness.

Such a team, however, can only be built with time and effort – it doesn't just happen overnight. To maintain good relationships with family, colleagues, contemporaries or old friends takes effort and time. With the fast-paced lives that many of us lead today, we may be too overwhelmed to make this time. Several years of ignoring old relationships or past hurts may end up dismantling a relationship altogether. It is important, then, to spend some time nurturing relationships if you believe they are important. **The presence of close and authentic connections becomes even more essential as we age.**

Circles of Connections

We live within many circles.

Our **most intimate circle** may consist of just a handful of people and may perhaps include your partner, a few very close friends, siblings or parents. This is our 'go-to' circle in times of need and the people we feel the deepest connection with. These are the people with whom we can really allow ourselves to be vulnerable. These are the people we feel completely safe with. This is the circle that remains with us as we grow older. We form strong bonds with them and feel a deeper sense of connectedness with them as we experience life together. The need for this intimate circle cannot be over-emphasized.

The next is our **circle of acquaintances**, consisting of those we connect with more casually but who are equal in importance to the first circle. These are the larger social circles we move in, people whose company we enjoy, who we are loosely associated with in some way. They may be old family friends that we share memories with, childhood buddies we spent years with in school, cousins we grew up with, colleagues we work with, people who belong to the same club or organization who we meet frequently and so on. Some people are better at maintaining these relationships than others. Of course, it takes effort and time to sustain such relationships and some may not believe it to be a wise investment, but it may be prudent to remember that these are also important associations that keep the wheels of society well oiled. We will find that, as we get older, we tend to sustain these more superficial relationships with greater ease. Perhaps we become more adept at managing our own expectations of them and, therefore, mange these relationships better.

The **third circle** consists of the people you know but are least intimate with. These could be people you just met, your colleagues whom you don't work with closely, someone you chat with at a store you visit often, certain Facebook friends, distant relatives, and so on.

The **circles beyond this** are all the people you don't (yet) know but are still connected to, like those belonging to your city, your country and the world.

All these connections are important, obviously in varying degrees. As I said, how much effort you put into sustaining connections depends a lot on your time, personality and needs.

Most of us put in an effort on special occasions, say on birthdays or festivals, to pick up the phone to call an acquaintance. These days with social media, Whatsapp groups and such it is far easier to keep in touch or at least stay connected (albeit superficially) and in the general know of things. This is not to say one makes any real meaningful connections on social media alone, but it certainly has its uses.

The Art of Listening

Relationships are primarily about communication. Since good relationships are necessary for human beings to flourish, it makes sense for us to master the art of good communication. Without effective communication, there could be many crossed wires and misunderstandings would be inevitable. Not everyone is adept at communication; it is a learnt art. Knowing how to ask the right questions in the right tone of voice, managing to curtail anger or irritation and reserving judgment when required can be extraordinarily difficult tasks that we can, however, learn to do with time.

One of the most important ways to improve connections with people is to master the art of listening. What is the big deal with that, you may ask? You just listen, right? Wrong. **There is hearing and there is real listening.**

Listening is more than just a passive act. Have you ever been with someone who stays on his or her phone, texting, while you talk about your day? Have you had your mind wander while your friend described his/her first day at work? Have you put someone on speakerphone as they talked while you went about doing something else with half an ear to what they were saying? I think all of us have been guilty of this at some point! Guilty of half-listening or daydreaming while someone speaks; not really paying attention and thinking of our responses instead;

judging the person and their words before really understanding what exactly they are saying or listening with only one's own agenda in mind. To really improve a relationship, it's important to not just listen but to actively reciprocate when someone is speaking. This is called **active reciprocal listening.**

Being there for someone doesn't mean you are there for him or her only in times of need. In fact, research has shown that it is important to stay connected and involved during times of joy and happiness as much as in times of crisis. This is something we don't always recognize. Sharing life events is what it's all about, whether they are good things or unpleasant ones.

What Kind of a Communicator Are You?

Given below are four different ways in which people respond. Can you identify how you respond?

1. **The Joy Multiplier:** Your friend comes to you with news about his/her project being accepted/successful. You set aside everything you are doing at that moment, turn towards them and engage fully, physically and emotionally. You ask questions to have them elaborate and savour their story. You help them relive their happiness and excitement. This creates a powerful bond. This is the ideal listening style.
2. **The Joy Thief:** Your partner comes to you with some significant news about his/her career success. You immediately begin to enumerate the problems you foresee. Perhaps he/she has to travel more; perhaps the workload will be greater and that may compromise on your time together. There are so many relevant problems that you already envisage! While all these reasons may be valid and you may be justified in thinking of them, this is not the

time to enumerate them. It will rob your partner of the opportunity to feel the joy and fulfillment of the moment. Focus on the positive and leave the analysis for later.

3. **The Conversation Hijacker:** Your friend comes to you with news about his/her project being successful. You immediately remember your great success with the deal you sealed that very day! You excitedly tell him/her all about it. Might as well make this into a share fest and share all the wonderful news right away is what you are thinking.

   Hold your horses. He/she has just told you something of great significance to him/her. It's vital you set aside your own excitement for your achievement (however big or small), and allow them their moment of glory and excitement. Share in it by asking the right questions. Allow the moment to linger. The opportunity to talk about your success will come later. Given that you have made them feel good about themselves, they will also be in a better position to share your joy.

4. **The Conversation Killer:** Your partner comes to you with news about their project being accepted/successful. You are busy answering a mail on your phone. You hear what they say, partially; you nod, smile vaguely even pat their knee and say, 'Oh, how wonderful!' and go back to that very important mail. Nothing can be as crushing as a brush-off like that. While that mail may be urgent, so is appreciating your partner's piece of good news.

   There are two ways to deal with this situation. One, you put your phone away and respond appropriately. Two, if it is imperative that you finish that mail that very minute, then tell them, 'I would really like to hear your story in detail, just hold on for a few seconds while I send off this mail and I am with you.' Then proceed to do just that. Finish sending that mail right away (if it's going to take more than a few minutes, you will seriously need to weigh the importance of sending that mail as opposed to listening to your partner at that crucial moment), put away your phone, turn to your partner and respond appropriately.

A successful relationship is often based on good communication. **For it to be effective, communication has to be authentic and empathetic.** Respect for the other, paying attention to what is really being said, suspending judgement and truly listening to what is being communicated are all important to ensure thriving, happy relationships.

Connections Within a Marriage or An Intimate Relationship

Marriage and intimate relationships can be complicated.

The institution of marriage itself puts a great deal of pressure, particularly of expectations, on the couple involved. It is up to the individuals concerned to re-evaluate and shape their own rules for their marriage to see it work. In our country, marriage is often not just between two people, but also between two families. This can be both constructive and detrimental, depending on how it is viewed. Having family support, especially to take care of the children is immensely helpful. At the same time, having to live within the constraints and the rules of a large family may be oppressive for some.

Many couples choose not to (or perhaps may not be able to) enter into a traditional marriage. Some women make a conscious choice to remain single for various reasons, and then there are relationships of different sexual orientation. Each of these relationships faces similar problems, though they may be to different degrees. In the end, it comes down to the intimate relationship between two people. How that relationship is negotiated will largely depend on the wisdom and maturity of the two people involved.

Some of the most crucial ingredients within such relationships would be trust, regard and respect for the other's views or ideologies, love, compassion and a basic consideration for the other as a human being.

Expectations Within a Relationship

A couple within a marriage or relationship is expected to feel romantic love. That is, after all, what a marriage is supposed to be all about, isn't it? There may also be an unprecedented need for fulfillment from the romantic partner, something they may find challenging to live up to.

The term 'Suffocation Model of Marriage' was coined by Finkel and colleagues in 2014.[6] They have explained the different kinds of marriages that have existed over the ages. Although this was with reference to American couples, we can see similar patterns (though perhaps not quite so ubiquitous) in our own country.

- **The Institutional Era** (1776–1850): Marriages were practical in function, serving as a source for fulfillment of social and economic needs.
- **The Companionate Era** (1850–1965): Marriages began to have a more emotional purpose, fulfilling needs for loving and belonging.
- **The Self-Expressive Era** (1965–present): Marriages today are expected not only to fulfil belonging and love needs, but also support personal growth and self-actualization.

This could apply to marriage or a romantic relationship outside of marriage. Your relationship may fall into any of the above categories. Mostly, though, we see that today relationships have gradually adopted the ideology that the partners are responsible for each other's happiness and self-realization. A relationship that provides this in some way is, therefore, beneficial to overall well-being while one that doesn't live up to these high standards may be detrimental to health and happiness.

While this high expectation exists within a relationship, we are also exceedingly hard-pressed for time, with the many roles we play making demands on our time and effort through the day. So how much we give to our partners and to the relationship itself becomes that much more challenging even with best intentions in mind. This is why it is called the Suffocation Model. While we may want more from our relationships, it turns out to be quite a challenge to achieve this as an ideal.

When I talk to people over 40, many speak of a decreased feeling of romantic love for their partner. Many feel disillusioned, unfulfilled or frustrated by their expectations. It is possible to lose the intensity of (what is commonly understood as) love with time. It takes work to keep fires burning, something many don't quite appreciate. Some find a wonderful new balance with their partner. They become friends in addition to being romantic partners. Each one of us has to find our own way of making it work to the benefit of both partners without affecting our own well-being.

Brain scans of people done after a week into a relationship and then a year later found differences in the areas of the brain that were active. In long-term relationships, the areas of 'attachment' became more active. What you share with someone over the long term are memories, nostalgia, shared responsibilities and a deeper kind of love and respect. Infatuation, which perhaps existed in the early days of a marriage or a relationship, is sure to fade, to be replaced, ideally, by a deeper, more mature love for one another. When you are over 40, it is more likely than not that you've been in a long-term relationship which has evolved over the years into something more mature and mellow but also, hopefully, more meaningful. Over time, you have learnt to adapt and manage your expectations.

Having a good marriage or relationship has been found to be beneficial for the heart, to prevent diseases by improving immunity, to stave off depression, reduce stress and generally increase well-being. A bad marriage (or relationship), on the other hand, has quite the opposite effect on our health. Hostility within a relationship can be a source of great suffering, even giving rise to heart attacks, depression, cancer, obesity, hypertension and a susceptibility to all kinds of diseases due to lowered immunity. Who would have thought having a good relationship with our partner was all that important? Well, it is.

Maintaining Your Relationships

Here are a few things that could help you maintain healthy and long-lasting relationships:

Don't feel automatically entitled to happiness: Being married or being in a relationship does not make the partner automatically responsible for your happiness. That is an inside job. It is not the responsibility of your partner to make you happy. It works well if both partners focus on a common goal for life satisfaction. Even if that is not the case (as I often see in many relationships where both partners pretty much lead separate lives), your own well-being is in your hands.

Make the relationship a priority: Knowing that a good relationship within a marriage is beneficial for you should give you incentive enough to *make* it a priority.

Carve out time for each other: In our daily lives, our time is taken up by innumerable things. Making time for your relationship will not just happen; you have to *make* it happen if you truly want to.

Revisit the rules of your marriage: As you get older, with the children possibly gone from home, the time you have with each other can be either a relief or a source of frustration! Retirement is another milestone that marks more time together. What do you do with this time? How do you invest it well with each other? These may be questions to explore.

Provide support: To receive support you also need to be able to give back. This is a primary tenet of any relationship. Provide support needed for your partner's growth. He/she may also want to do other things as he/she ages, just as you do.

Care to listen: Listening attentively to your partner is of paramount importance. Go through the communication styles listed above and identify how you listen and communicate. If you want to be heard, then you also need to listen and be interested in your partner. Ask pertinent questions. Discuss options and be open to having disagreements if need be.

Forgive to move on: Sometimes it so happens that there may have been some indiscretions or ill-treatment by or from your partner in the past. If you truly want to make it work, forgiveness has to be a priority, not just for the relationship, but also for your own well-being. It is said that harbouring anger or resentment is like consuming poison and expecting the other person to die!

Stop being passive-aggressive: Sometimes, in an attempt to 'get back' at your partner for some hurt that has been caused, you may act out passive-aggressively by doing small things to annoy your partner or express displeasure instead of actually saying what has upset you. Remember, no one can read another person's mind, so even though you may feel vindicated by acting out passive-aggressively, the problem will remain unsolved.

Learn to communicate: Communication is the most important aspect of any relationship. It's not something we are taught in school (but honestly, I think it should be!) so we often miscommunicate our wants and needs, only to be annoyed that they are not met or understood. It is far better to express clearly what is going on in our minds if we want to be understood. Having differences of opinion is completely natural in any relationship, but one must learn healthy ways of making up and communicating effectively. In a healthy relationship, one recognizes this and respects the other's perspective and you agree to disagree.

Acknowledge your partner: It's important to acknowledge your partner's presence, achievements, virtues, effort to keep things together and so on. While all of this is expected, expressing it openly (just like expressing love openly) makes your partner feel appreciated and he/she will be appreciative in return.

Respect your partner: According to psychologist John Gottman, known for his work on marital stability and relationship analysis, *contempt* is the one emotion that is sure to deflate a relationship. The opposite of contempt is respect for the other. Practising healthy respect for your partner will put him/her (and his/her actions) in a different perspective.

Don't judge: Being mindful means practicing being non-judgemental.[7] It's hard to know what it is like to be in another's shoes, as much as we may try or want to. The best we can do, therefore, is not to pass undue judgement. It is also tempting to be judgemental in order to feel vindicated when there is a problem. This serves no purpose, however, as the problem itself will not be solved with your judgment call. In all likelihood, you will only feel more frustrated and that will lead to more strife.

Find your own happiness: Working on yourself (rather than obsessing solely over the merits and demerits of your primary relationship) will enhance your chances of life satisfaction irrespective of the relationship. Find your own outlets for joy and meaning. They do not have to be tied to your partner's at all times.

DIVORCE AND SEPARATION

Sometimes relationships or marriages don't work out. People may struggle on, trying to remain together because of children, finances, family and societal pressures, and so on. There should be no excuse to stay on in toxic situations, but that's often easier said than done and one cannot and should not judge another's position. Domestic abuse, for instance, is very prevalent in our country, with about 40 per cent of women admitting to being abused. Many stay on despite the indignity of it, however, while others manage to move on despite the complications involved.

A serious effort by both partners to make things work is an equitable reason to stay within a relationship or marriage. But if no attempt is being made to sort things out, you are better off out of it.

Divorce or separation is like bereavement. The loss of a partner starts a grieving process much like the death of a loved one. You go through similar stages of denial, anger, bargaining, depression and, finally, acceptance. The wrecking of a relationship can lead to depression and ill-health. Researchers say there is such a thing as Divorce Stress Syndrome, which has been compared to

Post-Traumatic Stress Disorder or PTSD. The emotional stress of divorce can cause both physical and mental health complications like depression, substance abuse, social isolation, obesity, diabetes, heart disease, hypertension and anxiety.

For women, in particular, in addition to financial and emotional difficulties faced, society often offers little support at this time of need. Younger people who divorce may face the problem of living and managing singly, or being single parents and having to struggle with child care, while older people may experience resentment and bitterness at having wasted 'the best years of their lives'. Having a family and close friends who provide adequate emotional support (the support team I talked about earlier) can be a great relief.

If the decision to divorce has been made and carried out, then coping strategies must fall into place with the help of the support group of close friends and family, a therapist, lawyer and perhaps even a financial advisor.

The strategies for coping should include:

- Regular exercise, meditation and yoga to calm the mind.
- Spending time with close family and friends to feel connected.
- Work or career to keep the mind occupied.
- Therapy sessions to work through anger or resentment issues.
- Hobbies to keep you engaged.

All these will play a role in getting through this difficult time.

Talking to people who have been through the ordeal, I often hear a mixture of deep sadness, relief, anxiety and fear. Most survive with admirable fortitude, though some continue to feel betrayed and bitter long after the event. Residual grief or anger over the years are highly dependent on the personalities of the couple, the coping strategies undertaken, the availability of genuine support and the way things played out during the whole process.

There are some, of course, who not only survive but go way beyond their potential and thrive after the grieving period. Much of what held them back is now behind them and they spread their wings to new horizons. It's good to remember that divorce, however difficult, is certainly not the end of the world and may even prove to be a healthier choice for many.

Relationships with Friends

Friendships differ greatly within and between sexes. Friendships between men tend to be less intimate and emotional, and more dependent on commonly shared interests and activities. Men's friendships also tend to be more 'transactional' as they work towards common goals or reciprocate favours. Most men don't seem to feel the need to constantly 'stay in touch' or invest too much time in their friendships. Relationships between women are far more intimate but more fragile. By and large, women tend to invest more time and energy in friendships.

Having said that, each friendship is different and should be viewed as such. Deep friendships, science has found, does not stop at just common interests or 'being there for each other'. They seem to share the same brain waves and neural responses to events and subjects. A study done by Carol Parkinson, a cognitive scientist at the University of California, showed that brain waves of subjects exposed to videos on various topics were extremely similar among those who were close friends when compared to those who were not. This seems to suggest that people who are friends share something very deep, like the very structure of their brains. This could also explain why you feel that certain deep level of comfort when you are with your best friend. It's because your brains are in sync.

People with strong social ties appear to have less fibrinogen (a protein in the blood that makes the blood cells 'sticky', causing clotting and inflammation). Social connectedness and deep friendships protect you from heart disease, depression and loneliness.

Evaluating the merits and depth of a friendship should help put things in perspective when the going gets tough. Just like the love in a marriage, friendships are also sometimes difficult to sustain due to paucity of time and effort. They are as susceptible to disintegration as a marriage or any other important relationship. We all need friends to live wholesome lives, and investing time and energy in positive, nurturing relationships is very important. To sustain friendships, we need to:

- **Make time:** It's not always convenient to make time for our friends, especially with all our various obligations, but a conscious effort to do so, keep in touch and share and enquire about our friends' well-being is a must. The memories you make when you share happy times with a friend – whether it's a meal or a shared hobby or an enjoyable conversation or even a heart-to-heart – can sustain a feeling of well-being for a length of time. And then there are the memories of those times to fall back on too.
- **Reach out:** Sometimes all it takes is a phone call. We should be able to reach out on a regular basis to our friends even if just to touch base and update each other about our lives.
- **Stay authentic:** This is one of the keys to any meaningful friendship. How can it be called a friendship if both or either person involved is not authentic? If you feel the

need to put up a façade, cover up or make excuses, perhaps it's time to re-evaluate the friendship altogether. This is not to say that one has to bare one's soul to every friend, but what is shared needs to be genuine and honest.

- **Work at it:** We often take relationships for granted. While that is certainly the prerogative of any good relationship, constant neglect will surely erode it at some level. Make the effort to work at a relationship you value.
- **Don't judge:** Just as in a marriage, this is probably the one thing that keeps a relationship healthy. One has no right to judge another harshly. We mostly never have all the facts about another person's life, which makes it difficult to truly comprehend another's behaviour and responses. Judging them, therefore, is not helpful or constructive.

We sometimes allow relationships to decay or die a natural death over trivialities. If it is an important relationship, it's worth resurrecting even if that means having a painful conversation. Allowing yourself to be vulnerable is not easy. But that's what it takes to overcome barriers, especially those built up when the ego comes into play.

Female Friendships

There is a wide range of research that reinforces the importance of healthy female friendships. The benefits of such friendships go far beyond shared enjoyable experiences. If you have one or a few really good girlfriends, I am sure you will unequivocally agree. We can have deep, meaningful conversations with our girlfriends, be supported in times of need, laugh uproariously at the silliest of things, holiday together, get advice when needed (and also when unsolicited), and feel wanted and valued for just being who we are with all our imperfections.

I know I couldn't have survived some very stressful times in my life without my friends. There's something about a female friendship that is especially heart-warming.

An important study done at the University of California, Los Angeles (UCLA), suggests what we always knew – that friendships between women are very special and play a significant role in combatting stress. Dr Laura Klein, the author of this study, explains that the hormone oxytocin is released as part of the stress response in a woman. Oxytocin appears to buffer stress or the fight-or-flight response and also enables women to bond with other women. This bonding creates a calming effect on the body. Estrogen, she adds, seems to enhance this effect. Men, on the other hand, respond to stress differently and tend to cut off from people. As mentioned earlier in the book, the term **'tend and befriend'** was a notion that was coined by Dr Klein and her associate, Dr Shelley Taylor, to denote such female bonding, especially during stressful times.

Another study found that women who had no friends had an increased risk of death. The large-scale, very famous Nurses' Health Study conducted at the Harvard Medical School found that the more friends women had, the less likely they were to develop ailments as they aged, and the more likely they were to be leading joyful lives. In fact, the results were so significant that the researchers concluded that not having close friends or confidants was as detrimental to your health as smoking or carrying extra weight.

While the above is true, I believe the opposite problem also exists. Women can also be their own worst enemies. Women are by nature more judgemental and critical of each other, tend to feel envy or jealousy, and can be intertwined in highly toxic relationships. Such relationships can be enormously detrimental to health. If we are guilty of behaving badly for no reason towards other women, we need to ask ourselves why. It is often our own insecurities that lead to such behaviour.

Relationships With Parents and Siblings

Our relationship with our parents and siblings are the very first social interactions we ever experience in our lives and these will surely change over time. We need to renegotiate the terms of these relationships with age.

You will, in all probability, be your parents' caregiver in their later years, which takes on a whole new dynamic. As you do this, you may be able to carve out a wonderful, mature closeness. This is especially true if it has been worked on over the years. You may, for instance, realize just how similar you are to your mother or your sibling, something you may have denied all along. There will also surely be tensions as you lead different lives with different priorities and perspectives.

In a study published in the journal *Psychology and Ageing*, researchers at the University of Michigan Institute for Social Research (ISR) studied the relationships of adult children with their parents. They found that certain topics like basic personality differences and unsolicited parental advice were the most likely to cause tensions. Interestingly, daughters appeared to have greater conflicts with their parents than sons, perhaps because daughters were closer to the parents to begin with.

All families have their idiosyncrasies. Learning to live with them is a part of life. Much of it may not bother you when you are an adult, especially if you don't live under the same roof as your parents. Distance makes some compatibility disputes non-issues. If you do live with your parents for whatever reason, then it becomes important to reinvent the rules of your relationship. Siblings could become your greatest allies or turn into strangers, depending on personalities and early childhood experiences.

There is also the possibility that some relationships may not pan out so well. In some cases, the best that can be achieved may be a cordial association and in others a truly nurturing association.

Holding on to childhood hurt with parents and their parenting, or with siblings and their conduct, is not healthy or productive. They may not even remember it the way you do if you do confront them with it. In order to move on, it's important to forgive and make peace. This is crucial for one's own well-being. Various modalities like psychological counselling, cognitive behavioural therapy (CBT) and meditation can help with this.

RELATIONSHIPS WITH CHILDREN

As we grow older, so do our children. The evolution from the vulnerable infant to an independent human being is sometimes hard for a parent to accept and internalize. Some parents find it harder to let go of their children and the umbilical cord is far from severed in many mother/child relationships. I come across many women who come to me for their ante-natal checkups with their mothers (rather than their husbands) in tow. They allow their own parents to make important decisions for them, their child and their pregnancy, and have stronger bonds with their mothers, essentially going back to being a 'child' to their own parents. These days, however, children develop some distance from their parents as the generation gap widens, causing mutual understanding to diminish and growing individualism to increase. Exposure to the world at large has escalated and technological development has advanced to such a degree that even young children don't need you quite as much any more for counsel or comfort. They have the Internet! The best you can hope for is that you have laid a strong foundation for your child to make his/her own way through the vicissitudes of life.

Forging a mature relationship with your child as he/she grows older is an art and takes a lot of patience. While you may be tempted to hover and protect, there is only so much you can control in their lives. Ultimately, they would need to survive without your constant supervision. The rules on the subject of relationships with parents and siblings mentioned above apply in the reverse where you are the parent. Some tips to guide you in your relationship with your child as they grow older are:

- Reinvent the rules of your relationship
- Treat your child with the respect he/she deserves
- Don't use financial support to control your adult kid
- Don't force your dreams and ideals on your children, they have to come up with their own
- Don't feel offended if they turn down your support.

An area of concern may be when you become a grandparent and believe you have a copyright to the rules of parenting. Much argument ensues from differences of opinion with your children on 'how to bring up their child'. This kind of advice is usually unsolicited so it may be best left unsaid. It's far better to enjoy the privilege of being a grandparent and leave the parenting to your children.

Toxic Relationships

Some relationships become acrimonious and painful over the years. The energy within the relationship is quite literally so toxic that it is damaging to the health and well-being of those involved. You could either be the recipient in a toxic relationship or the cause of it. It takes great insight to be able to recognize this and then deal with it.

A toxic relationship is not only terribly draining of energy and resources, but is also extremely detrimental to both the physical and psychological health of everyone involved.

How Do You Identify a Toxic Relationship?

Toxic relationships may have some or all of the following characteristics:

- You can't be yourself when you are around the other person.
- You never feel heard or listened to.
- You or the other person behaves in a passive-aggressive manner (where you are not able to or will not say what is really going on and will instead resort to sulking and manipulative tactics). This is an indication of a lack of authenticity and comfort within the relationship.
- You fight/argue all the time and there never seems to be a resolution to these disagreements.
- You find it difficult to or are afraid to communicate effectively.
- You constantly feel misunderstood, disrespected, unappreciated or ill-treated.
- There is physical or emotional abuse in the relationship.
- You feel negative, anxious or tense when the other person is with you.
- It is always a one-way street with one or the other doing all the compromising or giving.
- You just don't feel happy in the relationship.
- You are constantly criticized or treated with contempt or disdain.
- You are not allowed to grow or change.

If such a relationship cannot be fixed, and you must stay in it, the only solution is to get outside help. A good therapist could be a stepping stone to resolving issues if they can be resolved. Leaving the relationship is, of course, the other option, but that is a decision that can only be yours.

A more subtle and perhaps unrecognized kind of relationship is the **ambivalent relationship**.

This is a relationship where you don't exactly know where you stand. You're not sure if you like the person or not, not sure if you should be together or not. You're not sure if your values work with the other's or not. It could be with a friend, spouse, parent, co-worker or sibling. There may be much second-guessing as to the intent and vacillation over your feelings for the other person, leaving you confused and frustrated. The most common question you ask yourself in this relationship is, 'Should I stay or should I leave?' This is compounded by friends who are free with their advice on the matter. The truth is, only you can decide. It's a difficult situation and is best handled with the help of a good therapist or some deep insight.

Relationships are complicated. Depending on how much we value them, we can either put in the effort to make them work or walk away. We also need to recognize if a relationship is actually good for us or is, in some way, deleterious to our well-being. Most importantly, we need to understand the great importance of having good relationships in our lives, even if they are just a few close ones.

twenty

Keeping the Brain Healthy

Keeping the brain healthy is as important as staying fit physically. What would be the point of possessing a perfectly healthy body if the mind is deteriorating? Our intellect and cognition are dependent on the neurons or nerve cells in our brain just like pretty much everything else in our bodies, including our breathing, digestion, cardiac function, emotions and so on. Keeping these neurons healthy is fundamental to maintaining cognition and brain health.

I know many people in their 70s and 80s and even 90s who are amazingly active, alert, enthusiastic, energetic, thrilled to be alive, feisty and inspiring, and I believe it is utterly possible to not just live a long life but to be truly 'alive' right through it.

My mother, for one, has now entered her eighth decade and she remains a trailblazer, if ever there was one. She continues to practice medicine, even if not as actively as she used to. She savours her time in her garden, which is always a glorious riot of colours. She is wedded to various commitments related to community causes. She also participates in various other social activities and is engaged with her friends and family, who take up much of her time. Her active, engaged life at such an advanced time keeps her young in spirit.

At the same time, I know people in their 30s and 40s who behave like they have given up on living a healthy, productive life. They don't make any effort to grow, learn or stimulate their brain – and it is not for a lack of time or resources. There are also those who are so busy trying to make ends meet that they truly don't have the time to think about things like cognitive decline.

Some of the symptoms of cognitive decline, or deteriorating brain health, are:

- Forgetfulness
- Difficulty in maintaining focus or getting distracted easily
- Decreased problem-solving capacity
- Decreased levels of understanding
- Feeling confused

Women will recognize these symptoms as being very similar to those of menopause. The good news is that the menopausal symptoms disappear once the body switches over completely to a post-menopausal state and adapts to a new, low estrogen milieu. However, when cognitive decline is a result of the brain's diminished functioning, these facilities continue to deteriorate even after menopause. That is a cause for concern and needs to be addressed and treated.

The 40s are a decade when many people begin to peak on the work front, as I've already mentioned. Being engaged with work keeps the mind differently absorbed, especially if you enjoy your work and find it challenging. It can sometimes prove stressful when the pressures at work come in conflict with family obligations, children growing up and a spouse who has (or does not have) to contend with a growing career. Many women decide not to have a career, and many men these days choose to retire early, of course. Some women may also be forced to opt out of a career, however flourishing, as they automatically become the 'caregivers' at home. These adjustments can be quite challenging and stressful. Nevertheless, not being a part of the workforce should not be reason for cognitive decline.

Some women also attempt to get back to their career in their 40s or even 50s, after their children have grown up or responsibilities at home have somewhat reduced. This is a challenge in itself. If you have been away from work for a while, it's not easy to get back to it. Yet, feeling independent and purposeful has a significant effect on one's well-being, and there are always ways and means of adjusting.

Keeping the brain active and engaged is important to prevent its deterioration. The brain is often compared to a muscle. Training and challenging it will aid its upkeep and development. Allow it to degenerate with disuse, and it will decline and atrophy. **For mental well-being, intellectual growth is just as important as creativity.**

We know from research that our brain continues to change physically, with the number of neurons and the connections or synaptic junctions between them changing right till the day we die. This is called **neuroplasticity**.

In the course of the normal aging process, shrinkage and death of neurons, and reduction in the number of synaptic spines (the area where one neuron connects with another) and functional synapses occurs. This decline is dependent on various factors:

- Decreasing hormones like estrogen, as experienced during menopause;
- Oxidative stress, which is the damage to cells in the body, including neuronal cells, due to inflammation caused by external factors like smoking, alcohol, drugs, etc.;
- Obesity;

- Lack of physical exercise;
- Poor nutrition;
- Diabetes and insulin resistance;
- Loneliness and lack of social connections;
- And, most importantly, lack of proper stimulus to the brain cells.

The good news is that this decline can be arrested, and the brain tissue and its functioning preserved. Simple lifestyle changes like switching to a better diet with higher-quality fats, more fruits and vegetables, and fewer processed foods, and adding exercise and stimulating the brain are immensely helpful.

Preservation of cognitive function is also largely dependent on how much we challenge and stimulate the brain by the things we allow it to assimilate or be exposed to. Actual physical changes in the brain, like the increase in synaptic junctions, more activity between cells and maintenance of brain tissue, have been found to occur when the brain is stimulated enough. Today, we have FMRIs, or Functional MRIs, which can register and record the changes in the brain following different stimuli, thoughts, meditation and so on. Through these FMRIs, researchers have found that there are tangible physical changes within the brain cells depending on what they are experiencing.

Preventing Cognitive Decline With Age

Several dietary and lifestyle changes can help reduce age-related cognitive decline. Some of these are:

- **Change your diet:** Switch from a diet high in simple sugars, carbs, hydrogenated fats and processed foods with additives to a diet that includes whole foods and simple ingredients and in which the food is (preferably) freshly made. A diet high in mono- and polyunsaturated omega-3 fats, fibre and polyphenols, fruits, vegetables, nuts, seeds and good fats is exactly what you need to keep your brain nourished and healthy.

- **Eat less:** Calorie restriction may improve learning and memory. **Intermittent fasting** with a focus on restricting total calories is one way of doing this. '*Hara hachi bu*' is a term commonly used in Okinawa, an island in Japan. The Okinawan people's habit of eating only till they are 80 per cent full is thought to be one of the secrets of their extraordinary health and longevity. In addition to having the highest percentage of living centenarians in the world, Okinawans appear to be less prone to heart disease, diabetes and obesity. Several short-term human trials have shown that **calorie restriction** can improve many health markers such as body weight, blood pressure, blood sugar, insulin levels, blood cholesterol and triglyceride levels, and inflammation. In a study on calorie restriction and memory led by the neurologist Agnes Floel and her colleagues at the University of Munster in Germany, it was found that those subjects who ate a restricted number of calories seemed to have better memory recall.

- **Engage in cognitive stimulation and training:** Activities such as playing chess and speaking more than one language can enhance **cognitive reserve** and provide protection against loss of brain function. Learning something new, like a new language, skill or musical instrument has been seen to be especially helpful in creating new pathways in the brain and keeping it young. The key is learning something the brain was never exposed to before, rather than trying to retrieve old information that it may have stored. People who speak more than one language have to constantly think of words and phrases and switch rapidly between languages, a process called 'code-switching'. This helps the brain multi-task better. We are fortunate that in our country most of us speak more than one language and fluently so.

- **Exercise:** Besides making you feel good, exercise is also great for the brain. It is known to increase levels of Brain-Derived Neurotrophic Factor or BDNF, which can lead to enhanced cognitive function. Bathed in serotonins and endorphins, the brain feels good and functions optimally. Clarity of thinking, decision-making and other cognitive functions have been seen to improve following exercise.

- **Moderate your consumption of caffeine and alcohol:** Restricting yourself to three to four cups of coffee (or about 400 mg of caffeine) a day appears to provide protection against cognitive decline. More than that, coffee is a stimulant that can lead to jitteriness or muscle tremors, lack of concentration, anxiety, migraine, insomnia, restlessness, an upset stomach and gastritis. As for alcohol, one to two drinks per day is plenty (one drink is equal to 12 ounces of beer, 5 ounces of wine or 1½ ounces of spirits). Drinking in moderation has been found to reduce the risk of stroke and heart disease. However, consuming more than this on a regular basis leads to risks that far outweigh the benefits. Your risk of intoxication, liver disease, cancer of the throat, esophagus and liver, clogging of the arteries and heart attack, as well as dementia (characterized by memory loss) increases.

- **Stay connected socially:** Nurturing meaningful relationships and staying connected is also found to benefit brain function. Social isolation is known to be connected to rapid decline of brain function, depression and loneliness. **Social disengagement**, defined as having very few or no social relationships, is a strong risk factor for cognitive decline, whereas social integration, enhanced by marital status, volunteer activity and frequency of contact with children, parents and neighbours, has a memory-preserving effect on elderly adults. In one study held over a six-year period, memory among those with the lowest level of social integration declined at twice the rate of subjects with higher levels of social integration.

In India, we still have the opportunity to remain socially connected quite easily, unlike in many Western countries. We can call up a friend, have an aunt drop in, have cousins stay over, friends visit and so on at frequent intervals to keep us connected. In many homes, the grandparents or an aunt live with the family. This is a wonderful way of exposing younger people to the older generation, and nurture among them a sense of responsibility and connection. All of this has countless benefits, and though it can also be intrusive or overwhelming at times, taken in the right spirit this kind of connectedness can be highly beneficial for the brain.

- **Break the monotony:** The monotony of daily life leads to a certain level of apathy and disengagement of the mind. Find ways to challenge yourself with interesting conversations, attending talks and workshops, watching inspirational videos or enrolling in an online course.
- **Change your routine:** In his book *Keep Your Brain Alive*, Lawrence Katz, professor of neurobiology at Duke University, lays out 83 neurobic exercises to improve brain function and prevent 'senior moments'. According to him, doing things like brushing your teeth with your non-dominant hand, taking a new route to work and breaking everyday routines creates new circuits in the

brain. This is like doing mental sit-ups to strengthen brain function.
- **Take up gardening:** A research study by Australia's Permaculture Research Institute found that people who garden regularly are 30 per cent less likely to develop dementia or Alzheimer's disease when compared to those who do not engage in this activity. Gardening is known to relax the mind. It may also have something to do with growing and caring for living things. If you haven't started gardening already, it may be a good idea to start now.
- **Spend time in nature:** In Japan, *shinrinyoku* or forest-bathing is a short, leisurely visit to a forest. A Japanese study of men and women who went on a three-day/two-night trip to a forest that included short walks each day, has showed that a monthly trip in the lap of nature can increase natural killer cells (which are a particular kind of immune system that act as a first line of defense against cancer cells and viral infections). Breathing in the antimicrobial compounds found in the essential oils of trees increases relaxation and helps in stress management, resulting in increased vitality and less anxiety, depression and anger. Time in the lap of nature may also decrease the risk of psychosocial stress-related diseases. Spending 15 to 30 minutes in the proximity of nature every day is highly beneficial in improving well-being.[8]

I can attest to this as I've lived most of my life in a hill station surrounded by natural beauty (though much of it has been destroyed lately due to increasing population and tourism). Going out for an early morning walk amidst nature is truly rejuvenating and cannot compare to training indoors.

Exposure to the sun is also known to elevate the mood

besides helping you make enough vitamin D for your body. In a study at South Korea's Chonnam National University, FMRI scans showed that when people saw images of nature, like mountains, forests and other landscapes, they experienced heightened activity in the anterior cingulate gyrus, the part of the brain linked to positive outlook and emotional stability, and the basal ganglia, an area that has been linked to the recollection of happy memories.

- **Adopt a pet:** Taking care of a pet or pets is a sure-fire way of elevating your mood, giving you purpose, reducing loneliness, keeping you entertained and having fun! Pets are extraordinarily caring and the unconditional love they provide is a wonderful boost for well-being.
- **Exercise in open air:** A 2011 study published in the medical journal *Medicine & Science in Sports & Exercise* found that people who walked on an outdoor track moved at a faster pace, perceived less exertion and experienced more positive emotions than those who walked on a treadmill indoors.
- **Manage stress better:** While a certain amount of stress is a stimulant, chronic stress can lead to cognitive decline over a period of time. Excessive stress leads to cognitive dysfunction as well. In a study involving 36 women between the ages of 25 and 53, those with the highest work-related stress levels displayed decreased attention and visuo-spatial memory. Managing stress better is a matter of learning the skill. It helps to have a wide repertoire of stress-alleviating strategies at hand to use when required. I find that some alone-time and a walk always help to alleviate stress. A review of eight research studies highlighted a strong association between post-traumatic

stress disorder (PTSD) and smaller brain size (that is, the total brain volume). The duration of PTSD influences the extent to which the brain deteriorates. Developing effective coping strategies as soon as possible may help to limit PTSD-induced decreases in brain volume.

- **Get enough sleep:** Six-to-eight hours of good quality sleep is essential for good brain health. The brain gets rejuvenated during sleep. One of the ways this happens is by the removal of certain toxic peptides called amyloid beta from the brain during sleep through the cerebrospinal fluid, a clear fluid that connects the brain and spinal cord. The system is called the glymphatic system and has been seen to play an important role in the prevention of accumulation of amyloid plaques in the brain, which are connected to Alzheimer's disease. Memory, alertness and cognition improve with good quality sleep and adequate sleep brings about less susceptibility to irritability and stress.
- **Manage high blood pressure:** Small, delicate capillaries that preserve the flow of blood throughout the brain are particularly susceptible to damage caused by elevated blood pressure. Chronic uncontrolled hypertension leads to the breakdown of these cerebral capillaries, a condition associated with the development of neurodegenerative diseases and cognitive impairment. Evidence suggests that blood pressure of 115/75 mmHg and below significantly reduces the risk of cardiovascular disease, and may, therefore, be an ideal target for those who wish to maintain optimal cognitive performance.
- **Manage blood sugars:** Due to the high metabolic demand of the brain, even small abnormalities in glucose metabolism can noticeably impact cognitive performance. Diabetes (with its typically abnormal blood sugars) has been linked

with lower levels of neuronal growth factors, decreased brain volume and higher incidence of all types of dementia. If you have been diagnosed with diabetes, ensure your sugars are maintained within a normal range with diet and exercise besides medication, if you are on any.

- **Maintain your optimum weight:** Adipose tissue or fat cells secrete molecules that directly influence multiple functions within the brain. There is a clearly established reciprocal relationship between adiposity (amount of body fat) and overall brain volume and cognitive function. In other words, as body weight increases, brain volume drops and cognitive function worsens.

  In a study utilizing MRI brain imaging technology to explore the link between obesity and brain volume, researchers have discovered that visceral abdominal obesity in particular was associated with deteriorating brain structure. This was true even in individuals without pre-existing cognitive deficits.

- **If you suffer from depression, get help:** An intimate relationship exists between depression and cognitive dysfunction. Many studies have closely examined this link and indicate a close connection between these two conditions, rather than a causal effect of one on the other. Interestingly, depression seems to worsen cognitive dysfunction and poor cognitive health. Research has also delineated a specific condition called 'depression-associated reversible dementia', which is cognitive impairment associated with depression that subsides upon treatment of depression. In a study of 57 elderly subjects with major depression, those who displayed depression-associated reversible dementia were found to be nearly five times more likely to develop true dementia over a three-year period.

- **Meditate:** This is one activity that has enormous benefits for the brain. There is scientific evidence to show that meditation results in an increase in activity in the brain area that controls metabolism, heart rate, working memory and attention. It has also been found to reduce stress and blood pressure and to even improve your creativity. A scientific study conducted in Massachusetts General Hospital in the United States found that people who have been meditating for a long time have an increased amount of grey matter in certain areas of the brain like the hippocampus (which is associated with memory, emotions and cognition), the posterior cingulate gyrus (associated with mind wandering and focus), the temporal parietal junction or TPJ (associated with perspective-taking, empathy and compassion) and the pons (where many regulatory neurotransmitters are produced). In other words, meditation seems to actually change the physical structure of the brain. Even 15 minutes of meditation a day is known to have positive effects. The good news is that these changes seem to become evident after just eight weeks of regular meditation. There are different kinds of meditation. A few include some rituals or the use of a mantra, while others focus only on the breathing and visualization. You can try them out and find the one most suited for your personality.
- **Read:** Reading is an important (and perhaps highly underused) way of improving brain health. Reading stimulates the imagination, improves memory, encourages analytical skills and expands vocabulary. Reading literary works has been found to improve a skill called 'theory of the mind', which is the ability to understand another person's thoughts and feelings better. Reading is also a

great de-stressor and helps you sleep better. One of my favourite things to do at the end of a day is to curl up with a book and fall asleep reading it.

Unfortunately, the habit of reading has been rapidly diminishing. Most people choose, instead, to watch a video or a movie or listen to a podcast. While these are also excellent ways to increase your ability to engage and stimulate the mind, reading requires a greater and different kind of effort, as we have to create thoughts about the content of the material read, activating our mental structures. Reading requires the production of an 'inner voice', which increases our attention span. This means that careful reading is certainly not an automatic or passive process, but rather it occurs when we actively process and understand what we are reading. It is a much more engaging activity as compared to watching a movie. Being a part of a book club where you read and discuss books is a wonderful way to keep reading and keeping your brain active and interested.

Just as the desire to maintain a fit and functional body into your later years demands the implementation of regular physical exercise, ensuring vibrant mental capabilities and cognitive acuity requires constantly pushing the brain in new directions to produce changes that strengthen existing synaptic connections and encourage new ones. This becomes clear when considering that individuals with mentally demanding careers appear to be at a significantly decreased risk of developing Alzheimer's or dementia later in life, compared to those whose work primarily centres around physical labour. Neuroplasticity is an intrinsic property of the brain and is maintained throughout life. Cognitive stimulation or challenging the mind enhances cognitive reserve and provides protection against loss of brain function regardless of age.

twenty-one

Ageing Meaningfully

I have the privilege of seeing many men and women go through many milestones in their lives, both personally and professionally. I meet women of all ages and different walks of life in my line of work. Many of them come back to me through the years with diverse problems, or when their daughters grow up and need my care. Working as an ob-gyn, I have delivered babies who then grow up and have their own babies. (This says something about the number of years I have been doing this, I suppose!) Recently, I had a 24-year-old young woman come up to me to say, 'Doctor, you delivered me!' Undoubtedly, I felt privileged, but I was also subtly reminded of my own age!

We all get older, there's no getting away from that. The question is, how do we plan to age?

Do we want to:

- End up with all kinds of physical infirmities?
- Suffer from several physical illnesses, especially those that are lifestyle-related?
- Be depressed, regretful or lonely?

OR

Do we want to:

- Feel more content now than when we were younger?
- Feel passionate about life and how we are living it?
- Feel more confident and self-assured?
- Feel satisfied and fulfilled with our lives?
- Be prepared for our future and excited about the years to come?

The first chapter of this book titled 'How are you doing so far?' would have given you an idea about how to measure where you are at this point in your life and how to go forward from here on.

As you grow older, the strife of your twenties and thirties is behind you. You are hopefully more financially secure, the children are more or less settled, you are moving on in your career and, most importantly, you are less concerned about others' opinions and more focused on your own well-being. I saw this reflected in a questionnaire I sent out to a hundred women over the age of 40 asking them questions about their life experiences. A majority (70 per cent) said they were more content and confident now than they had been in the past.

Crossing your 40th birthday is by no means an indication that you are 'old', certainly not in today's day and age when human life expectancy is about 80 years and being a centenarian is not unusual. It is, however, a milestone to consider as many physical and emotional changes materialize around this time. In the previous chapters, I've explained the physical and emotional changes that take place in our bodies and minds as we turn 40 and older, and the ways in which we need to adapt and prepare for the most fulfilling of our years.

Growing older is a natural and inevitable process, and there are ways in which we can ensure that we enter and live through these years comfortably and contentedly.

So, what does it mean to age well and how do we go about it? Here are a few pointers:

- **Create a 'wellness mindset':** While we certainly must work out regularly, following a fitness routine that suits us, and must eat appropriately, we need to also look within ourselves and work simultaneously on increasing self-awareness and understanding, explore our strengths, work on them, recognize our weaknesses and accept ourselves for who we are. It makes the journey of growing older that much more appealing and, at the same time, eliminates the pressures put on us by external factors. The mistake most of us make is to focus heavily on maintaining ourselves physically, but concentrating on the physical body is really only touching the tip of the iceberg. There is so much more to us than that. This is not to say that staying fit and healthy, especially as we age, is not important; of course it is. But what I'm saying is that it should not be our only priority. A **wellness mindset**, therefore, should include the various aspects of wellness we have discussed in chapter 1.
- **Identify what you can and cannot control:** What immediately comes to mind in this regard are the lines from the Serenity Prayer attributed to the American theologian Reinhold Niebuhr: 'God, grant me serenity to accept the things I cannot change, courage to change the things I can and the wisdom to know the difference.'

  It is 'the wisdom to know the difference' that is important. Without that wisdom, we remain forever conflicted, trying to figure out what is and what is not in our control.

  Frustration arises when we fight against or long for things that are clearly beyond our control. Being able to differentiate between the two gives way to acceptance and peace. This goes both for our physical bodies and our personal lives. We cannot, for instance, change our genes, which might have a propensity for diseases such as diabetes or cancer, but we can control how we live our lives right now to mitigate or at least minimize the effects and expression of those genes, not just for ourselves but also for our progeny. This is called **epigenetics**.

Epigenetics

Epigenetics is a fairly new and exciting field that explores just how our environment affects our genes. We don't only inherit our genes from our parents; these very genes can undergo alterations after they are inherited. This means that external factors like our lifestyle or what we are exposed to can alter our genes by turning them 'on' or 'off' but not really affecting the DNA sequencing. There may be external alteration of the gene structure. One example is what is called DNA methylation, where a methyl group is added to part of the DNA, thereby preventing certain genes from being expressed. What this means is:

- While you may have inherited the gene for a particular type of cancer, external factors like the food you eat, your exercise and so on can turn 'off' this gene, preventing its expression and thus the development of that cancer.
- What you eat and how much you exercise can influence your progeny through epigenetics. That is, kids can inherit the parents' eating habits through epigenetic mechanisms.
- A mother's diet during pregnancy will determine the child's metabolism later on in life, setting him/her up for the development for diabetes and obesity, for instance.

External substances that can affect the structure of gene are diet, exercise, tobacco smoke, heavy metals, diesel exhaust, pesticides, certain hormones, radioactivity, and even viruses and bacteria.

- **Change your perspective:** Growing older comes with experience to draw from and, hopefully, with that experience comes perspective – or that is how it should be. Developing the right perspective should be a priority for each of us as many things are a matter of how we view them. Some of our relationships with others, for instance, may be acrimonious or stressful. They may need to be viewed through a different lens, not just for the sake of the relationship itself, but also for our own well-being. I've already explained the importance of good-quality connections in the chapter on relationships. Our definition of success may need to be altered, our prioritization of time reworked. We should be able to edit our own lives to retain what is important and leave behind that which isn't.
- **Let go of expectations:** Letting go of expectations happens partly from experience and partly due to the shift in our own thought process. When we are younger, we may attribute our happiness to those around us and expect them to make us happy. As we grow older, this changes. We are able to see that other people cannot make us happy or provide us with satisfaction, and that expecting them to do so is foolish as that is an 'inside job'. Happiness and satisfaction need to be cultivated from within. There is no external agency that can do this for us. Expectation and entitlement can be detrimental. We may, for instance, work very hard and then expect certain results (for example, a promotion) from our efforts. Perhaps we even feel entitled to them – and not without good reason! Sometimes, however, there are many other things at play that are beyond our control. In this instance, the efforts put in and the qualifications of our colleagues who may

be at an advantage for that promotion, office politics, the priorities of the decision-makers and the financial position of the company may all play a role in who gets the promotion. When we don't get what we expect or feel entitled to, we become disappointed, which leads to frustration, dissatisfaction and heightened stress, and for some it may even affect their close relationships. Our efforts, therefore, should be focused on doing the best we can (as that is very much under our control) and not becoming embittered if things don't go our way. Working hard and leading a good life without thinking of the results is much easier in theory than in practise, of course. It takes a lot of discipline to remain calm about results and expectations. This is true of not just work but pretty much everything else in life, like relationships, family, finance and even one's health.

- **Depend less on the opinions of others:** Needing validation from others, including family, friends and society at large, is not unusual. Many people make pleasing others their priority. With age, hopefully, comes the ability to differentiate between the chatter around us and focus more on what we need for ourselves. Depending less on others' opinions of us (which are often tainted by their own beliefs), and doing the best we can to live up to our own standards is helpful in dealing with unnecessary pressure.
- **Pursue something you always wanted to do:** Many obligations in your younger days (like family and the need for career enhancement) may have kept you from pursuing your own passions. As we grow older, this becomes possible and, if we are motivated enough, it becomes a reality. Julia Child didn't learn to cook until

she was almost 40, and only launched her popular show when she was 50. Vera Wang, the world-famous figure-skater, switched careers to become a world-famous fashion designer after the age of 40.

- **Plan ahead:** Planning ahead should very much be a part of every decade of our lives. The plans may be for furthering our career, following a passion, retirement, where we will spend our lives and with whom. We don't have complete control over what the future holds. Nevertheless, being prepared with a plan, however short-term, makes for a more cohesive life.
- **Stay fit:** Physical well-being is crucial for a better life experience. It is possible to stay fit way into old age. It is even possible to start exercising at any age (see the chapter titled 'It's never too late'). Being physically fit not only keeps one independent, but also helps you do all the things you always wanted to, like travelling or starting a new career.

Fitness is one aspect of well-being that produces discernible and remarkable benefits, both physically and mentally, and that too in a remarkably short time. We all know the importance of staying fit by including cardio, strength-training and flexibility in our workout routines. The positive emotions that result from exercising may not be quite so evident unless you are aware of them. A simple walk in the park can considerably improve the mood. A better mood also enables us to do all the other things necessary for meaningful aging. Those who exercise regularly not only remain younger physically (with more stamina, strength and flexibility), but also healthier mentally and emotionally. Regular exercise has so many benefits that there is no valid reason not to include it in our day.

- **Explore spirituality:** Spirituality is about connecting with something much larger than ourselves. This is an exciting time to ask larger, big-picture questions. In fact, sometimes life brings us experiences at just this time that compel us to search for a deeper awareness of ourselves and our place in the universe. If you are religious, perhaps your religious beliefs answer those questions for you; if not, you may want to turn to philosophy, nature or literature for a deeper understanding and to figure out your relevance in this world. Spirituality may even take the form of contributing to society or the lives of others in some way. Whatever your take on it, this is something you may want to explore further.
- **Become more self-aware:** Our ability to grow and explore what we want, how we want to live out our advancing years, how we choose to contribute to society and others is related to our own level of self-awareness and self-disclosure. While it is possible, of course, to go through life with scant regard for who we truly are or what we really want from life, the experience of living is much more enjoyable when we understand our core and are honest with ourselves.

The question to ask is, who are we trying to please or live for – ourselves or other people? Once we are able to answer that question truthfully, we can move forward with honesty towards ourselves and have a keen awareness of our requirements for growth. This is not to say we disregard the people we care about. It may just be a paradigm shift in our priorities that makes it possible to pay closer attention to our needs and live a better life.

- **Embrace gratitude:** One of the foremost qualities one can develop to improve their quality of life via increasing life satisfaction is to inculcate the practice of gratitude.

  We tend to become blasé about the things and people in our lives. Overcome by a sense of entitlement, we take things for granted. This is more evident in affluent cultures where running water, electricity, medical care and solid infrastructure are so much a part of day-to-day existence that they are taken for granted. Psychologists call this concept 'hedonic adaptation'. The problem is that there is no guarantee that these conditions will last and, even if these material things do, people don't. It's important, therefore, to be **actively grateful** for what and whom we have in our lives. Research in the field of positive psychology has shown that gratitude is strongly and consistently associated with greater levels of life satisfaction and happiness. It may be something as simple as expressing gratitude to your partner or your employee, or writing a gratitude journal. This is a way of appreciating what we already have instead of being unhappy with what we don't.

- **Build resilience:** Have you noticed how some people manage to beat the odds and come out on the other side stronger and better? Others seem to flounder and sink, often taking others down with them. It's hard to predict who will survive a tragedy, who will be able to use their strength and keep their heads above water, and who will succumb to the pressures. All of us have various trials in our lives. How we deal with them establishes how well we live our lives.

> **Daily Exercises**
>
> - **Plan ahead:** Invest a little time in the mornings looking at the day ahead. Have a plan, anticipate hiccups, think through solutions and be prepared.
> - **Revisit your day:** Invest a little time every evening in contemplation of the day gone by. Ask yourself what went well, what didn't and what else could have been done. This is not to beat yourself up with self-criticism, but to reflect, learn necessary lessons or feel satisfied, and prepare better for the following days.
> - **Remember to show gratitude:** Write a gratitude journal. Every night list three things you are grateful for. It could be something as simple as the wonderful meal you shared with your family or partner, or the time you spent with a friend, or the sudden rain on a hot day. Don't stop with just writing about gratitude. Make sure you express it to the people concerned. So if someone spent time listening to you or helped you plan something, voice your appreciation. If your partner was considerate, don't forget to express your gratefulness.

In the 1960s, a Polish psychologist and psychiatrist, Kazimierz Browski, developed a theory called the Theory of Positive Disintegration. On the surface this seems like an oxymoron. How can disintegration be positive in any way? The very word 'disintegration' denotes a breakdown. What this means, however, is that, sometimes, following a tragedy or difficulty, our previous sense of self or identity may disintegrate so that we are at our greatest potential for **further growth**.

When we begin to truly question who we are, we are able to retrieve those bits of ourselves that we want to save, or disregard or downplay the ones we don't, and construct a new identity that is more authentic to our true selves. This can be seen as a form of **post-traumatic growth**. Some have this ability to grow while others may break down. For instance, having gone through a terribly trying time, you may emerge stronger despite the pain. What you would want to do is retain that strength you developed as a result of the pain to flourish from there on.

This is resilience – the ability to grow from difficulty. Being resilient entails not just bouncing back after a setback, but actually going beyond the point where we started to superior potential, strength and capability.

Of course, it is not imperative that we encounter tragedy for this to happen. We can, of our own accord, choose to keep the pieces of ourselves that we wish to and that are beneficial for growth and leave behind the undesirable things that don't serve us well. This could include attitudes, dogmas, and even life philosophies as a whole. This can be achieved through deep self-exploration and insight. Alternatively, this can happen through counselling, therapy or by opening up to and seeking help from those close to you who support and cherish you.

All of us face tragedy and struggle as we age. As our years advance, we are inevitably going to be exposed to the whole gamut of the human experience. Building resilience to help us through trying times is, therefore, important if we want to continue to live purposefully through our lives instead of falling apart at every crossroad.

Resilience is a skill that can be developed even if you don't inherently have it. So what do you need to do to cultivate and enhance resilience?

- **Make connections and sustain them:** Meaningful relationships with close family members and friends are important in times of difficulty. Meaningful social connections are the key to a healthier and happier life. It is easier to bounce back from a setback when you have a supportive squad around you. It may just be a couple of dear friends or a larger group you belong to. This team has to be nurtured consistently for it to be there when you need it.

- **Accept that change is inevitable:** Accepting that everything, including the good times, change is the best way to avoid frustration and negative thinking.
- **Learn optimism:** In his book *Learned Optimism*, Martin Seligman, the founder of the Center of Positive Psychology at the University of Pennsylvania, talks about the importance of having an optimistic outlook. We can actually learn not to view bad events as insurmountable problems that are all-pervasive. Optimism, Seligman says, is a skill that can be learnt.
- **Set realistic goals:** You are never too old to set goals and pursue them. The goals, however, need to be realistic. Setting unrealistic goals will only set you up for discontent. This applies to physical wellness as much as emotional well-being.
- **Be appreciative of what you have achieved so far:** In trying times, it's easy to wallow in self-pity and self-deprecation. Recognizing and giving yourself credit for just how much you have already achieved, how you may have changed as a result of trauma or stress, how well you have dealt with daily impediments or how you have used a negative experience to grow are all worthy of appreciation.
- **Develop practices and rituals for self-care:** Our exercise class, meditation, spiritual rituals, music, hobbies, holidays,

challenging work and connecting with friends are all self-sustaining practices to improve well-being. Preserving these practices through difficult times is especially important for our emotional well-being. Often, we tend to neglect our rituals during hardship or due to a perceived lack of time. This may be from sheer exhaustion or it may be despondency that prevents us from doing what we love or enjoy. But these are the very rituals that help us keep our heads above water.

USE MILESTONES TO FOSTER CHANGE AND BUILD RESILIENCE

If there is fear of growing older, you are less likely to embrace it fully. The more you consent to this inevitable process, the better prepared you will be for the various changes you will experience.

While it is an individual's prerogative to combat the signs and symptoms of ageing and prevent ill health or disease with the various procedures, treatments and lifestyle modifications (like exercise and diet) available, it is also important to remain open to and explore thoughts about your own mortality and the ageing process itself.

It is a privilege to be able to age. Not everyone shares that privilege. Ageing itself is riddled with stigma and often poorly understood. We are uncomfortable discussing it and anticipate incapacitation without really understanding how to circumvent or deal with it. Research has shown, however, that the 20s and 30s are actually fraught with uncertainty and angst (financial, relationship, career and so on) and with ageing comes a certain level of equanimity, comfort and peace within oneself and the world around us. Youth is often revered but it is not only young people who can 'grow, evolve and mature'. One can continue to evolve, grow and learn right up to the end of our lives. It all depends on one's mindset. So, ageing is actually something we should look forward to!

As we age, we should come to realize that time is a scarcity and value it passionately by seeking out positive experiences, fostering stronger relationships and building resilience. We should become very selective of how we choose to spend our time. Our social circle should tighten and deepen. We should try to minimize negativity and experience deeper, more meaningful lives. This will, of course, include pain and loss, but that's part of the human experience that nobody is exempt from.

Milestones are important for many reasons. They help you keep track of your life and tell a story of important events. Turning 40 is an important milestone for many. The 50s, 60s and 70s may be other significant milestones that bring on more change like your child's graduation, a wedding or a birth in the family. They will all be memorable in different ways. A narrative of our life story, stringing together all these memories defined by milestones is important for us to make sense of our lives.

Let us not stop with just celebrating the big birthdays. Let us instead look at each day and year as significant. Let these milestones be used to foster change by reflecting on your life and asking the question: *What do I want my life to look like from here on?* Once you formulate or begin to formulate an answer, work towards achieving that vision for yourself.

Let us not wait for disease or infirmity to befall us. Let us prevent them instead and manage them effectively and lead better quality lives.

Let us not stop at just dreaming. Let us wake up and chase those dreams instead, whatever the age, because we do, after all, want to be **healthier, happier, stronger!**

appendix

Medical Conditions That Develop after 40

There are several medical conditions that become more prevalent with age. Most of them can be prevented and even reversed altogether through lifestyle management. However, when they are present, they need to be addressed properly by including the necessary lifestyle changes along with medication when necessary. If approached properly, many of these diseases can be managed with making lifestyle changes alone, eliminating the need for medication altogether. All this, however, has to be carefully managed by a doctor adept at lifestyle medicine. Tapering off drugs, monitoring blood chemistry and keeping things on an even keel as the disease reverses is critical.

I have talked about the most common ones in this chapter, which may read like a textbook with lists of risk factors, symptoms and possible treatment methods. There isn't much I can do to make it a fun read, as these are dreary facts that must be told! Reading through, you will find that many of the risk factors are common to many diseases. Obesity, for instance, predisposes people to diabetes, hypertension, cancer and heart disease. Some other risk factors are conflicting, seeming to protect you from one disease while putting you at a higher risk for another. Having multiple pregnancies and deliveries, for instance, may put you at a higher risk for cervical cancer, but protect you from ovarian cancer – hardly a pleasant choice!

The human body is fascinatingly complicated and it is clear that we cannot control the countless things that go on within it. We can, however, control much of our own lifestyle and, to that end, we must do the best we can.

When one talks about diseases, the question arises: Do you believe you are inevitably at risk for a disease if you have a family history of it?

In a questionnaire I sent out to many women asking them about their understanding of their own health risk for a particular disease that they had a family history of, many believed they were the prisoners of their genes. This is not necessarily true. You don't have to be a victim of your genes. How you lead your life in terms of what you eat, how much you exercise, your stress levels, life satisfaction, emotional well-being and so on are important determinants of your risk for several diseases. In fact, these are *more important* than your genetic inclination. Although the gene for a disease may be present, whether it is 'expressed' or not – in other words, whether it leads to the development of the disease or not – can be controlled to a large extent by lifestyle.

A change in lifestyle habits can alter the genes themselves; this is called epigenetics.

Type-2 Diabetes

This is the kind of diabetes that used to be found only in adults. However, even teenagers and people in their 20s these days are being diagnosed with diabetes. **India has the dubious distinction of being called the diabetic capital of the world.**

We've been told that type-2 diabetes is a chronic, irreversible condition. However, it can be managed very effectively with the right diet and lifestyle. It is possible to get off diabetic medication completely with the appropriate change in lifestyle. If not, at least the medication can be kept to the absolute minimum.

Type-2 diabetes is clearly lifestyle-related. If you have a genetic history for this disease, you do have a higher propensity to develop it, but you can likely starve it off with the right exercise, diet and lifestyle plan started as early in your life as possible.

What Does It Mean to Have Diabetes?

What we eat gets converted into various sources of energy that are essential for the proper functioning of the body. Foods like carbohydrates, when consumed, get converted to glucose, which is either used for energy by the muscles, brain and so on, or stored in the liver for further use or, if in excess, converted to fat and stored in the fat cells.

Diabetes affects how your body processes glucose. Glucose is extremely important for your overall health. It serves as a source of energy for your brain, muscles and other tissue cells. Without the right amount of glucose, your body and brain will have trouble functioning properly. Too much of it, however, is detrimental.

Insulin is the hormone secreted from the pancreas that manages the glucose in the body by either storing it as fat in the fat cells or glycogen in the liver. In this way, it maintains the blood glucose levels on an even keel. In type-2 diabetes, the body secretes enough (or even excess) insulin but the cells of the body become 'resistant' to the insulin signalling. This means the insulin is unable to perform its function of maintaining the blood glucose level, as it cannot do its job of diverting the glucose from the blood to where it is required. The high level of sugar in the blood then begins to affect various organs like the kidneys, eyes, heart, nerves and blood vessels.

Essentially, this is a disease of **insulin resistance**.

Risk Factors of Type-2 Diabetes

You can get diabetes at any age, but it is most definitely more common post 40. This is especially true if you have other risk factors for diabetes, which are:

- You are over 40 years old.
- You are overweight with a large waistline.
- You eat a poor diet (high in processed sugars).
- You don't exercise enough.
- You smoke tobacco.
- You have high blood pressure.
- You have a family history of diabetes.
- You have a history of gestational diabetes (diabetes in pregnancy), which puts those women at a greater risk of developing diabetes after childbearing age.

Symptoms of Type-2 Diabetes

Some common symptoms of type-2 diabetes are:

- Fatigue
- Extreme thirst
- Increased urination
- Blurred vision
- Weight loss for no apparent reason
- Tingling in your hands or feet
- Tender gums
- Slow-healing cuts and sores

Sometimes you may be completely asymptomatic (without symptoms). It's important, therefore, to keep a tab on your blood sugar through annual check-ups.

Prevention and Management

The management of diabetes should be lifestyle-centric so while you may require medication to control your sugar levels, a proper diet and exercise routine is also imperative in the management of diabetes and goes a long way in preventing the progression of the disease to its morbid complications.

- **Cut your carbs:** Your intake of carbohydrates from the bread, cereal and grains group needs to be cut down to the absolute minimum. I recommend eliminating it altogether from your diet when possible. It's not hard to do this once you get used to eating in alternate ways. Substitute these carbs with a lot of leafy and water-based vegetables instead. Low glycemic fruits like citrus fruits, pears, berries and other tart fruits and apples are acceptable. So no more loading up on your rice, pasta, noodles, potatoes, corn or rotis; instead, focus on proteins like lentils, legumes, dairy, nuts, seeds, meat, eggs and fish.

    You don't necessarily need to eat many small meals for fear of becoming hypoglycemic (an attack of low blood sugar). Including good quality fat, fiber (from vegetables) and protein in your two or three main meals will ensure that your blood sugar doesn't drop erratically.
- **Train with weights:** Building muscle mass is essential in the management of diabetes. I've talked about it at great length in my book, *Gain to Lose*. Muscle is a metabolically active tissue that uses both fat and glucose as fuel. Building muscle, therefore, enables more of the glucose to be

utilized effectively. In one study published by researcher Eriksson in the *Journal of Sports Medicine*, participants who had type-2 diabetes completed a three-month progressive resistance programme that consisted of two days a week of circuit weight training. The researchers found that circuit weight training was responsible for improvements in blood glucose level control and that these improvements were related to training-induced muscle hypertrophy or muscle growth. This study also showed that an increase in muscle mass from strength training is important in the management of diabetes, as well as in decreasing the risk of developing complications associated with diabetes.

- **Include HIIT in your cardio workout:** High Intensity Interval Training (HIIT) was found to be more effective in the management of blood glucose. Long duration, lower intensity cardio sometimes causes blood sugars to drop precipitously. A shorter duration HIIT twice a week should, hence, be incorporated into your workout schedule. Research done in the University of Turku in Finland and published in April 2017 found that HIIT is very effective in the management of blood sugar levels and also has a rapid impact on the metabolism. It is a highly time-efficient way of staying fit, especially if you are diabetic.

If you are a diabetic, please consult your doctor when starting an exercise programme and always inform your trainer/instructor about your condition.

Regular monitoring of blood sugars is essential. Your doctor will also check your kidneys, eyes, neurological function, feet and heart to ensure that your diabetic condition does not affect these organs.

The objective of using exercise to manage diabetes is:

- To maintain your blood sugar on an even keel;
- To maintain cardiac health by performing the right kind and amount of cardio;
- Prevent further progression of the disease;
- Maintain muscle mass with weight training.

A diagnosis of diabetes may be devastating. Many people feel helpless and unhappy when they are told of their condition. Your diet and exercise, however, is pretty much **under your control**. This should give you a sense of control over the disease and make you very proactive in its management.

Heart Disease

We are familiar with men being susceptible to heart attacks. The truth is, women, after menopause, are as much at risk as men to a cardiac event. Prior to menopause, the hormone estrogen, which is known to protect the heart, helps mitigate the risk. Hormone Replacement Therapy, with estrogen and progesterone, used to be commonly prescribed for this very reason. A large study called the Women's Health Initiative or WHI, however, revealed that this was not necessarily the case, and now we prescribe short courses of HRT, only if required, for the relief of postmenopausal symptoms.

Many of us tend to neglect the symptoms of heart disease, though they may be diverse and unusual. The archetypal pain on the left side or the chest, radiating down the left arm may be replaced by:

- Chest pain on any side
- Discomfort
- Numbness

- Nausea
- Shortness of breath
- Unusual fatigue
- Light-headedness
- Sweating
- Palpitations

All of the above symptoms are often overlooked and mostly trivialized as a 'gastric' problem and treated with a generous dose of antacid. Meanwhile, many women with symptoms of heart disease fall between the cracks because of the lack of awareness and diminished degree of suspicion of the very real existence of heart disease in women.

Diabetics are at an even greater risk and a heart attack for a diabetic person may be 'silent' or painless. It is important, therefore, to be hyper-vigilant.

In men, any pain or discomfort in the torso area raises alarm bells. As mentioned earlier, we tend to think of men being more prone to heart attacks, but the risk factors and lifestyle management are the same for men and women.

Risk Factors of Heart Disease

The various risk factors associated with heart disease include:

- Obesity
- Smoking
- Diabetes
- Hypertension
- Family history
- Lack of exercise
- Chronic stress
- Depression

- Menopause
- Acute stress or Broken Heart Syndrome or Cardiomyopathy (TCM): The Japanese word '*takotsubo*' means 'octopus trap' (as, during an attack, the ventricle of the heart resembles the fishing pot used to trap octopus). This is believed to be triggered by **extreme emotional or physical stress**. Women are more likely than men to experience the sudden, intense chest pain, a reaction to the surge of stress hormones released by an emotionally stressful event. It could be the death of a loved one or even a divorce, break-up or physical separation, betrayal or romantic rejection. You could, therefore, quite literally 'die of a broken heart'. TCM is treatable, however, and the repercussions can be reversed with timely management.

Prevention and Management

- **Maintain a healthy weight:** Obesity, especially abdominal obesity is linked to heart disease. So while weight loss is often sought for cosmetic benefits, it is great for the heart too.
- **Exercise regularly:** This does not mean not excessively or in bouts as is common with the 'weekend warrior'. Exercise should include cardio (both moderate intensity cardio like walking for 45–60 minutes and a couple of sessions of HIIT in the week) and strength training.
- **Eat a heart-healthy diet:** You should have a diet that includes good quality fats from olive oil, avocado, walnuts and flaxseed. Eat more vegetables, fruit, nuts, legumes and seeds. Keep your grains whole and unprocessed and consume them in small quantities. As I mentioned earlier, the 'whole-food plant-based diet' is the only diet that has actually been shown to reverse heart disease as seen

in a study by Dr Dean Ornish. This would be a vegan diet that includes plenty of vegetables, fruits legumes and whole grains but excludes all animal products including diary and is very low in fat. Can everyone follow such a diet? That, I think, is for the individual to decide.

If you don't follow such a diet and are still interested in staying healthy, it's important to stay clear of processed food (and that includes processed meats) and trans fats (hydrogenated fats seen in packaged cookies, pastries and foods fried in reused oil). Eating simple meals, preferably made from scratch from whole foods, including plenty of fresh vegetables and legumes, and small quantities of whole grains is the way to go. If you eat meat, fish and poultry, then that is your source of protein. Do continue to include legumes and beans in your diet by substituting them for meat as often as you can. The incredible benefits of legumes and beans should not be underestimated.

A related question here is the role of saturated fat and cholesterol in heart disease. Currently, there seems to be some controversy over the connection between cholesterol and saturated fats in the development of heart disease. Suffice to say that, while it is completely safe to eat whole eggs and animal protein, it is certainly advisable not to go overboard with foods that are high in saturated fats on a regular basis. Your diet needs to be seen as a whole rather than as individual food items. So even if you eat eggs every day but also consume lots of vegetables, legumes and fruit as a part of your diet, include exercise, movement and some relaxation/meditation techniques in your day, you are doing perfectly fine.

- **Stop smoking:** Cigarette smoking is one of the highest risk factors for heart disease. Quit if you smoke.

- **Manage your co-existing diseases well:** Diabetes, hypertension and metabolic disease are risk factors for heart disease. If you suffer from any of them, ensure that they are well under control with medication (if required) and, more importantly, lifestyle.
- **Learn to deal appropriately with stress:** Stress management strategies like meditation, breathing and relaxation have been found to be useful strategies in improving heart health. Stress is closely related to heart disease and if you have a tendency to unravel easily when stressed, you need to find ways to de-stress.
- **Practice forgiveness, optimism and gratitude:** Researchers have found that heart attacks occurred more frequently among men who measured as **hostile** on a personality test rather than in men who clearly had the more traditional risk factors like smoking, hypertension and obesity. There is strong evidence for the physiological reactions brought on by stress, anger and the heart-damaging effects of hostility. Theodore M. Dembroski was credited with proposing that **'hostility' was the most likely to be the 'toxic' component** of the typical Type A personality. Numerous studies have found that hostility is a highly reliable predictor for heart disease. Women were studied in the Heart and Estrogen/ Progestin Replacement Study (HERS) and those with the highest hostility scores were found to be at twice the risk for a cardiac event. Combating hostility and anger, therefore, is an important aspect of heart health. Practising forgiveness, gratitude and optimism is one way of dealing with hostile feelings.
- **Treat depression:** Much evidence is focused on depression as a significant risk factor for heart disease. It is also responsible for poor recovery following major cardiac

events. While you may think that depression is only about the mind and emotions, it affects the workings of the heart, too, and can significantly affect convalescence following any kind of illness.

Hypertension

Hypertension or high blood pressure is a deadly disease that is often asymptomatic (without any symptoms) and, therefore, overlooked and untreated. It appears that, just like cardiac disease, the risk for hypertension is higher over the age of 40. The onset of hypertension can cause a variety of symptoms that are often attributed to menopause in women. **Some of the symptoms of hypertension like chest pain, sleep disturbances, headaches, palpitations, hot flushes, anxiety, depression, tiredness could be mistaken for menopausal symptoms and ignored** by women of that age and this becomes additionally problematic. Both men and women with a family history of hypertension and women with a history of hypertension during pregnancy are at increased risk to develop it during this time. Systolic blood pressure (the higher value of your blood pressure) rises more steeply in ageing women compared with men, and this may be related to the hormonal changes per se during menopause. It appears as if menopause itself could be a risk factor for hypertension!

Risk Factors of Hypertension

The various risk factors associated with hypertension include:

- Smoking
- Early menopause in women
- Lack of exercise and a sedentary lifestyle
- Obesity, especially abdominal fat
- Diabetes

- Family history of hypertension
- Hypertension during pregnancy
- Kidney disease

Prevention and Management

- The official diet to manage hypertension is the DASH diet or the Dietary Approaches to Prevent Hypertension diet. The focus of this diet is on fruits, vegetables, low-fat dairy, poultry, fish and eggs. It recommends lowering red meat and sugar, including sweetened drinks.
- Include potassium-rich foods like bananas, fruits and vegetables in your diet. A calcium- and magnesium-rich diet including dairy, vegetables, legumes, peas and beans, along with leafy vegetables appears to be beneficial in preventing hypertension.
- Garlic, which is very commonly used in Indian cuisine, also seems to protect against hypertension.
- Maintain a healthy weight.
- Exercise regularly.
- Quit smoking if you do smoke.
- Manage your stress by including yoga, meditation and relaxation techniques in your routine. These can help calm the sympathetic nervous system, which is responsible for the 'fight-or-flight' response activated during stress. **In women of menopausal age, the sympathetic nervous system seems to be particularly overactive.** Consciously calming it with yoga, breathing and meditation appears to help immensely.
- If you have a family history of hypertension or if you had high blood pressure during your pregnancy, consult your physician to have a lower salt diet and monitor blood pressure regularly.

- Limit alcohol to not more than one drink a day.

Hypertension can affect several other organ systems in the body like your heart, kidneys, eyes and brain. It is a silent and malicious killer, so it is important to have a physician check your blood pressure regularly.

Thyroid Disease

The thyroid is a small butterfly-shaped gland situated in the front of your neck. It produces hormones that are important for your reproduction, metabolism and the functioning of the muscles, heart, brain and kidneys.

While you could have both hyper and hypothyroidism, (hyperactive or hypoactive gland) as you age, hypothyroidism is more prevalent.

There are many factors that can trigger thyroid imbalances in a person, **including stress, nutrition and hormonal changes during andropause or menopause.** Women, in general, are more prone to thyroid disorders than men. One of the reasons hypothyroidism is more common in older women is that **autoimmunity (a condition in which your own cells attack the thyroid gland)** develops with age. The premenopausal levels of estrogen appear to help our immune system 'tolerate' our own cells, and a decline in estrogen with menopause makes this function less effective. An underactive thyroid gland will then present with hypothyroidism or, in other words, the thyroid glad will produce lower levels of the hormones it is supposed to produce and lead to a range of symptoms.

The symptoms of a low-acting thyroid gland are:

- Unexplained weight gain
- Intolerance to cold

- Constipation
- Hair loss or dry, coarse hair
- Fatigue
- Memory lapses
- Dry, coarse skin
- Depression
- Difficulty concentrating

Borderline thyroid disorders are easily managed and not major causes of concern. Thyroid imbalances, if severe, could produce various other problems in the body such as cardiovascular disease, atherosclerosis, heart attack, peripheral vascular disease affecting the small blood vessels of the extremities, increased cholesterol, cognitive decline and bone loss. It's important, therefore, to keep the thyroid hormones on an even keel. Testing your thyroid function post 40 is necessary.

Risk Factors of Thyroid Disease

- **Age:** Those over 40 are at a greater risk of developing thyroid problems.
- **Thyroiditis:** Hashimotos thyroiditis is an autoimmune disorder where the body attacks the thyroid tissue. The gland tissue eventually dies and stops producing hormones.
- **Cancer of the gland:** Although rare, cancer of the thyroid gland can produce an imbalance of thyroid hormones.
- **Thyroid goiter:** Nodules in the thyroid may also cause malfunctioning of the gland. If you notice a swelling at the front of your neck, it is important to have it investigated.
- **Removal of the thyroid gland:** The thyroid may have been surgically removed or chemically destroyed.

- **Lithium:** This drug, which is given in some psychiatric conditions, has also been implicated as a cause of hypothyroidism.

Prevention and Management

- **Stress:** Excessive cortisol from another gland in the body, the adrenal gland, can blunt the response of the hormones of the thyroid gland – i.e., the Thyroid Stimulating Hormone or TSH – and result in hypothyroidism. Too much or too little cortisol can also impair the conversion of the thyroid hormones T4 to T3. Chronic stress over time can fatigue our adrenals, making it difficult for them to keep producing cortisol on demand. Stress management is important for thyroid health as well, besides its other numerous health benefits.
- **Nutrition:** Nutrients like vitamin A, vitamin D, zinc, iodine and selenium, as well as omega-3 are important for the proper functioning of the thyroid gland. The idea is to eat a well-balanced diet with plenty of vegetables, some fruit, some whole grains and ensure there is protein from legumes, nuts, seeds, fish and poultry. More importantly, avoid processed food. Your gut health (which has been explained in chapters 7 and 8) is key to keeping not only your weight in check, but also your hormones in balance.

This tiny gland in the neck is all important in the proper functioning of our body. It can malfunction, but the good news is that treatment is often simply thyroid pills. Taken every day, they can normalize the levels of the thyroid hormones so that the body functions optimally.

I sometimes have people claim that the reason for their being overweight is the result of a thyroid problem. Point is, if you have an underacting gland and are being treated for it, then your hormone levels should be normal and you can't blame your thyroid anymore for your weight. You need to stay on your medication and start exercising!

Cancer

Cancer is probably one of the most feared words you can hear from your doctor. The very mention of it is enough to send you into panic. Management of cancer, however, has evolved rather rapidly in the past two decades. The disease, which used to be seen as a death sentence for the person diagnosed, has now become more manageable, thanks to the passionate efforts of researchers and oncologists all over the world. All cancers become more prevalent with age. I will discuss the most common ones that are gender specific here – cancer of the breast, uterus and ovaries for women and prostate cancer for men.

Breast Cancer

Breast cancer is, of course, more common in women, but not unheard of in men.

Most breast lumps are not cancerous, but if you feel a lump during a breast self-examination (which you should learn to perform from your ob-gyn), do consult your doctor. You should also beware of other significant symptoms like:

- Discharge from the nipples;
- Skin dimpling or puckering;
- Nipples turned inward (retraction);
- Redness, scaling hardness on the skin of your breasts;
- Change in size, shape or appearance of the breast.

Guidelines in the United Kingdom say that women aged between 40 and 49 years who are at an increased risk of developing breast cancer because the disease runs in their family should be offered annual mammographies. Those at highest risk of developing breast cancer should also get the chance to have a genetic test for the disease and the option of preventive surgery. The American Cancer Society advises starting mammograms at age 45 and continuing annual mammograms till age 54.

The need for mammography, however, needs to be individualized. You should speak to your gynaecologist to decide what is best for you.

Risk factors of breast cancer

The various risk factors associated with breast cancer include:

- **Genetics:** 5 to 10 per cent of breast cancers are linked to genetics and gene mutations that are passed through generations in a family.

    The most common genes are breast cancer gene 1 (BRCA1) and breast cancer gene 2 (BRCA2), both of which significantly increase the risk of both breast and ovarian cancer. If you have a strong family history of breast cancer or other cancers, your doctor may recommend a blood test to help identify specific mutations in BRCA or other genes that are being passed down in your family. Paradoxically, the majority of people diagnosed with breast cancer have no family history of the disease. It still holds as a risk factor, however.
- **Being female:** This is definitely a risk factor. Although men also do develop breast cancer, it is much more prevalent in women.
- **Age:** Your risk of getting breast cancer increases with age.

- **A past history of breast cancer:** If you've had breast cancer in one breast, then you have an increased risk of developing cancer in the other breast.
- **Obesity:** Being obese increases your risk of breast cancer.
- **Starting your period at a younger age:** Beginning your period before age 12 increases your risk of breast cancer.
- **Menopause at an older age:** If you attain menopause at an older age, the likelihood of developing breast cancer increases.
- **Age at your first childbirth:** Older women who give birth to their first child after age 30 may have an increased risk of breast cancer.
- **Having never been pregnant:** Women who have never been pregnant have a greater risk of breast cancer than women who have had one or more pregnancies.
- **Post-menopausal hormone therapy:** Women who take hormone replacement therapy medications that combine both estrogen and progesterone for prolonged periods of time have an increased risk of breast cancer.
- **Drinking alcohol:** Drinking alcohol increases the risk of breast cancer. The allowed limit of one drink a day for women is set for various reasons, including the increased risk of breast cancer with regular higher consumption.
- **Radiation exposure:** If you received radiation treatment to your chest as a child or young adult, your risk of breast cancer is increased.

Often, a lump is detected by the woman during a breast self-examination. Consult your gynaecologist at about the age of 40 to understand the preventive and screening measures you need to take. Breast cancer is treatable provided it is diagnosed early enough.

Cancer of the Uterus

The uterus is shaped like an upside-down pear; the body of the uterus can develop a cancer separate from the mouth of the uterus, which is called the cervix. The inner layer of the uterine body is the endometrium and the outer layer is muscle or the myometrium. The body of the uterus can develop a cancerous growth often from the inner lining of the organ. Both these cancer cells (from the body of the uterus and the cervix) can be picked up on a Pap smear. **The Pap smear is a screening test of a scrape of the mouth and inner lining of the mouth of the uterus (the cervix).** This screening procedure is minimally invasive, relatively painless and is done as an outpatient procedure. It is recommended for all women who are sexually active.

Risk factors of cancer of the uterus or endometrium

The various risk factors associated with cancer of the uterus include:

- Obesity;
- Diabetes;
- Hypertension;
- Certain drugs like Tamoxifen, given for the management of breast cancer, can also lead to cancer of the uterine body;
- History of polycystic ovaries;
- More years of menstruation, as happens when you start your periods young and have a late menopause;
- Never having been pregnant, and therefore being exposed to cyclical hormonal exposure throughout your reproductive life. Being pregnant prevents this exposure of the endometrium to the direct effects of hormones, especially estrogen for the period of the pregnancy.

Any condition that causes the uterus to be exposed to continuous effects of the hormone estrogen, without a counterbalance with the hormone progesterone, can increase your risk of endometrial cancer. Examples include irregular ovulation patterns, such as those that can occur in women with polycystic ovary syndrome, obesity and diabetes. Taking hormones that contain estrogen but not progesterone after menopause increases the risk of endometrial cancer.

Symptoms of cancer of the uterus

Symptoms of this cancer include:

- Unusual vaginal bleeding, especially around the time of menopause. If, following the cessation of your menstrual bleeding, as happens in menopause, you start to have vaginal bleeds, however erratic or minimal, it is essential you go in to see your gynaecologist and be investigated further. Bleeding after menopause is not normal;
- Abnormal bloody discharge;
- Pain or bleeding during urination;
- Back or pelvic pain;
- Painful sexual intercourse.

Sometimes there may be absolutely no symptoms and the cancer cells may be seen only after a routine Pap smear. Treatment could be in the form of surgery, chemotherapy, radiation or hormone therapy, depending on the stage of the cancer and the response of the cancer cells. If diagnosed early, endometrium cancer is manageable and completely treatable as it is slow-growing. It is important to pay attention to early symptoms and to not ignore post-menopausal bleeding or disregard Pap smears.

Cancer of the Cervix

A virus called human papillomavirus or HPV causes most cancers of the cervix. You can get HPV by sexual contact with an infected person. There are many different types of HPV, and not all HPV viruses cause cervical cancer. Some of them cause genital warts while others may not cause any symptoms at all. An HPV infection will cause the cells of the cervix to change very slowly to a cancerous stage. If these cells are detected early enough, as they can be with the Pap smear, further growth of the abnormal cells can be thwarted and effectively treated. It is important, therefore, for women to have regular Pap smears.

Some of my recommendations for Pap smears are:

- Any woman over the age of 21 who is sexually active needs regular Pap smears.
- The recommended amount is every three years till the age of 65.
- You can stop having Pap smears if you have three negative Pap smear results in a row.

Risk factors of cervical cancer

The various risk factors associated with cancer of the cervix include:

- Infection with high-risk HPV (most cervical cancers are caused by HPV 16 and 18).
- Women who smoke are about twice as likely as non-smokers to get cervical cancer. Researchers believe that the byproducts of tobacco damage the DNA of cervix cells and may contribute to the development of cervical cancer. Smoking also makes the immune system less effective in fighting HPV infections.

- Long-term use of oral contraceptive pills.
- Multiple pregnancies and deliveries.
- A weakened immune system.
- A family history of cervical cancer.

Symptoms of cervical cancer

Symptoms of this cancer include:

- Abnormal bleeding that may be heavy, irregular or malodourous.
- Pain in the lower abdomen.
- Abnormal vaginal discharge between periods.
- Pain or bleeding during intercourse.
- Cancer of the cervix is completely treatable if detected early enough. In the later stages of the disease, radiation and chemotherapy are available.

Cancer of the Ovaries

Cancer of the ovaries comes in a variety of forms. Some are more aggressive (faster growing) than others. Many ovarian cancers are unfortunately detected too late because there are such few reliable symptoms in the early stages. Unlike cancer of the uterus and cervix, ovarian cancer cannot be detected with a simple screening test like a Pap smear, though a routine ultrasound may sometimes pick up the disease.

Surgery and chemotherapy are the forms of treatment available and are successful only if the cancer is diagnosed early.

Risk factors of ovarian cancer

The various risk factors associated with ovarian cancer include:

- A family history of ovarian cancer must make you more vigilant for the disease.
- It is more likely to occur in those above 50 years of age.
- If you start your period at an early age and attain menopause very late, your chances of contracting ovarian cancer increase.
- Smoking.
- Long-term use of hormone replacement therapy.
- Never having been pregnant.
- Polycystic ovarian syndrome.

Symptoms of ovarian cancer

In the early stages, ovarian cancer may not produce significant symptoms. As the cancer grows, some or all of the following **symptoms** may arise:

- Abdominal bloating or swelling.
- Early satiety or feeling full even after eating small quantities of food.
- Unexplained weight loss.
- Discomfort or pain in the pelvis area.
- Changes in bowel habits, such as constipation.
- A frequent desire to urinate.

Ovarian cancer is treated with surgery and chemotherapy. Once again, the success of treatment is dependent on the stage of the disease and the type of cancer. Some are more aggressive than others. If detected very early, surgery with chemotherapy and close follow-up are often successful in managing the disease. Unfortunately, the symptoms are so vague that they are often overlooked or missed, leading to a late diagnosis and poorer patient outcome.

Prostate Cancer

The prostate gland is a small gland, about the size of a walnut, that lies just below the bladder in front of the rectum in men. It surrounds the urethra or the urinary outlet. The gland is a part of the male reproductive system producing the fluid present in semen. Prostate cancer is the most common type of cancer in older men. The good news, however, is that most prostate cancers are treatable as they are very slow-growing. Non-cancerous enlargement of the gland may also occur with age and this may cause similar symptoms to cancer. An enlarged prostate, therefore, needs to be investigated further.

Risk factors of prostrate cancer

The various risk factors associated with prostate cancer include:

- **Age:** Prostate cancer is rare in men younger than 40. The risk increases with age.
- **Family history:** Prostate cancer may have a genetic basis as it seems to run in families. Having a father or brother with prostate cancer doubles the risk of the disease as per the American Cancer Society.
- **Diet:** The exact role of diet in prostate cancer is not established but it appears that men who eat a diet high in red meat or high fat dairy seem to be at a higher risk. Eating less fruits and vegetables and a lower fiber diet may also be a contributing factor.

Symptoms of prostrate cancer

Symptoms of this cancer include:

- **Urination:** The main symptoms of an abnormal prostate gland (which may be just a benign enlargement or cancer)

are related to urination. So frequency of urination, blood in the urine, difficulty in urination or incontinence may present as signs of an enlarged prostate gland.
- **Constipation:** An enlarged prostate may present with constipation. Once a poor diet as the cause for constipation has been ruled out, the prostate needs to be looked at to identify if it is enlarged.
- **Low back or pelvic pain:** A deep aching kind of pain that persists needs to be investigated further. The pain may radiate down the thighs or hips.

Prevention and management

- Observational studies (studies that just made observations in cohorts of people as opposed to intervening in their lifestyle) found that men who ate more vegetables, fruits and soy were less likely to get prostate cancer. It is unclear if the protective effect is the soy or the increased vegetable intake. So eating three to four cups of vegetables appears to protect against cancer in general, including prostate cancer. Include cruciferous vegetables (cauliflower, broccoli, cabbage), tomatoes, soy, beans and legumes in your diet.
- Being physically active through the day, including exercise into your routine and thereby staying at a healthy weight is a general recommendation for preventing not just cancer but all kinds of chronic diseases.
- Early detection of cancer plays a critical role in the management and prognosis of the disease. Staying vigilant to recognize the early symptoms is, therefore, crucial.
- Early diagnosis is possible by regular physician visits, a physical exam or an ultrasound when required.

- A cancer marker called Prostate Specific Antigen or PSA is used to detect prostate cancer. It is also used for follow up after treatment.
- Once diagnosed, the management of the cancer depends on various factors such as the stage and type of the tumour, age of the person and so on. Since most tumours are very slow-growing, one option in management is what is called 'active surveillance', which involves close follow-up and regular check-ins with your doctor without resorting to surgery, radiation or chemotherapy.
- Other options for treatment include radiation, chemotherapy, surgery, cryotherapy and so on, which need to be individualized after a discussion with your doctor.

With progression in treatment for prostate cancer, men live long, healthy lives when the problem is detected early and managed appropriately. Continuing with the right lifestyle changes following treatment such as exercise and including more vegetables in your diet becomes even more important. Regular follow-ups with your doctor are, of course, critical.

Osteoporosis

The risk of osteoporosis, which is the thinning and weakening of bones leading to fractures, increases with age. Normal bone is composed of protein, collagen and calcium, all of which give bones their strength. Bones that are affected by osteoporosis can fracture even with relatively minor injuries that normally would not cause a bone to break.

Osteoporosis is more common in women. The hormone estrogen is also known to protect bones, hence the lowering of this hormone, starting in the 40s, predisposes women to osteoporosis.

Risk Factors of Osteoporosis

Risk factors of osteoporosis include:

- Age over 50.
- Smoking.
- Eating a nutritionally poor diet, devoid of calcium, vitamin D, magnesium and potassium.
- Excessive alcohol consumption.
- Excessive caffeine consumption.
- A family history of fracture or osteoporosis.
- Extremely low body weight. People who are underweight are at a higher risk of developing the disease.
- History of rheumatoid arthritis.
- Lack of exercise and a sedentary lifestyle. This is especially true if weight-bearing exercises like strength training, walking or running have not been a part of your life.
- Deficiency of vitamin D as a result of poor exposure to sunlight or if your body is unable to absorb the hormone (yes, vitamin D is really a hormone, not a vitamin) due to an intestinal problem like malabsorption syndrome.
- Early menopause in women.

Symptoms of Osteoporosis

- Osteoporosis often does not cause symptoms until the bone breaks. A fracture can occur with relatively little injury in which case pain can result. Such a fracture is called a **minimal trauma or stress fracture**. It may happen with something as trivial as walking or climbing down the stairs.
- With age and progression of the disease the spine may become more and more collapsed leading to a severely bent posture.

- Chronic back pain may be the only symptom and an X-ray might reveal you have osteoporosis.

Your health professional may advise a dual-energy X-ray absorptiometry or DEXA scan to determine if you have osteoporosis. This determines the degree of severity of osteoporosis in your bones.

Prevention and Management

The objective of the treatment of osteoporosis is the prevention of bone fractures from falls and preventing further reduction of bone loss and increasing bone density and strength. Although early detection and timely treatment of osteoporosis can substantially decrease the risk of future fractures, none of the available treatments for osteoporosis are complete cures. In other words, it is difficult to completely rebuild bone that has been weakened by osteoporosis. Therefore, **prevention of osteoporosis is more important than treatment**.

- **Training with weights** to build muscle mass and strength certainly helps in maintaining bones and strengthening the muscles, tendons and ligaments around joints. When this training is started early in life, the benefits are quite spectacular. However, it is never too late to start. Regular training to improve balance and core strength also goes a long way in preventing falls and injury.
- **Quit smoking** if you do smoke.
- Moderate your consumption of **alcohol**.
- Restrict your **coffee** intake to no more than two to three a day.

- Take the necessary **calcium supplements.** Calcium tablets are usually prescribed for people over 40. Vitamin D may be added if you are deficient.
- Eat a **calcium-rich diet.**

> **Foods to Prevent Osteoporosis**
> - Dark, leafy vegetables like spinach, broccoli, bok choy, Chinese cabbage, turnip greens, soybeans and kale
> - Fish like tuna, salmon, sardines and mackerel
> - Sweet potato
> - Grapefruit
> - Dairy products
> - Figs
> - Nuts like almonds
> - Prunes
> - Tofu

There are medications that stop bone loss and increase bone strength. Your physician may suggest these if you have been diagnosed with osteoporosis.

DEPRESSION

Women are twice as likely as men to be diagnosed with depression. Clinical depression is more common as women enter menopause and, again, hormonal fluctuations seem to be the cause, according to some studies. Depression can also occur in the perimenopausal period. Having said that, men are not immune to the disease. This is especially true as they age and the levels of their testosterone begin to fall.

There may be several reasons for this besides the lowering of hormones. Life circumstances during this stage in life, like children leaving home leading to '**empty nest syndrome**' and feeling lost with a lot of free time on hand can lead to depression. A change in career, retirement, aging parents or loss of loved ones, too, could all come together at around this time in your life, leaving you feeling stressed or depressed.

It is important to identify the condition correctly, as the term is often used freely and loosely. For example, you might say, 'I'm feeling really down or depressed,' when what you are actually experiencing is a passing emotion about a specific issue. This should be differentiated from clinical depression, which is the feeling of extreme sadness lasting for more than two weeks, often with no specific cause that can be identified, and which interferes with everyday life. Depression can be accompanied by suicidal thoughts.

Some of the symptoms include:

- Sadness or a low mood for prolonged periods of time;
- Loss of interest in things you used to enjoy;
- Loss of appetite or eating too much;
- Loss of sleep or sleeping too much;
- Thoughts of suicide;
- Difficulty concentrating;
- Fatigue;
- Feeling of guilt and worthlessness;
- Restlessness or feeling slow and sluggish.

Coping with Depression

Since this is a problem of the mind, it is often overlooked or brushed aside as being 'only in the mind'. Well, for starters, it *is* in the mind, both literally and figuratively. The point is that we should not neglect symptoms just because they are not obvious physical symptoms (such as abnormal blood sugars, or a high blood pressure or chest pain). Depression can be devastating and painful for the sufferer, made worse because it goes unacknowledged or untreated.

The way different people cope with depression may differ. Men and women deal with it differently, for instance. Some may be sad, crying with morbid thoughts and obviously depressed. Others may react with hostility, irritability, anger, isolation, alcohol or drug abuse or even risky, reckless behaviour. It's important, therefore, to be aware of unusual or changing behavioral patterns or tendencies in order to recognize what may be symptoms of a disease like depression.

Prevention and Management

Can you prevent depression? Yes, you can, to some extent, by the lifestyle choices you make.

- **Have a strong network of family and friends:** Nurture relationships through your life so there are people you feel close to and connected with. This is a deliberate choice. It is also an effort. Relationships take time and effort, and often when we are younger we are so busy working or tending to our own lives and families that we disregard other relationships. This may cause social isolation in our later years.
- **Exercise regularly:** Internalizing the habit of regular exercise can hold you in good stead in your later years. Exercise is a tonic for the brain, releasing endorphins, creating positive emotions and preventing depression.
- **Keep alcohol to the minimum:** Alcohol is a depressant. Over time, it can lead to severe depression, especially in those so prone.

- **Eat whole foods:** Complex carbs like fruits and vegetables and small quantities of whole grains increase serotonin activity in the brain. Foods like tuna, turkey and chicken have tryptophan, which clears your mind and boosts energy. A Spanish study, using data from 4,211 men and 5,459 women, found that rates of depression rose when levels of folic acid and B12 were inadequate. Legumes, nuts, many fruits and dark green vegetables have folate. Vitamin B12 can be found in all lean and low-fat animal products, such as fish and low-fat dairy products.
- **Get adequate vitamin D:** Vitamin D deficiency has also been linked to depression. If you are diagnosed to be deficient, a supplement will help. Getting out in the sun is helpful in producing vitamin D in your own body. Lack of sun and direct exposure can be a source of depression. This may be the cause for the disease more commonly diagnosed in the winter months when there is poor sunlight.
- **Ensure sufficient omega-3 fatty acids:** Scientists have found that societies that don't have enough omega-3s in their diet may have higher rates of major depressive disorder. Other studies show that people who don't eat fish, a rich source of these fatty acids, are more likely to have depression. Good sources of omega-3s are fatty fish, flax seeds, nuts (especially walnuts) and dark green leafy vegetables.
- **Maintain your weight within the normal range:** People who are overweight or obese may be more likely to become depressed. According to several studies, people who are depressed are more likely to become obese. Depression and obesity appear to be reciprocally related. Researchers believe that may be the result of changes in your immune system and hormones associated with depression.

- **Find meaning and purpose:** Finding your passion and doing things that are meaningful are important. Your work may be a part of it. Other activities like charities, voluntary activities, learning something new, helping other people, can all be a part of your repertoire of being more productive with your time.
- **Learn to manage stress:** Continuous stress can be a source of depression. This may be in the form of work stress, the stress of boredom, personal relationships or financial stress. Short periods of stress that are dealt with do not lead to long-term depression. Stress, therefore, needs to be dealt with in a timely and appropriate manner.
- **Find ways to relax and unwind:** Finding ways to relax and unwind is also important for your mental well-being. It may be a vacation, a book, a movie or just time alone. Find that one thing (or many things) that centre you and allow you to unwind at the end of the day.
- **Get professional help:** Seek help if you believe you suffer from depression. There are various forms of treatment including medication, psychotherapy and cognitive behavioural therapy, all of which are highly effective. In addition to medication and other forms of therapy, it is important to make the above lifestyle changes to sustain a positive mood.

Mitigate Your Risk of Contacting a Disease

With age, the risk of all kinds of diseases increases. We can mitigate some of this risk by adopting healthy lifestyle practices. Menopause itself predisposes women to some of these diseases like osteoporosis, heart disease and depression. Being aware of early symptoms and the lifestyle habits that put you at a higher risk are helpful in making you more aware of how to avoid them.

- You can start exercising regularly.
- You can maintain your weight at an optimum level.
- You can eat more vegetables and fruit.
- You can stop smoking.
- You can restrict alcohol to not more than one to two drinks per day, if you drink at all.
- You can meditate.
- You can have regular check-ups, especially if you are on contraceptive pills or an intra-uterine contraceptive device.
- You can be aware of your family history of disease and accordingly do screening tests and have regular check-ups.
- You can take calcium supplements.
- You can practise safe sex.
- You can improve your social connections and establish a few meaningful relationships in order to improve well-being.
- You can learn to forgive and erase hostility.
- You can learn to manage stress more effectively.

I do hope this chapter gave you a fairly decent idea of the various diseases you could face, especially as you age and how you can prevent and manage them more effectively.

Bibliography

ACE personal trainer manual: The Ultimate Resource for Fitness Professionals (Fourth Edition), *American Council on Exercise*, 2010.

Astrow, Alan B., Christina M. Puchalski and Daniel P. Sulamsy, 'Religion, spirituality and health care, social, ethical and practical considerations', *American Journal of Medicine*, March 2001.

Nordmann, Alian J., Abigail Nordmann, Matthias Briel et al, 'Effects of Low-Carbohydrate vs Low-Fat Diets on Weight Loss and Cardiovascular Risk Factors: A Meta-analysis of Randomized Controlled Trials', *American Medical Association*, 2006.

Logue, A.W., 'Evolutionary Theory and Psychology of Eating', 22 October 1998.

Seligman, Martin E.P., *Authentic Happiness: Using the New Positive Psychology to Realize Your Potential for Lasting Fulfillment*, London: Nicholas Brealey Publishing, 2003.

Biedermann, Luc, Jonas Zeitz et al. 'Smoking Cessation Induces Profound Changes in the Composition of the Intestinal Microbiota in Humans', *Plos One*, 14 March 2013.

Weinhold, Bob, 'Epigenetics: The Science of Change', *Environmental Health Perspectives*, March 2006.

Colberg, Sheri R., Ronald J. Sigal et al, 'Exercise and Type-2 diabetes', *Diabetes Care*, December 2010.

Clinical Exercise Specialist Manual: ACE's Source for Training Special Populations, 1999.

Mayorga-Vega, Daniel, Rafael Merino-Marban and Jesús Viciana, 'Criterion-Related Validity of Sit-and-Reach Tests for Estimating Hamstring and Lumbar Extensibility: A Meta-Analysis', *Journal of Sports Science and Medicine*, January 2014.

Epel, Elissa S., Bruce McEwan et al. 'Stress and Body Shape: Stress-Induced Cortisol Secretion is Consistently Greater among Women with Central Fat', *Psychosomatic Medicine*, October 2000.

Mardber, Emelie, 'Effect of Resistance Training in Patients with Type-2 Diabetes Mellitus: A Systematic Review', Orebro University, May 2014.

Berryman, Jack W. 'Exercise is Medicine: A Historical Perspective', *Current Sports Medicine Reports*, June 2010.

El-Khourry, Fabienne, Bernard Cassou et al. 'Effectiveness of Two Year Balance Training Programme on Prevention of Fall Induced Injuries in at Risk Women Aged 75-85 Living in Community: Ossébo Randomized Controlled Trial', *The BMJ*, 22 July 2015.

Seligman, Martin E.P., *Flourish: A Visionary New Understanding of Happiness and Well-being*, New York: Free Press, 2011.

Finkel Eli. J., Chin Ming Hui et al. 'The Suffocation of Marriage: Climbing Mount Maslow without Enough Oxygen', *Psychological Inquiry*, Routledge, 2014.

Gordon, B.A., A.C. Benson et al. 'Resistance Training Improves Metabolic Health in Type-2 Diabetes: A Systematic Review', *Diabetes Research and Clinical Practice*, February 2009.

Gregger, Michael, *How Not to Die: Discover the Foods Scientifically Proven to Prevent and Reverse Disease*, New York: Flatiron Books, 2015.

Hunter, G.R., J.P. McCarthy and M.M. Brammam, 'Effects of Resistance Training on Older Adults', Auckland: *Sports Medicine*, 2004.

Roeters, Jeanine E.H., Tineke Westerveld et al. 'Risk Factors for Coronary Heart Disease: Implications of Gender', *Cardiovascular Research*, Volume 53, 15 February 2002.

J.N. Morris and Margaret D. Crawford, 'Coronary Heart-Disease and Physical Activity of Work,' *British Medical Journal*, 1958.

Kabat-Zinn, John, *Mindfulness for Beginners: Reclaiming the Present Moment – and Your Life,* Colorado: Sounds True, 2006.

Cacioppo, John T. and William Patrick. *Loneliness: Human Nature and the Need for Social Connection*, New York: W.W. Norton and Company, 2008.

Eriksson, Johan G. 'Exercise and The Treatment of Type-2 Diabetes Mellitus', *Sports Medicine*, June 1999.

Kline, G.M., Porcari J.P. et al, 'Estimation of VO2max From a One-mile Track Walk, Gender, Age, and Body Weight'. *Medicine and Science in Sports and Exercise*, June 1987.

Escobar, Kurt and Len Kravitz, 'Resistance Training and Diabetes: The Importance of Muscular Strength', *Idea Health and Fitness Association*, 7 October 2016.

Konner, Melvin, 'What our ancestors ate', *New York Times Magazine*, 5 June 1988.

Lampio, Laura, Päivi Polo-Kantola, et al, 'Sleep During Menopausal Transition: A 6-Year Follow-Up', *Sleep*, Volume 40, Issue 7, 1 July 2017.

Levine, James A., 'Sick of sitting'. *Diabetologia*, 23 August 2015.

Kravitz, Len, 'Resistance Training for Clients With Diabetes', *Idea Health and Fitness Association*', 18 May 2010.

Pereira, Marta Inez Rodrigues and Paulo Sergio Chagas Gomes, 'Muscular Strength and Endurance Tests: Reliability and Prediction of One Repetition Maximum – Review and New Evidences', *Revista Brasileira De Medicina Do Esporte*, Volume 9, October 2003.

McBride, Gavin, Kalene Lynch et al, 'Effects of a Short Term, Short Duration, High Intensity Exercise Intervention on Body Composition and Intra-Abdominal Fat', 2014.

Mishra, Archan, Naval Vikram et al, 'Waist Circumference Cutoff Points and Action Levels for Asian Indians for Identification of Abdominal Obesity', *International Journal of Obesity*, January 2006.

Brian Wansink, *Mindless Eating: Why We Eat More Than We Think*, New York: Bantam Books, 2006.

Tse, Mimi M.Y., Anna P.K. Lo et al, 'Humor Therapy: Relieving Chronic Pain and Enhancing Happiness for Older Adults', *Journal of Ageing Research*. 2010.

Berek S. Jonathan, *Berek & Novak's Gynecology*, 15th edition, Philadelphia: Lippincott Williams & Wilkins, 2011.

Schneiderman, Neil, Gail Ironson and Scott D. Siegel, 'Stress and Health: Psychological, Behavioral, and Biological Determinants', *Annual Review of Clinical Psychology*, 2005.

Hovanec, Nina, Anuradha Sawant et al, 'Resistance Training and Older Adults with Type-2 Diabetes Mellitus: Strength of Evidence', *Journal of Ageing Research*, 2012.

Ornish D., Brown S.E. et al, 'Can Lifestyle Changes Reverse Coronary Heart Disease? The Lifestyle Heart Trial', *Lancet*, 21 July 1990.

Alhola, Paula and Päivi Polo-Kantola, 'Sleep deprivation: Impact on Cognitive Performance', *Neuropsychiatric Disease and Treatment*, October 2007.

Hall, Peter A., 'Executive-Control Processes in High Calorie Food Consumption', *Association for Psychological Science*, 6 April 2016.

Li, Qing, 'Effect of Forest Bathing Trips on Human Immune Function', *Environmental Health and Preventive Medicine*, Volume 15, 1 January 2010.

Christer, Robert and Len Kravitz, 'Aging and Cardiovascular Disease: Exercise to the Rescue!', *Idea Health and Fitness Association*, February 2017.

Akabas, Sharon R., Preface to *Journal* Supplement, 'Soy Summit: Exploration of the Nutrition and Health Effects of Whole Soy', *The Journal of Nutrition*, Volume 140, 1 December 2010.

Pollan, Michael, *The Omnivore's Dilemma: A Natural History of Four Meals*. New York: Bloomsbury, 2006.

Pollan Michael, *Cooked: A Natural History Of Transformation*, New York: Penguin, 2013.

Weir, Kirsten, 'The Exercise Effect', *American Psychological Association*, Volume 42, December 2011.

Taylor, Shelley E., Klein, Laura C. et al, 'Biobehavioral Responses to Stress in Females: Tend-and-Befriend, Not Fight-or-Flight', *Psychological Review*, 2000.

Granacher Urs, Thomas Muehlbauer and Markus Gruber, 'A Qualitative Review of Balance and Strength Performance in Healthy Older Adults: Impact for Testing and Training', *Journal of Aging Research*, 2012.

Vigil, Jacob M., 'Asymmetries in the Friendship Preferences and Social Styles of Men and Women', *Human Nature*, September 2007.

Weinstein, Richard, *The Stress Effect*, New York: Avery-Penguin Group, 2004.

Notes

1. Astrow, Alan B., Christina M. Puchalski and Daniel P. Sulmasy, 'Religion, Spirituality, and Health Care: Social, Ethical, and Practical Considerations', *The American Journal of Medicine*, March 2001.
2. Cooper Institute.
3. Hunter, G.R., J.P. McCarthy and M.M. Brammam, 'Effects of Resistance Training on Older Adults', *Sports Medicine*, 2004.
4. Konner, Melvin, 'What our ancestors ate', *New York Times Magazine*, 5 June 1988.
5. Boutcher, Stephen H., 'High-Intensity Intermittent Exercise and Fat Loss', *Journal of Obesity*, 2011.
6. Finkel Eli. J., Chin Ming Hui et al. 'The Suffocation of Marriage: Climbing Mount Maslow without Enough Oxygen', *Psychological Inquiry*, Routledge, 2014.
7. Kabat-Zinn, John, *Mindfulness for Beginners: Reclaiming the Present Moment – and Your Life,* Colorado: Sounds True, 2006.
8. Li, Quing, 'Effect of Forest Bathing Trips on Human Immune Function', *Environmental Health and Preventive Medicine*, Volume 15, 1 January 2010.

Acknowledgements

I am thankful to my publishers at Hachette and my editor, Prerna Vohra, for making this book a reality on the stands. I also want to thank my agent, Mita Kapur, for her support. My deep appreciation to all those who helped me pull this book together by providing valuable, much-needed feedback – Sunalini Mathew, Krithika Rajagopalan, Pradipta Sarkar, Uma Ram, Jayshree Gopal, Paul Ramesh and Sanjay Vijayraj. Many thanks to all the women who patiently answered my questions, filled in questionnaires and whose enthusiasm encouraged me to complete the book.

My deepest gratitude to every one of you who have shown me love and support in making my own journey through life more meaningful!

Sheela
www.drsheelanambiar.com